The Path to Dropping Out

THE PATH
TO DROPPING OUT

Evidence for Intervention

Melissa Roderick

Auburn House
WESTPORT, CONNECTICUT • LONDON

Library of Congress Cataloging-in-Publication Data

Roderick, Melissa R.
    The path to dropping out : evidence for intervention / Melissa
Roderick.
        p. cm.
    Includes bibliographical references (p.   ) and index.
    ISBN 0–86569–206–8 (alk. paper)
    1. Dropouts—Massachusetts—Fall River—Longitudinal studies.
2. High school dropouts—Massachusetts—Fall River—Longitudinal
studies.   3. Grade repetition—Massachusetts—Fall River—
Longitudinal studies.   4. Dropout behavior, Prediction of—
Longitudinal studies.   I. Title.
LC144.M4R63   1993
371.2'913'0974485—dc20   92–42905

British Library Cataloguing in Publication Data is available.

Library of Congress Catalog Card Number: 92–42905
ISBN: 0–86569–206–8

First published in 1993

Auburn House, 88 Post Road West, Westport, CT 06881
An imprint of Greenwood Publishing Group, Inc.

Printed in the United States of America

The paper used in this book complies with the
Permanent Paper Standard issued by the National
Information Standards Organization (Z39.48–1984).

10 9 8 7 6 5 4 3 2 1

To my parents and grandparents who
taught me the value of education, family, and community

Contents

Tables and Figures

FIGURES

Acknowledgments

This book began as my dissertation research at the John F. Kennedy School of Government at Harvard University and ended during my first year of teaching at the School of Social Service Administration at the University of Chicago. At the Kennedy School, I was fortunate to have an intellectual community that saw this project through its many stages of development. I owe my greatest thanks to Mary Jo Bane who, as my dissertation advisor and mentor, provided support and guidance in more ways than I could describe. I am equally indebted to David Ellwood for his advising and support. In the end, much of what I have learned as a researcher, teacher, and professional I owe to their guidance and example. I hope that I can give my students but a portion of the many gifts they have given me.

I would like to thank the graduate students and members of the faculty and staff of the Malcolm Wiener Center for Social Policy who supported this project and contributed comments and criticisms during numerous luncheon seminars and individual consultations. In particular, Paul Jargowsky, Marie Chevrier, and Naomi Goldstein, my fellow graduate students, provided feedback on my work and invaluable technical and substantive expertise, along with their always available friendship. I would also like to thank David Wise and Richard Freeman who served as members of my committee and offered helpful suggestions and comments.

During my time at the Kennedy School, I had the opportunity to meet and benefit from the many talents of Richard Weissbourd. Rick's contributions to this work are many. His qualitative research and our conversations regarding this study and the substantive problems facing at-risk youths were a constant source of insight and inspiration that supplemented my analysis and provided critical direction.

Many members of the University of Chicago community and The School of Social Service Administration offered advice and support while I was working on this book. It is a testament to the richness of the intellectual climate of the school that, in such a short period of time, I have so many to thank. Michael Sosin, Bill Borden, and Theresa Eckrich Sommer read and commented on chapters. Larry Lynn provided needed direction and motivation. I am indebted to Mark Testa for his always available technical guidance and problem solving. I owe a special note of thanks to Dean Jeannie Marsh for her advice and commitment to this work and to Sharon Berlin who made sure that I had the time during my first year of teaching to complete this project.

This book is dedicated to my parents and grandparents. Many authors thank their families. I could not have not conducted this research without the help of my parents, Marilyn Morin Roderick and Joseph Roderick. They provided the contacts that allowed me access to the Fall River public school system. Their knowledge of the school system and the city as educators and as public servants provided an additional source of information and insight that enriched this research. Their teaching experience and knowledge of at-risk youths guided this study through many hours of dinner table conversation and Sunday morning breakfasts.

I am grateful to the staff and administration of the Fall River public school system for all their assistance and patience. They were always willing to help me track down a lost transcript, find space to work, and respond to my many questions. I would particularly like to thank Superintendent John Correiro, former Principal James Panos, and Ms. Patricia Silvia for making this research possible.

Finally, I wrote this book with the support and input of my partner, Shelley Fried, and my brother, Jason Roderick. Jason and Shelley read and edited every chapter, provided suggestions and criticism, and helped me get over many difficult spots. Shelley's contributions to this book are too numerous to cite. She was untiring in her efforts to support me during this project, whether it be staying up late to listen to a new argument or spending days entertaining visitors so that I could work on weekends. Shelley has enriched my life and my work in many more ways than I could describe. These are but a portion of the gifts for which I will be forever indebted.

Introduction and Overview

Fall River, Massachusetts, is a moderate-size city of slightly over 90,000 residents located one hour south of Boston. It is a city of hills and of mills and a city of immigrants. Students in Fall River public schools attend neighborhood elementary schools beginning in kindergarten. They go to the Talbot, the Henry Lord, the Morton, or the Kuss for middle school, and then, in ninth grade, they come together on the north side of the city to attend BMC Durfee High School. BMC Durfee High School of Fall River, a modern facility, was opened in the 1970s next to the newly built Bristol Community College. At its opening, Durfee High's new pool and athletic facilities, music department, state-of-the-art auditorium, vocational program, special education classrooms, foreign language labs, and spacious grounds promised new opportunities for its largely poor and working-class students. Unfortunately, Fall River faces the same problem that many school systems share with the much larger, complex, urban school systems of Boston, Chicago, New York, and Los Angeles. Of students who do not transfer out of the Fall River schools, 48 percent will never graduate. The question is why, and what, if anything, should the school system do about it?

This book presents the results of a study of the Fall River public school's seventh-grade class of 1980–1981. Based on data obtained from school transcripts, I traced the school career paths of different groups of dropouts and graduates beginning in the fourth grade. I also looked more specifically at how the experience of repeating grades and the experience of students during the transitions from elementary to middle school and from middle school to high school influenced their chances of dropping out.

The Fall River study was designed to address an important gap between what the literature on school dropout can tell us about early school leaving, and what policymakers need to know in order to address the problem. It is, in fact, my answer to a question put to me over six years ago by an administrator in Boston's antipoverty agency as we sat in a room trying to design new dropout prevention initiatives.

In the 1980s, I worked on the Boston site of the Summer Training and Education Program (STEP), a national dropout prevention demonstration. As this project came to a close, members of the staff and coalition that sponsored STEP were called to a meeting to discuss what new direction this program would take, if it were to expand. The meeting included representatives of many of the various groups that were involved in STEP: Boston public school teachers, youth counselors, and administrators of city dropout and youth programs, all of whom had worked on youth and educational issues for many years.

At this meeting, a heated debate began to develop. On the one side, several people argued that our students were falling apart during the transition to high school, and that we should focus new efforts on the freshmen. On the other side, several people cited the focus on the middle schools by influential education groups such as the Massachusetts Advocacy Center and the Carnegie Council on Adolescent Development, as evidence that ninth grade was far too late to intervene. Instead, they argued, our efforts should be focused primarily on the middle schools. As this discussion became more involved, one administrator turned to me and asked: "Isn't there any research evidence on which period is more important?" It was a critical question—one to which I did not have the answer.

What I found as I began a review of research on school dropout was that the answer to this question did not lie in the numerous books and articles that had been written about high school dropouts during the 1980s. There was research showing that school transitions were difficult for youths. There was also an emerging consensus in the literature on adolescent development that the middle school years were an important period in the formation of attachment to school. But there was almost no research on what impact a student's experience during these periods had on his or her later school outcomes.

Indeed, I found little empirical research that could help in resolving many of the debates with which those involved in and around schools were grappling on a day-to-day basis. Should dropout prevention efforts be focused on the middle school years rather than the high school years? Is there a path to dropping out during which intervention would reduce the chances that a student would leave school? Are the causes of school leaving beyond the control of schools, making the best dropout prevention strategy early intervention? And, do school policies regarding grade retention, tracking, discipline, or attendance place youths at risk of school leaving, as the descriptive statistics that compare the characteristics of dropouts to graduates appear to suggest? Resolving these questions requires a knowledge of how poor school performance and disengagement develop over the course of students' school careers—questions that can only be addressed with longitudinal data on the experiences of youths prior to high school. In order to obtain this information, however, I needed to go beyond the traditional sources of data on school dropout.

Most of our information on school dropouts has come from several large longitudinal studies conducted over the past decade, such as the High School and Beyond Survey. In Chapters 1 and 2, I review the general findings of previous quantitative and qualitative research on early school leaving and discuss the current limitations of our research base. Previous research on school dropout has provided school systems with a detailed set of characteristics that distinguish dropouts from graduates at or around the time of dropping out and has provided insights into the academic, personal, and social correlates of early school leaving. Because these data sets do not include information on a student's experiences prior to high school, they cannot be used to identify how dropouts and graduates arrived at such disparate points in their school careers. Analyses of these national surveys, moreover, cannot allow researchers to identify which of the many differences in the school experiences of dropouts and graduates are reflections of their difficulties in school and which are experiences that increase the chances that some students would drop out.

THE FALL RIVER STUDY

The Fall River study represents an ambitious attempt to begin exploring the middle school and early high school antecedents to school leaving. In constructing this data set, I relied on hard copies of school transcripts, a method that allowed me to be confident of the accuracy of student outcome and transcript information. The cohort was initially identified from seventh-grade homeroom registers. I then collected transcript data for each student from fourth grade to dropout, transfer, or graduation. Slightly more than one thousand students were enrolled in the seventh-grade class. Thirty-five percent of these students dropped out of school before receiving a high school diploma; 38 percent graduated; and 22 percent transferred to another school system. I was able to obtain school transcript data on 757 youths—approximately 90 percent of dropouts and 95 percent of graduates in the initial cohort. Chapter 3 describes the Fall River data set, the background and school performance measures that were used in the analysis, and the statistical techniques and general methodological approach taken in this study.

OVERVIEW OF FINDINGS

The purpose of the Fall River study was to address several questions critical to the policy debate. What do trends in the school career paths of dropouts and graduates tell us about the characteristics of different groups of dropouts and graduates? Can we identify a path or paths to dropping out? And, is there any evidence that students' disengagement and the academic processes that lead to withdrawal can be linked to aspects of the organization, policy, or practices of schools?

Chapter 4 presents a descriptive analysis of trends in the grades, attendance, and incidence of grade retention of dropouts and graduates beginning in the fourth grade. This is an empirical study of early school leaving. In Chapters 5 and 6, I use both logistic and event history analysis to look more closely at how grade retention and the experience of students following school transitions influenced their chances of dropping out. To those unfamiliar with statistical analyses, these chapters may seem intimidating. I have tried to present results in a manner that is accessible to both researchers and policymakers who may not be expert in the statistical techniques, or in any of the particular disciplinary fields that I have drawn upon. Those readers who are not comfortable reading and interpreting the results of multivariate analyses should note that the main findings of this research can be understood in a reading of the descriptive statistics reported in Chapter 4 and from my discussion of the impact of school transitions and grade retention in the later chapters. Let me begin by providing an overview of the main empirical findings of this study.

Early versus Late Grade Dropouts

The first major finding of this study is that there are two very different stories to be told concerning the path to dropping out in the Fall River public school system. The first path to dropping out describes the school careers of students who dropped out prior to or during the first year of high school (seventh- to ninth-grade dropouts). As early as the fourth grade, the average grades of these early grade dropouts were significantly lower than those of their classmates. Over one-half of these students had experienced a grade retention by the fourth grade. In addition, the school performance of these early grade dropouts deteriorated quite rapidly as they moved into and through middle school.

I find, however, that the average grades and attendance of the majority of dropouts in the Fall River school system were not substantially different in the fourth grade than those of students who later went on to graduate in the bottom third of their class. Trends in the average grades and attendance of late grade dropouts and graduates, moreover, followed quite similar patterns as they moved through middle school and into high school. On average, students' grades decline following school transitions. In addition, I find that the average attendance of students declines throughout adolescence. While the overall patterns of trends in late grade dropouts' and graduates' school careers were quite similar, the degree to which a student experienced declines in grades and attendance differed widely across groups and was directly associated with later school outcomes. Indeed, what were periods of moderate declines in school performance and engagement for some students, were critical points for dropouts.

Trends in Grades: The Effect of School Transitions

The school transitions to both middle school and high school were critical junctures in the academic careers of early school leavers. For all high school dropouts, school performance and engagement dropped dramatically following the transition to high school. Similarly, dropouts, on average, experienced much larger declines than graduates in their school performance during the move to the middle school in the sixth grade. These students did not recover from the losses incurred during school transitions. It was in the transition to high school, in particular, that many dropouts fell into serious academic difficulty. For example, as we will see in Chapter 4, the percentage of late grade dropouts (tenth- to twelfth-grade dropouts) who failed 25 percent or more of their credits increased from 5.3 to 60.7 percent following the transition to high school in ninth grade compared to an increase for graduates from 2.6 to 8.3 percent.

Trends in Attendance: Increasing Divergence

Late grade dropouts and graduates did not differ in trends in their average grades during middle school. I find, however, that throughout adolescence, the school engagement of late grade dropouts steadily diverged from those of graduates—a level of disengagement that accelerated in late middle school and in the transition to high school. From the sixth to the eighth grade, the average attendance of late grade dropouts declined by thirteen days on average, compared to an average decline of 5.26 days for students who later graduated in the bottom third of the graduating class.

The Effect of Grade Retention

The experience of being retained or "held back" emerges as another important facet of the school careers of dropouts. In this study, students who were retained in grade were more than three times more likely to drop out of school than students who were never retained. Approximately one-third of the higher dropout rate among retained youths can be explained by differences in the pre- and postretention grades and attendance of retained and promoted youths. Even after controlling for grades and attendance through the ninth grade, however, students who repeated grades were substantially more likely to drop out than those who had never repeated a grade. I also find that students who experience grade retention were more likely to drop out regardless of whether they were retained early or late in elementary and middle school.

There is a widespread belief among teachers that early grade retentions are not harmful to students. Previous research has found that students who experience early grade retention do no better than comparable youths who are promoted. The results of the Fall River study lend further evidence to the propositions that both early and late grade retentions have long-term implications for subsequent school performance, engagement, and chances of graduating.

The Effect of Being Overage for Grade

In this book I argue that designing effective dropout prevention programs requires that educators and policymakers understand whether and which school experiences matter. Designing effective approaches to dropout prevention also requires that they understand how school experiences, such as being retained in grade, influence a student's school performance and engagement. Students who are retained in grade may be more likely to drop out because repeating a grade may have negative effects on their self-esteem and attitudes toward school. Students who are retained in grade may also face an increased risk of dropping out because a grade retention makes them overage for grade. Youths who are older than their classmates may feel isolated from, and different than, their peers, particularly during adolescence. Teachers may also treat youths who are older differently, regardless of their academic performance.

The results of this study suggest that much of the higher dropout rates among retained youths can be explained by the impact of being overage for grade. Students in the Fall River cohort who are older than their classmates, either because they entered the school system overage for grade or because they were retained in grade, faced an increased risk of dropping out. The implications of this finding for both research and policy concerning grade retention are discussed in detail in Chapters 6 and 8.

THE PATH TO DROPPING OUT AMONG LATE GRADE DROPOUTS: A DEVELOPMENTAL PERSPECTIVE

How can we explain the divergent career paths of late grade dropouts and graduates in the Fall River study? Throughout this book, I draw heavily upon two related theories of how student attributes interact with the institutional characteristics of schools to produce different outcomes. The first is Vincent Tinto's theory of school withdrawal from college, which focuses on the degree to which a student's interactions with the social and academic community of the school work to inhibit or promote attachment to the institution and to the goals of continued schooling. The second is an emerging literature on the influence of social context in determining adolescents' developmental trajectories. This research, based primarily on Brofenbrenner's theory of the ecology of human development, focuses on the degree to which a student's interactions with, and experiences in, school may inhibit or promote positive development. These two theories are related, I would argue, because school membership can be viewed as one important element of an adolescent's developmental trajectory.

Of the many stages in the life course, adolescence is a particularly important period in the formation of attachment to school. During adolescence, students develop an increased capacity for abstract thinking at the same time that they are expanding their social networks beyond the family. The confluence of these cognitive and social changes means that young adolescents become more aware of their abilities and relative status among their peers, and begin to define their roles, capacities, goals, and aspirations in relation to their social environment. There is an increasing consensus in the literature that this period of identity formation is marked by not one, but several, development paths, reflected in increased sorting between those on positive versus negative trajectories.

In Chapter 7, I argue that the school career paths of late grade dropouts and graduates in the Fall River study provide clear evidence that during adolescence (from roughly ages 10 to 15), we see an increasing divergence in students' academic performance and school engagement. In addition, the Fall River study provides strong evidence that the policies and organization of schools have important influences on the direction adolescents are most likely to take.

Development does not occur in isolation. It emerges from and is shaped by a student's experiences at home, at school, in the community, and with peers, as well as by the interrelationships among these domains. This study finds that the experiences of youths following the school transition to both middle school and to high school have an important role in shaping the course of their school careers. The disparate academic experiences of late grade dropouts and graduates in the year following a school move suggest that these students' academic and adjustment difficulties posed significant barriers to their school membership—barriers that would have long-term implications for their continued persistence.

An important question is: Why do some youths encounter greater difficulty than others following these school transitions? One explanation is that students vary in their ability to cope with school transition stress by virtue of their personal or situational characteristics. Another explanation is that the policies and practices that students encounter in these new schools treat youths differently, and pose significant barriers to school membership and educational progress. At each of these transitions, tracking and departmentalization increase—policies that send direct messages to young adolescents regarding their relative position at a time when students are beginning to define their abilities and aspirations on the basis of that relative position.

My findings on the impact of grade retention point to another set of policies that may negatively influence an adolescent's school attachment. Previous research on the impact of grade retention has largely focused on the short-term impacts of a grade retention on a student's self-esteem, attitudes toward school, and school performance. The Fall River study suggests that repeating a grade may influence a student's performance and engagement at the time a student is retained and, later, when that student is 15 years old and is sitting in a class of 14-year-olds. In particular, being overage for grade and the experience of grade retention may have an important impact on a young adolescent's identity formation and attachment to school.

POLICY IMPLICATIONS: THE TWO DROPOUT PROBLEMS

What are the policy implications of this study? One of the most important contributions of this study to our understanding of the nature of school dropout is that school systems with high dropout rates may face two very different dropout problems. The first dropout problem, characterized by the school career paths of early grade dropouts, is that of youths who encounter substantial difficulties early on in their school careers, and whose school performance deteriorates quite rapidly during middle school. For these students, early intervention programs to improve their early school performance and to reduce the likelihood that they will be retained in grade appear to be the most appropriate policy response.

The second dropout problem, characterized by trends in the school career paths of the majority of dropouts in this study, is that of youths at the margin between dropping out and going on to graduate in the bottom third of their class. This path to dropping out may be best portrayed as the educational course of those students who experienced the greatest difficulty traversing the academic and development hurdles that are normally stressful for all students. This book presents evidence that school systems' policies and practices have an importance influence on what direction at-risk students' careers are likely to take. Taken together, then, these results suggest that, in looking for ways to reduce school dropout, school systems could look to their own policies that affect the way that youths experience school. In short, the difference between a 15 and 35 percent dropout rate in an urban school system may be that one school system has a higher proportion of youths who are highly at-risk. The differences between a 15 and 35 percent dropout rate may also result from the extent to which these school systems' policies and practices promote or inhibit school membership for those students who are at the margin.

This study identifies two specific school policies that have important influences on the chances that a student will drop out of school. In Chapter 8, I discuss the policy and research implications of my findings regarding both school transition and grade retention. I outline a variety of different program options for intervening following school transitions. I discuss changes in school systems' promotional policies during the 1980s and what my findings would imply for how school systems may begin to address the increasing incidence of grade retention.

A final contribution of this study, I would argue, is that it provides a framework for addressing the question that was put to me six years ago. My answer is that the appropriate question is not when the best time to intervene is, but how we should be intervening across students' careers, and for whom. There is an emerging consensus in the literature on the effects of a student's social context, including the findings presented in this book, that the way we structure, organize, and teach in middle schools has important influences on youths' developmental and educational trajectories. At the same time, one of the most important findings of this research is that the ability of students to adapt and form positive attachments in high school is as critical for their persistence as is their adjustment to middle school.

I hope that this book, as a first cut at examining the school antecedents to school dropout, will provide an empirical basis and an analytical framework to move the policy debate around school dropout to a more focused and informed investigation of the school's role in the dropout process. Clearly, analysis limited to school transcript information on one cohort of youths in one school system cannot provide a definitive answer to the question: What is the relationship between school experiences and school dropout? In the chapters that follow, I point out several of the more important limitations of this analysis and discuss the research and policy questions that are raised by my findings. As school systems begin to think about the potential implications of this study for their own programs and practices, they must consider the extent to which these findings are applicable to their population of students and the structure of their schools.

Many school systems are experimenting with alternative arrangements in both middle schools and high schools to reduce their rates of grade retention and their reliance on tracking, and to reduce the bureaucracy and anonymity of urban schools that place youths at risk of feeling isolated and marginal. These initiatives, often included under the larger rubric of school restructuring, are promising. The Fall River study provides evidence that these types of interventions may be an effective approach to dropout prevention. Critical next steps for research and policy regarding school dropouts, then, will lie in determining the robustness of these findings across school districts, investigating further how school policies influence students' school membership and academic development in both middle schools and high schools, and determining whether these new reform initiatives provide effective and feasible alternatives to our current practice.

Chapter 1

The Policy Context: A Profile of the High School Dropout Problem

We are headed for the usual cycle of events in education—the iden-
tification of a problem, a "movement" to attack the problem without
an adequate analysis, a problem-solving approach that fails, disil-
lusionment and hopelessness about public education. (Comer, 1986,
p. xvii)

To many involved in education reform, James Comer's critique of the
standards-raising movement could just have easily been directed at the
myriad of dropout prevention initiatives begun in the last decade. The
rate of early school leaving was not featured as a critical policy concern
in the first wave of education reports that ushered in the reform movement of the 1980s. But, by the end of the 1980s, virtually every major
school system in the country had instituted programs and policies to
reduce school dropout.

Reducing dropout rates requires a commitment on the part of school
systems to direct resources to and to prioritize dropout prevention initiatives. School systems must also have a base of knowledge with which
to design interventions, and to resolve debates over the appropriate
direction of prevention efforts. Should dropout prevention efforts be
focused on the middle school years or on the high school years? Should
initiatives be focused on system-wide changes or on the development
of targeted programs for at-risk youths? Or, are early school experiences
so formative that dropout prevention efforts aimed at changing school
experiences in early and late adolescence are misguided and ineffectual?
These questions will become even more important in the decade ahead
as educators struggle with understanding the critical elements of suc-

cessful and unsuccessful programs, and as the school-restructuring movement, advocates of early intervention, and the emerging focus on the middle schools provide alternative directions to serving at-risk youths.

When schools look to the research on school dropout, however, they often find that policy prescriptions do not, for the most part, follow from our current research base. Resolving these debates will require that we understand how poor school performance and disengagement develop over the course of a youth's school career. Previous research has been unable to identify how school experiences and the institutional characteristics of schools affect the decision to drop out, primarily because of the lack of longitudinal data on dropouts' and graduates' school careers prior to high school. This chapter discusses how and why early school leaving became a nationally recognized education concern, and school systems' response to this call for action. It ends with a discussion of how this gap in the research on school dropouts has affected the development of school policy. It is the gap between what previous research could tell us about dropouts and what school systems needed to know in order to design policies that motivated the Fall River study and that is the primary focus of the chapters that follow.

A beginning point for any book on school dropout is the question: How large is the dropout problem? Data on national dropout and graduation rates come from different sources, which provide a variety of information on high school attainment. I begin with a discussion of what national dropout and graduation statistics tell us about the magnitude of the dropout problem. I then review historical trends in various measures of high school attainment.

DROPOUT AND GRADUATION STATISTICS

In an average school system in the United States over one-quarter of students will leave high school before graduation. Many will later return to school. In the High School and Beyond Survey, for example, as many as 46 percent of dropouts went back to school to earn high school diplomas or high school equivalency degrees, such as GEDs.[1] Because of these high return rates, the educational attainment of young adults rises with age. For example, by age 24, approximately 86 percent of young adults will have a high school diploma or equivalency degree.

In this section, I will look separately at measures of dropout rates, which provide a gauge of the holding power of our school systems, and measures of educational attainment, which provide us with estimates of the educational qualifications of our population. Having students graduate without ever dropping out is clearly preferable to having them drop out and then later return to school or alternative programs. GED certificates do not provide the same economic returns as high school diplomas. In one study, Stephen Cameron and James Heckman found that labor market outcomes for males who earned GEDs were much more similar to those of high school dropouts than to those of high school graduates (Cameron and Heckman, 1991). In addition, a student who drops out and returns to school incurs costs that may have been avoided or mitigated if he or she had stayed in school. Quite simply, youths return to school because they realize that there is a large cost to dropping out. The longer they stay out of school, the higher these social and personal costs may be.

Comparing the dropout rate to the proportion of young adults who eventually obtain a high school diploma gives us two different measures with which to evaluate school systems and trends in education. In the 1980s, as we will see in this section, national statistics indicate that between 25 and 30 percent of each year's high school cohort dropped out before graduating. By their late 20s, 14 percent of these young adults would have not yet attained their high school diploma or GED. These rates of high school attainment have remained relatively unchanged since the mid–1970s.

Measures of the National Dropout Rate

What do we know about how many youths drop out of school? Unfortunately, there is no one agreed upon statistic that will provide a definitive answer to this question. In the 1980s, concern over dropout rates also gave rise to debate over how we should best measure these outcomes (Catterall, 1986; Kaufman et al., 1991; Rumberger, 1987). Three measures of the national dropout rate that are available over time are: the number of graduates compared to the population 17 years of age in any given year; the number of public high school graduates compared with public school ninth-grade enrollment four years earlier; and the percentage of 18- and 19-year-olds with a high school diploma or equivalency degree (see Table 1.1).

Appendix 1-A discusses the sources of information that are used to calculate these dropout statistics and the strengths and weaknesses of each measure. For example, comparing the number of public high school graduates to the number of ninth-graders four years earlier is intuitively appealing. This measure, however, does not provide a reliable estimate of the national dropout rate since it is not corrected for transfers into and out of the school system, earlier dropouts, or rates of early school leaving in private schools.

Comparing the number of youths who graduated from regular elementary and secondary schools each year with the number of 17-year-olds may provide the most reliable, historically available measure.

Table 1.1
A Comparison of Estimates of the National Dropout Rate for the High School Class of 1988–1989

	Uninterrupted Completion	Dropout Rate
High school grads/Pop 17	74.1%	25.9 %
High school grads/Ninth-grade class	71.2%	28.8 %
% 18- to 19-year-olds High school grads in October	71.9%	28.41%

Sources: National Center for Education Statistics, U.S. Department of Education, unpublished tabulations, U.S. Bureau of the Census (1991); National Center for Education Statistics (1992).

Youths who never failed a grade would be approximately 17 years of age at the beginning of their senior year. If there are not large year-to-year fluctuations in the population, or in the proportion of youths who are "held back" and graduating late, then this measure probably captures noninterrupted completion.

These three measures are surprisingly consistent in their estimates of the national dropout rate. Taken together, they suggest that between 26 and 29 percent of the class of 1988–1989 had dropped out of school before attaining their high school diploma. For the graduating class of 1988–1989, dropout rates calculated from each estimate are presented in Table 1.1. The dropout rate calculated as high school graduates as a percentage of the population 17 years of age provides the lowest estimate. If we divide public high school graduates by the number of ninth-graders four years earlier, we would obtain the highest estimate of the dropout rate.

Measures of Educational Attainment

We can expect that many of the dropouts from the class of 1988–1989 will make the decision to return to school. As noted earlier, up to 46 percent of dropouts in the High School and Beyond Survey had returned to school and completed their diploma or an equivalency degree within four years of when they should have graduated from high school. Data from the Current Population Survey allow us to examine what these high return rates mean for the eventual educational attainment of older cohorts of youths. For example, in 1989, 86.4 percent of 24-year-olds in the October Current Population Survey reported that they had not completed a high school diploma or equivalency degree. Six years earlier, the uninterrupted completion rate for this cohort was 75.2 percent when measured as the number of high school graduates compared to the population 17 years of age.[2]

Estimates of the Level and Trend in Early School Leaving

High school dropout rates vary significantly across school districts and regions. In 1989–1990, the high school dropout rate, as measured by the number of public high school graduates compared to ninth-grade enrollment four years earlier, ranged from a low of almost 8 percent in Vermont to a high of over 40 percent in South Carolina.[3] Students in urban areas are more likely to drop out of school than students in suburban or rural areas.[4] In large urban school systems, in particular, dropout rates often exceed 40 percent (Boston Public Schools, 1986; Catterall, 1986; Hammack, 1987; Hess, 1991).

High school dropout rates vary significantly by ethnicity, race, and gender.[5] Table 1.2 shows the average percentage of 19-year-olds and of 20- to 24-year-olds with less than a high school education in the years 1985 to 1987. A sample average of three years was calculated to remove year-to-year fluctuations often occurring in the Current Population Survey. In the last several years, approximately 22 percent of 19-year-olds, and 15 percent of 20- to 24-year-olds, reported that they had not graduated from high school or obtained an equivalency degree. The dropout rate among blacks is higher than among whites. The low level of high school attainment among Hispanic youths is particularly alarming. In the late 1980s, almost 40 percent of 20- to 24-year-old Hispanic young adults had not graduated from high school or obtained a GED compared to only 14 percent of whites. And, finally, as seen in Table 1.2, males are more likely than females to drop out. In the years 1987 and 1989, 26 percent of males compared to 18.6 percent of females had not graduated from high school or obtained equivalency degrees by the time they were 19.

Males, in particular black and Hispanic males, are more likely to return and complete schooling than their female counterparts (Cameron and Heckman, 1991; Kolstad and Owings, 1986). The higher return rate of males is reflected in Table 1.2. Among 19-year-olds, females are 7.3 percent more likely to be high school graduates. Among 20- to 24-year-olds, however, females are only 2.5 percent more likely to have a high school diploma or equivalency degree.

In historical perspective, these national dropout and graduation statistics represent a transformation in the educational attainment of America's young adults. From 1940 to 1975, the percentage of 25- to 29-year-old adults who completed twelve years of education rose steadily from 37.8 to 83.2 percent (see Table 1.3). Graduation rates have changed little

Table 1.2

Percentage of 19-Year-Olds and of 20- to 24-Year-Olds with Less than a High School Education; 1987–1989, by Gender, Race, and Hispanic Origin

	Average Percentage of Youth with Less Than a High School Education or Equivalency Degree; 1987-1989	
	19 Year Olds	20- to 24- Year Olds
Total	22.2%	15.0%
White	20.0	14.2
Black	33.5	20.4
Hispanic	46.5	38.6
Male	25.9	16.3
White Male	23.8	15.7
Black Male	38.6	21.3
Hispanic Male	n.r.	42.0
Female	18.6	13.8
White Female	16.5	12.8
Black Female	24.7	19.7
Hispanic Female	n.r.	34.8

Notes: n.r. = not reported, sample sizes too small. Averages reported for 19-year-olds are based on the average proportion of 19-year-olds with less than a high school education or its equivalent in 1987 and 1989. Averages reported for 20- to 24-year olds are based on the average proportion of 20- to 24-year olds with less than a high school education or its equivalent in 1987, 1988, and 1989.

Source: U.S. Bureau of the Census, Current Population Reports, Series P-20, Educational Attainment in the United States (Reports No. 428 and 451) (Washington, D.C.: U.S. Government Printing Office)

Table 1.3
Historical Trends in Uninterrupted Completion and Educational Attainment

High School Graduates as a % of Population 17 Years of Age

Year	HS Grads/Pop 17	Change	% Change
1929-1930	29.0%		
		21.8%	75.2%
1939-1940	50.8		
		8.2	16.1
1949-1950	59.0		
		5.9	10.0
1959-1960	64.9		
		11.8	18.2
1969-1970	76.7		
		- 3.1	-4.0
1974-1975	73.6		
		- 2.2	-3.0
1979-1980	71.4		
		1.8	2.5
1984-1985	73.2		
		- .3	-.4
1986-1987	72.9		
		1.2	1.6
1988-1989	74.1		

SOURCES: U.S. Department of Education, National Center for Education Statistics, <u>Digest of Education Statistics 1991</u> (Washington D.C.: U.S. Government Printing Office)

Proportion of 25-to 29-Year Olds With 4 or More Years of High School or High School Equivalency

Year	Graduating Classes	Percent	Change	% Change
1940	1929-1933	37.8%		
			13.9%	36.77%
1950	1939-1943	51.7		
			9.0	17.41
1960	1949-1953	60.7		
			14.7	24.22
1970	1959-1963	75.4		
			7.8	10.34
1975	1964-1968	83.2		
			2.6	3.12
1980	1969-1973	85.8		
			.3	
1985	1974-1978	86.1		
			- .1	
1987	1976-1980	86.0		
			- .3	
1989	1978-1982	85.7		

Source: U.S. Bureau of the Census, Current Population Reports, Series P-20, <u>Educational Attainment in the United States</u> u(various years) (Washington D.C.: U.S. Government Printing Office)

7

Table 1.4
Trends in the Proportion of 20- to 24-Year-Olds with Less than Four Years
of High School or High School Equivalent by Race and Hispanic Origin,
1970–1989

| | | | | Difference | |
| | | | | White/ | White/ |
Year	White	Black	Hispanic	Black	Hispanic
1970	17.3%	34.9%		17.6%	
1972	15.1	33.9		18.8	
1974	14.8	28.1	43.6	13.3	28.8
1976	14.3	27.5	40.9	13.2	26.6
1978	14.7	26.6	38.6	11.9	23.8
1980	14.9	25.1	39.3	10.2	24.4
1982	15.3	22.7	40.4	7.4	25.1
1984	14.7	19.9	41.1	5.2	26.4
1986	14.7	20.9	37.0	6.2	22.3
1988	13.9	20.6	36.5	6.7	22.6
1989	14.3	19.5	39.3	5.2	25.0

Source: U.S. Bureau of the Census, Current Population Reports. Series P-20, Educational Attainment
in the United States (various years) (Washington D.C.: U.S. Government Printing Office))

since the mid–1970s. From 1975 to 1989, the percentage of 25- to 29-year-old young adults with a high school diploma or its equivalent rose a mere 2.5 percent compared with an average increase of 23 percent in each of the previous decades from 1940 to 1980. This trend is also reflected in measures of uninterrupted completion (see Table 1.3). The leveling off of high school graduation rates over the past twenty-five years may signify that we have reached a plateau, or natural limit, in high school graduation rates given our current school systems, policies, and student population.

While high school graduation rates in the aggregate have changed little since the mid–1970s, the high school graduation rate of black young adults continued to improve. Table 1.4 compares trends in the percentage of 20- to 24-year-olds with less than a high school education by race and ethnicity. Throughout the 1960s and 1970s, the educational attainment of black young adults rose much faster than that of whites. As a result, the gap between black and white high school graduation rates has narrowed considerably. In 1970, black 20- to 24-year-olds were twice as likely as whites to have less than a high school education or GED. By 1989, the gap between the percentage of black and white 20- to 24-year-olds with less than a high school diploma or its equivalent had narrowed to slightly over 5 percentage points.

There has been very little improvement, however, in educational attainment among Hispanics. In 1974, the first year data were reported on Hispanics in the Current Population Survey, almost 44 percent of Hispanic 20- to 24-year-olds had not graduated from high school or received an equivalency degree. Since 1974, the level of high school attainment among Hispanics has barely improved. In 1989, the percentage of Hispanic 20- to 24-year-olds who did not have a high school diploma or equivalent was nearly 40 percent.

RECENT CONCERN OVER THE DROPOUT PROBLEM

In the 1980s, the dropout problem became a salient public policy issue. This resurgence of interest in further reducing high school dropout rates has emerged out of three connected concerns. First, the educational reform movement, begun with the publication of *A Nation At Risk*, focused attention on the failures of the American education system. Second, while youths were not more likely to drop out than they had been in previous decades, the cost of that decision has risen considerably. And, third, demographic projections that a larger proportion of the shrinking youth population will be comprised of minorities and youths from poor backgrounds—those most at risk of dropping out—generated concern centered in the business community that the quality of the American labor force is not, and will not, be adequate to meet the increased skill levels necessary to regain American competitiveness.[6]

The 1980s was a decade of scrutiny and pressure for reform in American education from virtually all levels of government. The decade began with the publication of the National Commission on Excellence in Education's *A Nation At Risk*, and ended with the election of a self-proclaimed "Education President." *A Nation At Risk* called attention to the failures of the educational system with its now famous declaration:

If an unfriendly foreign power had attempted to impose on America the mediocre educational performance that exists today, we might well have viewed it as an act of war. . . . We have, in effect, been committing an act of unthinking, unilateral disarmament. (National Commission on Excellence in Education, 1983, p. 5)

A Nation at Risk was soon followed by numerous reports documenting the mediocre performance of American students and the dilution of educational standards in American schools, particularly in American high schools.[7]

In the early 1980s, the emerging school reform movement did not highlight the dropout problem. The first group of reports focused almost entirely on the need for stricter standards, higher performance, and the establishment of minimum competency (Howe, 1985; Stedman and Smith, 1983). *A Nation At Risk* did not even mention early school leaving as one of its "indicators of risk" in American education. This omission led to concern that standard-raising reforms would adversely impact those students who were not prospering under the current mediocre system. Articles by researchers in the dropout area queried whether the standards-raising movement would exacerbate the dropout problem, while critics of the reports pointed to the omission of dropouts as evidence that concerns over excellence were being substituted for concerns over equity (Alexander and Pallas, 1984; Bastian et al., 1986; McDill et al., 1986).[8]

Counterreports, in comparison, emphasized dropout rates as a pressing educational problem. For example, in 1985, the National Coalition of Advocates for Students' report, entitled *Barriers to Excellence: Our Children At Risk*, called for a "more balanced debate" and rejected "the implication raised in current public debate that excellence in education for some children can be made available only at the expense of other children" (Edelman and Howe, 1985, p. xi). These counterreports featured school dropout rates as a primary indicator of failure. As *Barriers to Excellence* declared: "the rising number of school dropouts is the single most dramatic indicator for the degree to which schools are failing children" (Edelman and Howe, 1985, p. xi).

Children in Need, the Committee for Economic Development's (CED) influential report, began with the statement: "although much has been written on the need to improve our education system, recent reform efforts have largely bypassed the problems of the educationally disadvantaged" (Committee for Economic Development, 1987, p. ix). The CED report prominently featured school leaving as the third component of its three-part strategy for educational reform.

The CED report was just one example of the business community's increasing activism around school reform and educational issues in the 1980s. Business's involvement in educational reform was motivated by general concerns over the quality of education per se. Business's involvement, particularly around the issue of school dropouts, was also motivated by mounting evidence that the relative economic position of high school dropouts vis-à-vis graduates had declined dramatically during the 1970s and 1980s. In addition, demographic projections that those youths most at risk of dropping out would make up an increasing proportion of the school aged population and future work force lent an urgency to the problem of dropouts.

THE RISING COSTS OF EARLY SCHOOL LEAVING

Dropping out of school has become an increasingly costly decision. In 1990, the median earnings of adult men, aged 25 to 34, who had dropped out of high school was fully 35 percent less than those of adult men who had ended their education with a high school diploma or an equivalency degree.[9] Twenty-five- to 34-year-old men with some college, moreover, earned almost twice as much as men without high school diplomas in 1990. Women who drop out of school are also disadvantaged in the labor market. Among women, the median earnings of 25- to 34-year-old high school dropouts were over 40 percent lower than those of women who had graduated from high school or obtained an equivalency degree, and was fully 65 percent lower than the median earnings of their counterparts who had gone on to college.

High school dropouts have traditionally earned less than graduates. But, the current labor market problems faced by dropouts are the culmination of a two-decade-long decline in the relative economic position of lower skilled workers, a decline that accelerated in the 1980s. Young men and particularly young minority men have been the most affected by these trends (McKinley et al., 1990; Sum et al., 1988).

Trends in Male Earnings

During the 1950s and 1960s, the average income of male workers increased by 37 percent (Sum et al., 1988). Young adult men, regardless of their education, shared in this economic prosperity. For example, from 1959 to 1973, the average income of 25- to 29-year-old male high school dropouts increased by 23.6 percent, compared to an increase of 28.8 percent for high school graduates with no college education, and 25.6 percent for college graduates (Sum et al., 1988).

Beginning in the early 1970s, these earnings increases came to a dramatic halt (McKinley et al., 1990; Sum et al., 1988). From 1972 to 1987, the average earnings of all male workers declined by almost 13 percent. Young adult men were particularly affected by these trends. From 1972 to 1987, the median earnings of young adult male workers declined by over 21 percent. These large earnings declines were not shared equally within the young adult male population. Changes in the median earnings of young adult male workers during this period ranged from a decline of approximately 37 percent in the median earnings of high school dropouts to a slight decline in the earnings of college graduates. Minority youths and those with less education were the hardest hit. At the extreme, the median earnings of black male high school dropouts declined by 54 percent from 1972 to 1987. These changes in the relative

earnings position of young adult workers are documented in Appendix
1-B.

Trends in Female Earnings

Earnings trends among women during the 1970s and 1980s have not
been studied as carefully as those of men. Changes in women's earnings
over time are more difficult to interpret because their labor force participation has increased so dramatically. There is, however, little evidence
that during the 1970s and 1980s the earnings of young women declined
as dramatically over the past decade and a half as those of men. There
is also little evidence of growing disparity in the distribution of women's
earnings by race and education (see Appendix 1-B).

Young women have experienced dramatic declines and growing dis-
parities in their relative family income, largely due to changes in family
structure, government benefits, and earnings (Johnson et al., 1988). Several researchers have argued that declining marriage rates and the dramatic increases in the proportion of families who are headed by single
women can be linked to the declining earnings of men (Duncan and Hoffman, 1989; Sum and Johnson, 1987; Wilson 1987). Thus, women may have
indirectly experienced an increase in the costs of early school leaving.

How much of the changes in family structure that occurred during
the 1970s and 1980s, particularly in the black community, can be linked
to changes in the economic position of males is an ongoing debate (Ellwood and Crane, 1990; Ellwood and Rodda, 1991). What is clear, however, is that the economic status of female dropouts has gotten
considerably worse. For example, Greg Duncan and Saul Hoffman, analyzing the Panel Study of Income Dynamics, found that from the 1970s
to the 1980s, the poverty rate of the families of 25-year-old young women
more than doubled for black and white women who had either dropped
out of school or had an out-of-wedlock birth, rising from 10 to 22 percent
for whites and from 24 to 48 percent for blacks (Duncan and Hoffman,
1989). In contrast, the poverty rate of the families of young women who
had graduated from high school and had no out-of-wedlock birth remained relatively stable and comparatively low, increasing from 2 to 3
percent for white women and from 12 to 13 percent for black women.

In summary, during the 1980s, much of the evidence that the dropout
problem has gotten worse has not come from statistics that educators
have traditionally looked to. The increasing dropout problem has not
been increasing dropout rates, but severe increases in the cost of that
decision to both the dropout and society (Catterall, 1986; Natriello et al.,
1991). Just as important, current employment and occupation projections
predict that the labor market status of dropouts will continue to deteriorate in the decade ahead (Burtless, 1990; Kutscher, 1991; Silvestri and
Lukasiewisz, 1991).

TRENDS IN THE YOUTH POPULATION AND WORK FORCE

Demographic trends in the youth population and the work force have also lent an urgency to the problem of early school leaving. Those youths who are more likely to drop out and those facing the largest employment and earnings difficulties will comprise a growing proportion of the shrinking youth population and future work force.[10] Between 1960 and 1980, the population of 16- to 24-year-olds nearly doubled.[11] In the next decade, the youth population will decline in both absolute and relative terms. Between 1980 and 1996, our youth population—those between ages 15 and 24—will fall by 21 percent from about 43 to 34 million people. Young people as a percentage of the nation's population will also decline from 18.8 to 13 percent during this period. Beginning in the late 1990s, the number of young people will again begin to increase, albeit at a much lower rate than that projected for the overall labor force (Fullerton, 1991).

While the total number of American youths is falling, the proportion of that population who are minority is rising. Among blacks, the rate of population decrease is slower than among the general population. As a result, there will be fewer black youths overall, but the proportion in the total population will increase from 13.7 percent in 1980 to 15.3 percent in 1996. Perhaps the most dramatic change in the youth population is the increasing proportion of Hispanic youths. From 1980 to 2005, the number of Hispanic youths is expected to double from 3.1 to an estimated 6.2 million. By the year 2000, Hispanics, as a group, are predicted to be the largest single minority in the general population.

During the 1970s, the labor force increased rapidly. The baby boom generation entered the work force, and the labor force participation of women increased dramatically. In the decades ahead, the rate of growth in the labor force participation of women is expected to slow. As fewer women enter the employment pool and as the size of the youth cohort decreases, young adults will play a more important role in the economy. Minority youths, in particular, will be an integral part of our new work force. From 1986 to the year 2000, the labor force is expected to grow by nearly 21 million workers compared to an increase of 31 million workers from 1972 to 1986 (Fullerton, 1987). Black, Hispanic, and Asian Americans will make up 57 percent of the growth of the work force, with Hispanics accounting for nearly 29 percent of growth alone.

THE DROPOUT PREVENTION MOVEMENT

These trends were featured prominently in the W. T. Grant Foundation's report *The Forgotten Half: Non-College Youth in America* (Grant

Foundation, 1988). Examining the declines in the earnings of young adults, the changes in the composition and income status of young families, and the changing demography of the young adult population, the Grant Foundation report lent an urgency to the problems of youths with no college education, arguing:

The plight of the "forgotten half," never easy, has become alarming. This nation may face a future divided not along lines of race or geography, but rather of education. A highly competitive technological economy can offer prosperity to those with advanced skills, while the trend for those with less education is to scramble for unsteady, low paying jobs. (Grant Foundation, 1988, p. 1)

This influential foundation report critiqued the educational reform movement for its focus on the college-bound and called for a reduction in dropout rates at the state level to 10 percent or less by the year 2000.

The Grant Foundation report was just one of many reports from the business and foundation communities that focused on the rising social and personal costs of early school leaving. This voice, combined with reaction to the educational reform movement, placed school dropouts at the top of the educational agenda of cities and states and created an alternative focus to educational reform. By the late 1980s, virtually every major school system had grappled with the issue of high school dropouts—on the one hand, by trying to identify the extent of the problem in their communities, and, on the other hand, by committing resources to address the problem. "Dropout Prevention Plans," targeted prevention programs, the development of alternative school programs, and analyses of school practices that may place youths at risk of dropping out became common activities in urban school systems.

And, high school dropouts became a prominent, nationally recognized education concern. In 1987, under the sponsorship of the U.S. Department of Education's Office of Educational Research and Improvement, the Urban Superintendent's Network, including representatives of thirty-two major urban school systems, issued a report entitled *Dealing with Dropouts: The Urban Superintendent's Call to Action*. This report, stating that "the dropout problem has engaged the minds and hearts of Americans," outlined a variety of ongoing efforts in school systems to reduce early school leaving.

Local focus on the dropout problem was also emphasized by state governments and by the foundation sector. Dropout prevention programs and policies were included in many of the educational reform bills that were passed by state legislatures in the 1980s. For example, Florida's Dropout Prevention Act of 1986 obliged each local school system to submit dropout prevention plans (Finn, 1987). Activities at the state, federal, and foundation levels focused attention on the dropout problem by providing funds and incentives for communities to grapple with their dropout problem.

The history of Boston, Massachusetts's much publicized Boston Compact provides just one example of how the "dropout problem" captured the "minds and hearts of Americans," and became a major focus of community education reform. In September 1982, the Boston public schools entered into an agreement with Boston's businesses, universities, and foundations with the purpose of improving the Boston public schools.[12] This agreement was called the Boston Compact. As part of the compact, the Boston public schools agreed to take measures to raise student achievement, increase student attendance, and reduce the dropout rate by 5 percent each year. Each school was required to develop plans to help meet the goals of the compact. In return, the business community agreed to provide summer jobs, part-time jobs during the school year, and jobs to Boston's high school graduates through the Private Industry Council. Later, the university community pledged to take steps to increase college attendance. The foundation community, through the Boston Plan for Excellence, also committed $4 million to fund programs.

By 1986, the Boston Compact claimed success in raising attendance and in providing jobs for graduates and high school students. But, in May 1986, the compact, responding to a study on the dropout rate released by the Boston Public Schools' Office of Research and Development, declared that it had failed to reduce the dropout rate. According to this report, the dropout rate in Boston public schools had risen from 36.2 to 43 percent from 1982 to 1985, following the implementation of the Boston Compact (Boston Public Schools, 1986). This dropout study, reported on the front page of the *Boston Globe*, focused the efforts of the Boston Compact on the issue of school dropouts.

In May 1986, the Boston Compact held a conference to plan a community response. At this conference, the compact set a goal of reducing by one-half the number of students who drop out annually and of doubling the number of dropouts who return to regular or alternative education. The superintendent of the Boston public schools presented the draft dropout plan developed by the Boston Compact's Dropout Prevention and Reentry Task Force. The plan was primarily a compilation of existing programs including middle school programs, such as Project Promise; high school cluster programs, such as the Boston Compact's own Compact Ventures; alternative school programs; community organization support programs; GED and community-based high school diploma programs; and summer programs, such as the Ford Foundation's Summer Training and Education Program, in which Boston was a participant. These efforts in community-based organizations and the schools were also joined, in 1986, by the state's new dropout prevention initiative, Commonwealth Futures.

The draft dropout plan did not emerge as a successful, coherent, and implemented plan that gained the support of the schools. In this respect, the experience of Boston resembled that of many other cities, such as New York, whose dropout prevention initiatives were largely clusters of small programs and diffuse interventions that were not institutionalized (Grannis, 1991). The number of programs listed as dropout prevention initiatives in Boston's dropout plan, however, does represent the impressive array of dropout prevention and reentry efforts that were being conducted in and around the schools, most of which had emerged in the middle to late 1980s.

This level of activity around dropout prevention was not without its critics. Concerned that the focus on dropouts would direct attention away from and possibly impede the standards-raising movement, Chester Finn, former Assistant Secretary at the U.S. Department of Education, presented a cogent criticism of school systems' policy focus on dropouts in his 1987 article entitled "The High School Dropout Puzzle." In this article, Finn did not disagree with efforts to reduce school dropouts. He argued, however, that school officials had proceeded with dropout prevention efforts, focusing on school characteristics, with little evidence to support their claims.

When devising a policy response to the dropout problem, school systems had several policy options available to them. The most obvious policy option would be to make schooling compulsory, raising the legal age from the prevalent legal age of 16, to either a higher compulsory age or grade.[13] School systems could also have taken steps to raise the costs of dropping out. Indeed, punitive policies, such as not allowing youths who drop out to obtain drivers' licenses, or making public assistance recipiency contingent upon attendance in school, have gained popularity at the state level (Cohen, 1992; Toby and Armor, 1992). Ten states now link drivers' licenses to school attendance (Toby and Armor, 1992). Finally, school systems could have chosen to do nothing, relying on the proven high return rates for youths to make their own decisions to return (Toby and Armor, 1992).

In the 1980s, school systems often chose a fourth policy approach: changing the school experiences of youths that may contribute to the decision to drop out of school. This approach toward dropout prevention is based on the premise that school systems can either eliminate school attributes that contribute to early school leaving or can provide incentives for youths to stay in school. In short, school system policies assumed that school experiences affect the decision to drop out. As Finn argues, however, this approach was adopted by school systems with little evidence to support their claims. Finn raises the question: "Are we sure that the primary forces leading young people to drop out are rooted in the school or school system rather than in the young people themselves, in their personal environments, or in trends and developments in the larger society" (Finn, 1987, p. 14). Finn's critique of the dropout prevention movement identified a central problem facing school policymakers. The myriad of reports on school dropouts identified the importance of doing something to reduce the dropout rate. Research on school dropouts provided few, if any, answers to what that something should be.

THE RESEARCH/POLICY GAP

Reducing dropout rates requires a commitment by school systems, school administrators, and teachers to make dropout prevention a priority. Indeed, the failure of initiatives to reduce dropout rates has often been attributed to a lack of institutional support and to the inability of these initiatives to affect how schools operate (Grannis, 1991; Whelage et al., 1992). Reducing dropout rates also requires that we have a base of knowledge of the manner in which a youth's school experiences and the institutional characteristics of the school he or she attends influences the course of his or her school career.

Much of our information on dropouts and graduates has come from several large, longitudinal surveys conducted over the past several decades. One of the first of these national studies was the 1960 Project Talent Survey. Janet Combs and William Cooley, in an analysis of this survey, found that dropouts, when compared to graduates who did not go on to college, had lower measured achievement, lower occupational aspirations, poorer attitudes toward school, poorer self-esteem, and participated less in school in the ninth grade (Combs and Cooley, 1968). Jerald Bachman, Swayzer Green, and Ilona Wirtanen's analysis of the 1971 Youth in Transition study also found that sophomores who later dropped out of school looked substantially different from graduates on tenth-grade measures of school performance, participation in, and attitudes toward school (Bachman et al., 1971).

The more recent National Longitudinal Survey of Youth Labor Market Experience, begun in 1979, and the 1980 High School and Beyond Survey provided more detailed information on a youth's background, young adult experiences, and values and expectations, as well as information on the characteristic of a student's school.[14] These newer surveys have allowed researchers to gain a fuller understanding of how a youth's family background influences educational attainment. They have provided a great deal of information on the high school and adolescent experiences of dropouts and of graduates. They have allowed for analyses of variation in dropout rates across schools. And, these newer surveys have allowed researchers to gain a better understanding of the personal and social costs of dropping out. The results of these studies will be briefly summarized in the next chapter.

Analyses of these newer surveys have not, for the most part, moved us closer to an understanding of how school experiences affect the decision to drop out. Gary Whelage and Robert Rutter expressed their frustration over this gap in the literature in their article "Dropping Out: How Much Do Schools Contribute to the Problem?" In this article, Whelage and Rutter argue:

Implicit in much research on school dropouts is the assumption that a better understanding of the characteristics of dropouts will permit educators to develop policies and provide practices that will reduce the number of adolescents who fail to graduate. The intent is noble but the results have been negligible because the focus on social, family, and personal characteristics does not carry any obvious implications for shaping school policy and practice. . . . Since traditional research has tended to identify characteristics least amenable to change, the focus of new research might better be directed toward understanding the institutional character of schools and how this affects the potential dropout. (Whelage and Rutter, 1986, p. 72)

Why has research on dropouts not addressed questions relevant to the policy debate? One answer proposed by Whelage and Rutter is that research has asked the wrong set of questions. Early school leaving, as with teen pregnancy, is an easily measurable outcome for researchers interested in sorting out how family background affects later outcomes for children. Thus, a great deal of research on school dropout is a by-product of work that was primarily designed to identify how family and personal background characteristics are associated with bad outcomes for children, rather than to explore the nature and dynamics of early school leaving.

More important, however, efforts to examine the school antecedents to early school leaving have been constrained by the lack of longitudinal data prior to high school. As noted, the High School and Beyond Survey as well as other large surveys provide little detailed information on a student's school experiences prior to the sophomore year in high school. Thus, these data sets cannot be used to examine the impact of early school performance on later school outcomes or what role middle school and early high school experiences play in the process by which youths become disengaged and drop out of school. These data sets also cannot tell us which of the many differences in the school experiences of dropouts and graduates are reflections of their difficulties in school versus experiences that contributed to their academic problems and disengagement.

The gap in the literature on school dropouts has had, and will continue to have, important implications for the development of dropout prevention policy. First, school systems have generally proceeded with dropout prevention efforts with very little concrete direction from research as to the design, placement, targeting, or potential efficacy of programs and policies aimed at altering the in-school experiences of youths. The result, as evidenced in the Boston Compact, is that much of our policy response to dropout prevention has been diffuse and, often, inexact. For example, the Urban School Superintendent's "Call to Action" presented a quite typical list of "best bets" that were included in myriads of dropout reports. These six "best bets," which could probably apply to any educational problem, were: intervene early, create a positive school climate, set high expectations, select and develop strong teachers, provide a broad range of instructional programs, and initiative collaborative efforts (OERI, 1987).

Second, policymakers, in the absence of firm research evidence on the impact of specific school experiences, have tended to imbue descriptive statistics with causal interpretations. Perhaps the best example is the case of grade retention, a policy that I will examine in detail in this book. Across the various surveys, dropouts are much more likely to report that they have failed previous grades than graduates. In the 1980s, critics of grade retention often cited this association as evidence that retaining youths would increase their chances of dropping out. This conclusion may be correct. It may also be that youths who do poorly in school are highly at risk of experiencing both early poor school outcomes, such as failing a grade, and later poor school outcomes, such as dropping out. If grade retention policies place youths at risk of early school leaving, then developing effective alternatives to grade retention would be an efficacious use of a system's resources. If, however, retaining youths does not increase the chances of dropping out, then school systems would not be addressing the source of the problem.

Finally, and perhaps most important, policymakers do not currently have the information necessary to resolve debates over the appropriate direction for dropout prevention initiatives. To what extent should dropout prevention efforts be focused on the middle school years versus high schools? Do alternative high schools provide the solution to the dropout problem or should school systems focus on developing programs within the traditional schools? And, should dropout prevention initiatives be focused on system-wide changes or on the development of targeted programs for at-risk youths? These questions will become even more important in the decade ahead as both an emerging focus on the middle schools and the movement to restructure schools have provided alternative directions for dropout prevention (Carnegie Council on Adolescent Development, 1990; Grannis, 1991; Hess, 1991; Natriello et al., 1990; Whelage, 1992).

After a decade of school initiatives, we are just beginning to see some long-term results. Many of these results have not been promising (Toby and Armor, 1992; Walker and Vilella-Velez, 1992; Whelage 1992). For example, an evaluation of New York City's $40 million Dropout Prevention Initiative found that the program had little impact on dropout rates (Grannis, 1991; Public Education Association, 1990). These results raise several important issues. To critics of dropout prevention these unsuccessful programs are further evidence that dropout prevention initiatives aimed at changing the school experiences of youths are misguided and ineffectual (Finn, 1987; Toby and Armor, 1992). To advocates of school restructuring, these results are evidence that broader change is needed in schools and that short-term, targeted interventions are doomed to failure (Grannis, 1991; Whelage, 1992). And, finally, to others, the same results are evidence that the intervention was targeted at the wrong age group, used the "wrong" intervention, or was not long or intensive enough.

Resolving these debates will require a knowledge of how poor school performance and disengagement develops over the course of a youth's school career, as well as knowledge of how the structure of schools affects dropping out that goes beyond catalogues of successful and unsuccessful programs. The findings of this longitudinal study of the school careers of dropouts and graduates in one school system can be used to inform these policy debates.

Indeed, as I have argued throughout this chapter, much of the inability of research to inform school policy has stemmed from the lack of longitudinal data on dropouts and graduates. One of the advantages of longitudinal research is that it allows us to sort out how much of the differences in the school careers of dropouts and graduates are the result of early differences in school performance, and how much may be the result of differences in these students' later school experiences. Longitudinal studies allow us to identify heterogeneity within the dropout population that cannot be identified by looking at cross-sectional statistics; for example, two youths may arrive at the same point along two very different paths. Finally, by looking at the school career paths of different groups of youths, we face the question: How can we understand why youths go down various paths? It is in trying to answer this question that we may begin to develop an understanding of the school's role in the dropout process and a framework to guide approaches to dropout prevention.

SUMMARY

As we enter the 1990s, the need to reduce dropout rates has not gone away. On the one hand, school systems will become increasingly diverse in the next decade, and teachers and administrators will face a broadening array of problems. The children of the 1980s experienced more poverty and economic and social dislocation than perhaps any generation since the Great Depression. In 1992, over one-fifth of our nation's children live in poverty, with over half of children in some of our larger cities living below the poverty line. These children will enter school with even greater needs. On the other hand, the cost of failing to graduate these children is higher than it has ever been. There is a growing consensus that the skill level of the American work force must increase. This is a tall order for school systems. If anything, the experience of the 1980s has proven that reducing these seemingly sticky dropout rates will require an even greater commitment on the part of school systems and communities. It will also require that we learn from past successes and failures and develop new approaches based on a firmer understanding of the etiology of the problem we want to address.

NOTES

1. Analyses of the High School and Beyond Survey found that within two years of when youths should have graduated, approximately one-third of dropouts had earned their diploma or GED. Within four years of when their counterparts who stayed in school had graduated, approximately 46 percent of dropouts in the High School and Beyond Survey had attained a high school education or its equivalent (Borus and Carpenter, 1983; Frase, 1989; Kaufman et al., 1991; Kolstad and Owings, 1986).

2. In the cohort that should have graduated from high school in 1983–1984, the dropout rate was 26.8, when calculated as the number of high school graduates as a percentage of the population 17 years of age in 1983. In 1987, four years after these youths should have graduated from high school, the Current Population Survey estimated that only 14.5 percent of 21-year-olds had not yet attained a high school diploma or its equivalent. Thus, data from the Current Population Survey suggest that, by age 21, approximately 46 percent (12.3/24.2) of this cohort has returned and successfully completed their high school education or its equivalent. And by age 24, CPS estimates suggest that only 13.6 percent of the cohort had still not obtained a high school diploma or its equivalent. In sum, we would estimate that within seven years of graduation, approximately 49 percent of dropouts from the class of 1983–1984 had returned to school and completed their diploma or an equivalency degree (U.S. Bureau of the Census, 1991 and various years).

3. Data on state-by-state variations in graduates as a proportion of ninth-

grade enrollment were obtained from unpublished tables calculated by the National Center for Education Statistics, U.S. Department of Education.

4. Dropout rates calculated from High School and Beyond show dropout rates for urban areas of approximately 24.5 percent, for suburban areas of approximately 15.1 percent, and for rural areas of approximately 15.6 percent at the third followup (Frase, 1989).

5. This section discusses trends in the educational attainment of black, white, and Hispanic young adults as reported in the Current Population Survey. The Current Population Survey does not report yearly estimates of educational attainment for other racial/ethnic groups. The High School and Beyond Survey does provide estimates of dropout rates by race and ethnicity. In the High School and Beyond Survey, American Indians dropped out at the highest rate of any racial/ethnic group while Asian Americans dropped out at the lowest rates. At the third followup, dropout rates by race/ethnicity in the High School and Beyond Survey were: American Indians/Alaskans 35.5 percent; Hispanics 27.9 percent; blacks 22.2 percent; whites 14.8 percent; and Asians 8.2 percent (Frase, 1989).

6. My analysis of the emergence of the dropout problem relies somewhat on analyses presented by both James Catterall and Russell Rumberger in their review articles on dropout policy (Catterall, 1986; Rumberger, 1987).

7. A partial list of influential education reports in the early 1980s would include Adler's The Paideia Proposal (1982); Boyer's High School (1983); the College Entrance Examination Board's report entitled Academic Preparation for College (1983); Goodlad's A Place Called School (1983); Sizer's Horace's Compromise (1984); and reports from the Task Force on Education for Economic Growth (1983) and the Twentieth Century Fund (1983). For a good review source on the various reports and reactions to them, see Gross and Gross (1985).

8. While virtually all of the reports, specifically Boyer's High School (1983), emphasized the need for both "equity and excellence," reaction to the reports focused on the question of whether the new movement was ignoring the needs of disadvantaged youths. In addition, critics highlighted the extent to which the new reforms were motivated by concern that too much attention had been paid to disadvantaged students, particularly minorities. See Gross and Gross (1985) for a full treatment of the debate.

9. Data on the median earnings of young adult men and women in 1990 were obtained from U.S. Bureau of the Census, Current Population Reports, Series P–60, Money Income of Households, Families, and Persons in the United States: 1990 (Report No. 174) (Washington, D.C.: U.S. Government Printing Office).

10. This section briefly summarizes trends in the youth population and labor force. For a discussion of the implications that these demographic changes will have on the number of children in school who will be at risk of dropping out or of experiencing school failure, see Natriello et al. (1991), pp. 33–43.

11. Population data presented in this section, unless otherwise noted, were calculated from U.S. Bureau of the Census, Statistical Abstract of the United States: 1988 (Washington, D.C.: U.S. Government Printing Office, 1988); and U.S. Bureau of the Census, Current Population Reports, Series P–25, Projections of the Population of the United States by Age, Sex and Race, 1983 to 2080 (No 952) (Washington, D.C.: U.S. Government Printing Office, 1984).

12. Information on the Boston Compact was drawn from a variety of sources, including The Federal Reserve Bank of Boston's (August 1986) report *Boston Dropouts: Planning a Community Response* as well as from an interview with Jay Ostrower, director of the Center for Jobs, Training, and Education, Action for Boston Community Development in December 1989.

13. In 1989, thirty-three states including the District of Columbia required compulsory school attendance until the age of 16. Eight states require enrollment until the age of 17, while nine states have a compulsory age of attendance of 18. Mississippi is the only state where the age of compulsory attendance is 14. The average graduation rate of states does not differ dramatically by the age of compulsory attendance. When measuring the average graduation rate as the number of graduates as a percentage of ninth-grade enrollment four years earlier, the average graduation rate in the years 1988 to 1990 was 74.6 percent for states whose age of compulsory attendance was 16; 71.3 percent among states with compulsory attendance until age 17; and 78.7 percent among states with compulsory attendance to 18. Mississippi's average graduation rate in the years 1988 to 1990 of only 63.9 percent was statistically significantly lower than those of other states (National Center for Education Statistics, unpublished tables).

14. Both the National Longitudinal Survey of Youth Labor Market Experience and the High School and Beyond Survey were conducted by the National Center for Education Statistics. The National Longitudinal Survey of Youth Labor Market Experience includes a sample of 12,700 young men and women who were 14 to 21 years of age in 1979. The High School and Beyond Survey includes information on 58,720 youths, approximately half of whom were seniors and half sophomores in 1980. Each of these surveys contains information on youths' family, social, and demographic background characteristics; a youth's ability and achievement measured at adolescence; parents' and student's expectations and aspirations; and the employment, school, and social experiences of youths in late adolescence. Both surveys include high school transcript data and information on the characteristics of the high school.

Chapter 2

School Dropouts:
A Literature Review

Early school leaving is probably the most widely studied educational problem in America. In the 1980s alone, hundreds of books and articles were written on the topic of high school dropouts. What can this substantial literature tell us about the problem school districts face? This chapter presents a brief review of empirical and qualitative studies of school dropout. I begin with a summary of previous research on the personal and social correlates of early school leaving, the characteristics that distinguish dropouts from graduates at or around the time of dropping out, and the reasons students give for leaving school. I then discuss research findings on the extent dropout rates vary by differences in youths' family backgrounds and by the characteristics of the schools.

Empirical research on early school leaving has provided school systems with a detailed set of characteristics that can be used to predict school dropout. Qualitative research on school dropout provides a framework for understanding the interactive process by which poor school performance and social and economic disadvantage can influence school membership. This chapter ends with a discussion of the findings that emerge from qualitative studies of early school leaving.

HIGH SCHOOL DROPOUTS: SCHOOL AND ADOLESCENT OUTCOMES

School Performance and Engagement

When dropouts are asked why they dropped out, they are most likely to state that they left because they were doing poorly and disliked school (see Table 2.1). The more difficulties a youth has in school, the greater are his or her chances of dropping out. In the High School and Beyond Survey, over one-half of students who reported that they received mostly D's or less in their sophomore year left school before graduating (Frase, 1989). In comparison, 35 percent of youths who reported they received mostly C's and D's, 21 percent of those who reported receiving mostly C's, and less than 5 percent of those who reported that they received mostly B's or better in their sophomore year left school before graduating.

Repeating a grade previous to high school is perhaps the most dramatic indicator of the degree to which a student has experienced prior difficulty in school. Students who are retained in grade are much more likely to drop out. In the Youth in Transition study, for example, youths who had repeated grades previous to high school were 40 to 50 percent more likely to drop out than youths who were never retained (Bachman et al., 1971). Students who repeated two grades were 90 percent more likely to drop out than their counterparts who had never experienced a grade retention. This strong association between grade retention and early school leaving, discussed in more detail in Chapter 6, is found across studies (Barro and Kolstad, 1987; Fine, 1991; Grissom and Shepard, 1989). Indeed, whether youths are overage for grade by the time they enter high school has emerged as one of the most easily measurable and reliable indexes of their risk of school leaving (Dryfoos, 1990; Fine, 1991; Grissom and Shepard, 1989; Hess, 1991; Massachusetts Advocacy Center, 1986; PINS Advisory Committee, 1988).

As the statistics cited above illustrate, data from the various national surveys have found that by the tenth grade, youths who will later drop out of school are more likely than graduates to be doing poorly in school and to report a history of previous difficulties in school (Bachman et al., 1971; Barro and Kolstad, 1987; Combs and Cooley, 1968; Eckstrom et al., 1987; Frase, 1989). Analyses of these surveys have also found that dropouts show signs of disengagement from school prior to the decision to leave. In the High School and Beyond Survey, sophomores who later dropped out of school reported lower attendance and lower levels of participation in extracurricular activities than youths who later graduated (Eckstrom et al., 1987). Late grade dropouts were also less likely than graduates to report that they were interested in school or satisfied with the way their education was going in their sophomore year of high school (Eckstrom et al., 1987).

Dropouts' disengagement from school often becomes evinced in conflict with school authorities. In the High School and Beyond Survey, early school leavers were more than twice as likely as graduates to report that they cut classes in their sophomore year (54 versus 25 percent) (Eckstrom et al., 1987). Dropouts were also much more likely to report

Table 2.1

Reasons Given for Dropping Out of School in the High School and Beyond Survey and the National Longitudinal Survey of Youth

Major Reasons for Dropping Out of School : High School and Beyond Survey

	Total	Males	Females
Did not like school	.33[a]	.35	.31
Poor grades	.33	.36	.30
Offered job/chose to work	.19	.27	.11
Getting married	.18	.07	.31
Couldn't get along with teachers	.15	.21	.09
Had to help support family	.11	.14	.08
Pregnancy	.11	**	.23
Expelled or suspended	.10	.13	.05

Primary Reason High School Dropouts Left School by Sex, Race, and Ethnicity, 1979: National Longitudinal Survey of Youth

	Male			Female		
	White	Black	Hisp.	White	Black	Hisp.
School Related						
Poor performance	.09	.09	.04	.05	.05	.04
Disliked school	.36	.29	.26	.27	.18	.15
Expelled/suspended	.09	.18	.06	.02	.05	.01
School dangerous	.01	.00	.00	.02	.01	.01
Total	.55	.56	.36	.36	.29	.21
Economic						
Desired to work	.15	.12	.16	.05	.04	.07
Financial difficulties	.03	.07	.09	.03	.03	.09
Home responsibilities	.04	.04	.13	.06	.08	.08
Total	.22	.23	.38	.14	.15	.24
Pregnancy/Marriage						
Pregnancy	.00	.00	.00	.14	.41	.15
Marriage	.03	.00	.03	.17	.04	.15
Total	.03	.00	.03	.31	.45	.30
Other	.20	.21	.23	.19	.11	.25

a. Respondents could choose more than one category.

Sources: Eckstrom, Ruth et al. (1987, p. 59); Rumberger, Russell (1983, p. 201)

that they had discipline problems in school (41 versus 16 percent) and to report that they had been suspended or put on probation from school within the last year (31 versus 10 percent) (Eckstrom et al., 1986).

This section has reviewed the findings from national surveys on the extent to which dropouts and graduates differ in their performance and engagement in school prior to dropping out. Most research, as illustrated in this section, has characterized dropouts by identifying differences in the characteristics of dropouts and graduates and by identifying which students are the most likely to drop out. A focus on "more than" or "less than," however, may erroneously lead to the conclusion that all youths who drop out after the tenth grade were doing very poorly in school and were in trouble in school prior to dropping out. Youths who are doing very poorly in high school and who are substantially disengaged from school are, not surprisingly, the most likely to drop out, partly because they may have already left school, albeit informally. For example, 70 percent of students in the High School and Beyond Survey who reported that they missed twenty-one days of school or more in the fall of their sophomore year later dropped out. But, these students were only 7.2 percent of dropouts in the survey (Frase, 1989).

When reviewing the high school characteristics of dropouts and graduates provided by the various surveys, I am often struck by how many different pictures can be painted with these summary statistics. As noted above, dropouts were more likely than graduates (41 versus 16 percent) to report that they had discipline problems in their sophomore year. This also means that 59 percent of dropouts reported that they did not have discipline problems in school prior to dropping out. Indeed, if instead of comparing dropouts to graduates, or identifying who is most at risk of dropping out, we asked what characterizes the "majority" of dropouts, we would find that, in their sophomore year: (1) 56.6 percent of dropouts reported that they had missed less than four days of non-illness related absences in the fall; (2) 60.3 percent of dropouts reported that they received mostly "B's and C's" or better in their sophomore year; and (3) 60 percent of dropouts reported that they were interested in school (Eckstrom et al., 1987; Frase, 1989). Thus, it is quite possible to misrepresent or misinterpret what the findings of these various surveys tell us about the average dropout even as late as the tenth grade. The reasons youths give for dropping out, and their school characteristics, clearly suggest that doing poorly in school lays the foundation for school disengagement and school withdrawal. Yet, the data from High School and Beyond does not support the notion that, by the tenth grade, the majority of dropouts have become so disengaged from school that their withdrawal is inevitable.

Why would youths who are encountering difficulty in school drop out? Table 2.1 presents the reasons students gave for leaving school in both the High School and Beyond Survey and the National Longitudinal Survey of Youth. The reasons they gave for dropping out suggest several other important factors, including early pregnancy and marriage, discipline problems, and economic responsibilities.

Early Pregnancy and Marriage

Marriage and parenting play a particularly important role in young women's decisions to drop out. When asked what was their primary reason for dropping out, over 30 percent of white and Hispanic females and 45 percent of black females cited pregnancy or marriage. The link between early parenting or marriage and school dropout goes in both directions. Young women who become pregnant and marry while in school are much less likely to graduate (Hayes, 1987). Those who drop out are also more likely to marry or become parents before age 20. Indeed, research has consistently found that doing poorly in school is a strong predictor of both school dropout and early parenting (Abrahamse et al., 1988).

Having a baby, becoming pregnant, or marrying significantly decreases a young woman's chances of graduating from high school, even when controlling for differences in family background, educational aspirations and motivation, and school performance (Hayes, 1987; Rumberger, 1983; Waite and Moore, 1978). Young men who marry or become parents are also more likely to drop out of high school, although their educational attainment is not affected as severely as that of young women (Fernandez et al., 1989; Rumberger, 1983; Voydanoff and Donnelly, 1990).

Importantly, the impact of parenting or marriage appears to be greatest when these events are accompanied by a more general transition to adult roles. For example, youths who give birth after age 16 are at a higher risk of dropping out than younger parents (Hayes, 1987). Young women who have a child after age 16 are more likely to be simultaneously making the transition to adult roles, including establishing independent households, marrying, or getting a job (Hayes, 1987). Each of these transitions would make it more difficult to combine parenting and schooling. In comparison, teenage mothers who live with their parents are both more likely to stay in school and to return to school after the birth of their child (Hayes, 1987; Voydanoff and Donnelly, 1990).

Discipline Problems

For males, discipline problems and conflicts with school personnel emerge as important factors in the decision to leave school. Males were more than twice as likely as females to report that not being able to get along with teachers contributed to their decision to drop out. Males were also much more likely to report that expulsion or suspension contributed to their decision to leave. Fully 18 percent of black males cited expulsion or suspension as their primary reason for leaving school. Black students, and in particular black males, are more likely to experience expulsion and suspension throughout their school careers. For example, research on Boston's middle schools found that black students were much more likely to be suspended from school and were more likely to attend schools that relied heavily on suspension policies (Massachusetts Advocacy Center, 1986). This study found that suspension rates differed dramatically across Boston's middle schools. In 1984–1985, as many as 31 percent of students in one Boston middle school were suspended, compared to a suspension rate of 1.7 in the middle school with the lowest reported number of suspensions (Massachusetts Advocacy Center, 1986).

Interviews with dropouts reveal that the 'decision' to drop out of school is often made by school systems, either through expulsion due to disciplinary problems, dismissal for inattendance, or a directive from guidance counselors or school administrators (Fine, 1987, 1991; Selinker and Martin, 1992). There has been little empirical research on what proportion of dropouts are involuntarily dismissed from school, or what proportion drop out by bureaucratic fiat (youths who are dropped from attendance registers for nonattendance). There has also been little research on the extent to which suspension, as a policy, may contribute to overall disengagement from school and school failure. As Michelle Fine points out, policies that send those students who are doing poorly in school home to miss class and to be unsupervised when they are showing signs of needing more direction and supervision may actually exacerbate these youths' difficulties (Fine, 1991).

Economic Responsibilities

For Hispanic youths, economic responsibilities appear to have an important influence on their educational decisions. In the National Longitudinal Survey, Hispanic males and females were as likely to cite economic responsibilities as school-related reasons as their primary reason for leaving high school.

Regardless of ethnicity, students who drop out are more likely to be focusing on work while in school. Youths who drop out are not more likely to work while in high school than those who later graduate (Barro and Kolstad, 1987). Students who dropped out did, however, work more hours in their sophomore year than those who later graduated. Early school leavers were also much more likely to report that they found their sophomore year job more enjoyable than school (66 versus 54 percent) and were more than twice as likely (23 versus 10 percent) to report that their sophomore year job was more important to them than school (Eckstrom et al., 1987).

Research has found that working more than ten hours per week places adolescents at a higher risk of early school leaving even when controlling for family background, school performance, measured achievement, and other background characteristics (Barro and Kolstad, 1987). These findings suggest that part-time work while in high school may impair a youth's chances of graduating if he or she is trying to balance the competing roles of worker and student. For example, one study found that the number of hours a student worked was strongly associated with a student's grade point average (Steinberg et al., 1982). This study also found that part of the lower GPA of youths who worked long hours could be explained by the fact that they were absent more often from school, spent less time on homework, and reported that they enjoyed school less.

The results presented in this section are not surprising. By the tenth grade, students who will later drop out of school are, on average, having difficulties in school and look substantially worse than graduates on measures of achievement, performance, and involvement in school. Dropouts are very likely to point to these poor school experiences as their reason for leaving school. The findings presented in this section also suggest that adolescents who are prematurely making the transition to adult roles, as measured by hours worked, marriage, and parenting, face an increased risk of dropping out. For females, marriage and parenting play a central role in the decision to leave school. Males are more likely to cite their dislike of school, discipline problems, and conflicts with school personnel as ingredients in their decision to leave school. Finally, Hispanic youths of both sexes were much more likely to cite economic responsibilities as their primary reason for leaving school.

THE INFLUENCE OF FAMILY BACKGROUND

In *Schooling Disadvantaged Children: Racing Against Catastrophe*, Gary Natriello and his fellow authors define a youth as educationally disadvantaged if he or she has "been exposed to insufficient education" in either formal schooling, at home, or in the community (Natriello et al., 1990, p. 13). This section briefly summarizes what previous research can tell us about the manner in which a youth's family background influences the chances that he or she will drop out of school.

Youths from disadvantaged and poor families are more likely to encounter early problems in school, to be retained in grade early in their school career, and to fall behind in school as they get older. For example, a recent study in the Baltimore public schools found that the gap in math achievement between black and white children increased from 6 to 14 points from the first to the third grade (Entwistle and Alexander, 1992). This gap did not develop because black children learned less during the school year. Black children, children from households where their parent(s) did not graduate from high school, and children from single parent families in this study learned as much or more during the school year as children from other households. Rather, much of the learning gap between black and white children could be attributed to differential learning that occurred over the summer months—ground that was not made up during the school year. Doris Entwistle and Karl Alexander found, moreover, that the learning gap between black and white children could be largely attributed to differences in the income, parental education, and family composition of these students' families.

Adolescents may also be educationally disadvantaged if they do not receive encouragement to complete high school and if their parents do not monitor their education. In one study, Rumberger found that an important difference between students who were doing poorly in school and dropped out and those who were doing poorly and remained was the extent to which both the student and his or her parents were involved in the child's education and educational decisions (Rumberger et al., 1990). Children from disadvantaged families may be less involved in their education because they are not receiving encouragement and parental monitoring. They may also be less involved in their education because they are more likely to be balancing competing roles between home and school. For example, Fine found that children from poor families and, in particular, children from immigrant families, often miss school because they are needed in the home to assist their families (Fine, 1985).

In sum, research on the influence of family background on both school performance and the decision to drop out suggests that youths from disadvantaged families bring to school an array of characteristics that place them at a greater risk of early school leaving. In the High School and Beyond Survey, youths from families in the lowest socioeconomic quartile were more than three times as likely to drop out of school as those from families in the highest socioeconomic quartile. Youths from poor families, those whose parents did not graduate from high school, those from single parent families, and those from larger families are more likely to encounter problems in school, and are more likely to drop out (Bachman et al., 1971; Barro and Kolstad, 1987; Eckstrom et al., 1987; Hill, 1979; Howell and Frese, 1982; Lerman, 1972; Mare, 1980; McLanahan and Bumpass, 1988; Rumberger, 1983; Sandefur et al., 1989; Steinberg et al., 1984; Shaw, 1982; Waite and Moore, 1978). Early school leaving is also more common among youths who reside in urban areas, especially in the central city (Borus and Carpenter, 1983; Lerman, 1972; Masters, 1969; Rumberger, 1983).

The Rumberger study cited above illustrates a general finding in the literature on the influence of family background: the educational environment in the home is the most important determinant of whether a youth will graduate from high school. Across studies, parental education, measures of the presence of reading material in the home, a parent's educational expectations for his or her child, and the degree to which parents monitor their child's education have comparatively the largest and most consistent impacts on the probability of dropping out across all race and sex groups (Eckstrom et al., 1987; Howell and Frese, 1982; Rumberger, 1983; Rumberger et al., 1990; Sandefur et al., 1989; Waite and Moore, 1978). In the High School and Beyond Survey, for example, sophomores whose mothers did not graduate from high school were twice as likely to drop out as sophomores whose mothers graduated from high school but did not go on to college (Barro and Kolstad, 1987).

Parents who have graduated from high school may be more equipped to provide educational support for their child in the home. These parents may also be more likely to emphasize high school graduation. Frank Howell and Wolfgang Frese's longitudinal study of fourth- and fifth-graders found strong evidence that youths whose parents emphasized high school graduation were more likely to graduate, even when controlling for early school performance and achievement, such as IQ; later educational outcomes, such as high school grade point average; and, a youth's family background characteristics (Howell and Frese, 1982). This study also found that a mother's educational expectations for her child, parental encouragement to complete high school, the frequency of parental discussion about dropping out of school, and a youth's academic motivation were all significantly associated with the probability of graduation from high school.

Young adults from single parent families face a substantially higher risk of early school leaving. In the High School and Beyond Survey, for example, sophomores from female-headed families were over 60 percent more likely to drop out than sophomores from families where both parents lived in the home (Barro and Kolstad, 1987). Much, but not all, of this difference can be attributed to other differences in the characteristics of single parent versus dual parent households, such as low family income and low educational attainment (McLanahan, 1985; Sandefur et al., 1989). Yet, after controlling for income, parents' occupation and education, and other background characteristics, youths from single parent families in the High School and Beyond Survey were still 28 percent more likely to drop out than students from dual parent households (Barro and Kolstad, 1987).

Research on school dropout has found that most of the racial and ethnic variation in dropout rates can be attributed to differences in family background (Barro and Kolstad, 1987; Fernandez et al., 1989; Rumberger, 1983). Differences in parental education explain much of the gap in dropout rates between whites and Hispanics, while differences in parental education and family structure can account for the gap in dropout rates between whites and blacks (Sandefur et al., 1989). Black young adults are more likely to graduate from high school than whites when controlling for family background and tested achievement (Barro and Kolstad, 1987; Rumberger, 1983).

Finally, many Hispanic youths face an increased risk of dropping out because they are more likely to be immigrants to the United States and are more likely to come from homes where English is not the primary language, both of which are associated with higher rates of early school leaving (Rumberger, 1983). In general, research has found it is a youth's own English proficiency that is the important factor in early school leaving, and not the result of coming from a non-English speaking household per se (Fernandez et al., 1989; Steinberg et al., 1984).

THE INFLUENCE OF SCHOOL ORGANIZATION AND POLICY

The type of family a youth grows up in has an important influence on educational attainment. Recent evidence from the High School and Beyond Survey suggests that which high school a youth attends may also have an important impact on the chances that he or she will graduate. The High School and Beyond Survey improved upon earlier surveys by including information on the extent to which dropout rates differ across high schools. Analyses of these data have found that dropout rates are higher in larger schools, in public versus Catholic schools, and in urban schools (Barro and Kolstad, 1987; Bryk and Thum, 1989). Dropout rates are also, on average, lower in schools where students feel safe, where students report that there is a high school spirit, and where students and principals report that their teachers are committed (Bryk and Thum, 1989).

The more students in a school who are at risk of school leaving, the higher the school's dropout rate is likely to be. Dropout rates are higher in schools that serve a higher proportion of youths from low socioeconomic backgrounds. Dropout rates are also higher in schools in which a greater number of students have discipline problems, a greater number of pupils have academic difficulty, and there is less interest in school among the student body (Bryk and Thum, 1989).

One of the most surprising findings from the High School and Beyond Survey is that dropout rates are, on average, higher when there is a greater degree of differentiation within the school. Analysis of the High School and Beyond Survey has found that schools in which there is a greater variance across the student body in socioeconomic background, academic performance, student engagement, and concentration in academic courses have higher dropout rates (Bryk and Thum, 1989).

Anthony Bryk and Yeow Meng Thum, in a seminal paper analyzing the High School and Beyond data set, examined how these school characteristics affected a youth's individual likelihood of dropping out, when controlling for an individual's school performance and background characteristics (Bryk and Thum, 1989). Bryk and Thum found that low SES students are more likely to drop out if they attend larger schools, primarily because larger schools are more problematic environments. In particular, the researchers find that larger schools have more discipline problems, are schools where students feel less safe, are schools where there is a low degree of staff commitment, and, importantly, are schools where there is a high degree of tracking—measured by the level of academic differentiation within the school.

PIMP

In sum, Bryk and Thum's analysis suggests that the academic environment of a school may have an important impact on a youth's chances of graduating. Their analysis finds that when a student who is at risk of early school leaving attends a school that is safe, has committed staff, has high student and staff morale, and has a curriculum that focuses on academic instruction, she or he is more likely to graduate. Unfortunately, it is difficult to sort out the cause and effect of school climate. Does low teacher morale contribute to higher dropout rates? Or, as some researchers suggest, does teaching in schools where there are large numbers of students at risk, where there are many discipline problems, and where students do not care about their studies cause teachers to give up (Firestone and Rosenblum, 1988)? Regardless of cause and effect, Bryk and Thum, as well as other researchers, have found strong evidence that large high schools, particularly urban public high schools, are difficult environments that have negative influences on student outcomes (Garbarino, 1980; Newmann, 1989; Pittman and Haughwort, 1987).

An important finding is that students who are educationally at risk stand a greater chance of dropping out if they attend schools that have a high degree of academic and socioeconomic differentiation. One interpretation of this finding is that in schools that are characterized by high degrees of academic differentiation, at-risk youths are given less attention. Lower performing students may also receive fewer resources in large diverse high schools because they are more likely to be placed in nonacademic tracks (Bryk and Thum, 1989; Lee and Eckstrom, 1987; Oakes, 1985, 1992). For example, Valerie Lee and Ruth Eckstrom, in an analysis of the High School and Beyond data, found that students in noncollege tracks were less likely to have access to a guidance counselor in planning their courses and post-high school plans (Lee and Eckstrom, 1987).

Students in noncollege tracks are also more likely to drop out. In the High School and Beyond Survey, the dropout rate for sophomores enrolled in vocational programs was 19.7 percent, compared to 16.6 percent in the general program and 5.8 percent in academic programs (Barro and Kolstad, 1987). Despite a great deal of recent emphasis on tracking, there has been little definitive research on the extent to which tracking policies in middle schools and high schools influence a student's likelihood of withdrawal. One review of the literature concluded that these differences in dropout rates across educational programs can generally be attributed to differences in the characteristics of students in general, vocational, and preparatory tracks (Weber, 1986; Weber and Sechler, 1986).

To Bryk and his fellow researchers, the findings from High School and Beyond suggest that the degree to which a school operates as a community has an important impact on the chances that a youth will decide to remain a member of that community (Bryk and Driscoll, 1988). Qualitative research on early school leaving also suggests that when large high schools operate several different communities, students who are from disadvantaged backgrounds may be at risk of feeling isolated and marginal.

QUALITATIVE RESEARCH ON SCHOOL DROPOUT: TOWARD A THEORY OF STUDENT WITHDRAWAL

In *Leaving College: Rethinking the Causes and Cures of Student Attrition*, Vincent Tinto developed a theory of student departure from college that provides a framework with which to understand how doing poorly in school, particularly for youths from disadvantaged backgrounds, may lead to disengagement and then to the decision to withdraw. Tinto posits that a youth's likelihood of dropping out of college is determined by how strongly that student develops an attachment to the school as an academic and social institution (Tinto, 1987). A student's level of attachment, according to Tinto, is initially influenced by goals prior to entry. After a student enrolls in college, however, attachment to the institution is largely determined by a student's social and academic interactions with the school community. Positive interactions foster membership and attachment, while negative interactions produce alienation and raise the likelihood of withdrawal. Tinto goes further to argue that youths become at risk of experiencing alienation and withdrawal when they encounter one of four barriers to school membership: difficulty in adjustment; academic difficulty; incongruence or a mismatch between a student's perceived needs and interests and those of the institution; and, finally, feelings of isolation.

Middle school and high school participation is different in several important ways from participation in college. Attendance in high school is not voluntary until students become legally eligible to leave school. Most students do not choose the high school they attend. And, academic performance in high school does not, for the most part, carry with it the possibility of dismissal for academic incompetence.

Despite these differences, the qualitative literature on early school leaving provides evidence that Tinto's framework applies equally well to the case of the high school dropout. Tinto's model, particularly the concept of incongruence, allows us to integrate the various areas of research presented in this chapter. In particular, qualitative research on school dropout allows us to develop an understanding of the interactive process by which difficulty in school, particularly for those from disadvantaged backgrounds, would lead youths to leave a community of which they have decided they are not members.

Both the characteristics of dropouts and the reasons they give for leaving school suggest that academic failure and frustration is a primary reason for dropping out of school. In interviews with school dropouts, the most frequently cited school-related reasons for leaving school were boredom and not being able to accumulate credits needed for graduation (Tidwell, 1988). Case studies find that a common thread in dropouts' school careers are cumulative records of poor school experiences, which then lay the basis for other difficulties (Fine, 1987; Reich and Young, 1975).

But, few leave school simply on the basis of self-imposed academic dismissal. Indeed, the literature on early school leaving suggests that central to the process of school withdrawal is the development of incongruence between a youth's perceived needs and interests and those offered by continued education. Incongruence, as presented by Tinto:

refers to the general mismatch or lack of fit between the needs, interests and preferences of the individual and those of the institution . . . it springs from individual perceptions of not fitting into and/or being at odds with the social and intellectual fabric of institutional life. (Tinto, 1987, pp. 53–54)

Tinto argues that a youth may experience several forms of incongruence. Incongruence may arise because of a mismatch between the returns to continued schooling and a student's goals and expectations. Incongruence may also arise because the student feels marginal and isolated either socially or academically. Finally, a youth may experience incongruence because of role conflicts between school and his or her external communities. Students belong both to the school community and to an external community of home and family, both of which place demands and expectations on youth. Tinto notes that it is those from disadvantaged backgrounds who are most likely to be balancing several competing roles, and thus who are most vulnerable to experiencing this form of incongruence.

These three elements of incongruence—a goals/schooling incongruity, isolation and marginality, and role conflicts—are a central theme in qualitative research on school dropouts. Dropouts often perceive that the economic and personal benefits to continued schooling are minimal (Alpert and Dunham, 1986; Farrell, 1990; Fine, 1987, 1991; Reich and Young, 1975; Tidwell, 1988). Carol Reich and Vivienne Young argue that approximately 53 percent of dropouts could be defined as "work oriented" (Reich and Young, 1975). When compared to 'classic dropouts,' "whose withdrawal from school is merely a retreat from an unpleasant situation," 'work oriented dropouts' "have conceptualized an alternative life style they judge to be more compatible with their interests and abilities" (Reich and Young, 1975, pp. 7–8). Research on the influence of home environment would suggest that students who do not receive encouragement to complete high school or who do not receive parental monitoring of their education are more likely to perceive that there are few rewards to staying in school (Rumberger et al., 1990). This goals/schooling incongruity may also develop if young adults find the pedagogy and content of classroom learning irrelevant to their lives (Fine, 1987; Tidwell, 1988; Whelage et al., 1989).

A second form of incongruence arises when youths feel marginal to and isolated from the social and intellectual life of the school. When asked what was the worst features of their high school, dropouts in Romeria Tidwell's study most often cited boring and uncaring teachers and crowded classrooms (Tidwell, 1988). When asked for recommendations for high schools, these dropouts most often cited the need for more attention to the students, particularly those with academic difficulties. Dropouts' suggestions for improvements included: "teachers should give more assistance with math and reading and to students who have problems"; "help students with low grades"; and "I need for my teacher to teach and interact with me rather than just hand out material for me to read" (Tidwell, 1988, p. 951). In addition, dropouts in this study argued for better and more accessible counseling.

Bryk and Thum's analysis of the High School and Beyond Survey suggests that youths who are doing poorly in school may be particularly at risk of feeling isolated and marginal when they attend schools in which teachers are seen by their students as less responsive and caring. Tracking in high schools may also lead youths to feel that they are marginal to the intellectual life of the school (Bryk and Thum, 1989). Fine notes that isolation and marginality arise in large bureaucratic high school settings (Fine, 1985, 1987). Fine found that in large urban high schools youths are routinely discharged for nonattendance. Students' personal problems, moreover, are often ignored or treated as issues of discipline or inattendance (Fine, 1985, 1987). For example, Fine describes the case of Jose who gave his reason for leaving as: "I live with my grandmother and she just came out of the hospital for triple bypass in her heart. Now she needs a balloon put in. I can't concentrate and got to help her." In contrast, Jose's guidance counselor explained the cause for his leaving as "Jose got overinvolved and was irresponsible about his own education" (Fine, 1987, p. 96). Jose, however, was not asked by the attendance officer why he was withdrawing from school.

Fine's qualitative research supports Tinto's notion that youths from disadvantaged backgrounds are often balancing several competing roles—a balancing act that may lead to incongruity between the demands and expectations of a student's school and a student's external community. This balancing act arises from the lives of disadvantaged students who, as we have seen, are more likely to be making early transitions to adult roles. It also arises because school administrators and personnel, like Jose's guidance counselor, are not oriented toward helping youths overcome barriers to school membership (Whelage et al., 1989). Teenage parents are obviously the most at risk of experiencing incongruity between schooling and their external environment. In addition, many youths at risk of dropping out, like Jose, are often engaged in adult roles with significant familial responsibilities outside of school, whether it be caring for a sick relative, acting as a translator, or taking care of siblings (Fine, 1987).

In summation, qualitative research on school dropout suggests that adolescents who are educationally disadvantaged at home and at school face an increased risk of experiencing incongruities that weaken their attachment to school. As described in the literature, youths who have done poorly in school, and particularly those who are assuming adult roles outside of school, develop a sense that continued schooling does not meet their needs. Dropping out, as described in this literature, is an act of rejecting membership in a community in which a youth feels marginal, gains little self-esteem, perceives the institution as offering few rewards, and which she or he experiences as personally rejecting them.

CONCLUSION

This chapter attempted to synthesize what the large body of quantitative and qualitative research on school dropout could tell us about the nature of early school leaving. This literature has provided school systems with a detailed set of characteristics that can and are used to identify those students who are at risk of early school leaving. Youths who are doing poorly in school, who are showing signs of disengagement from school, who are in conflict with school authorities, and who repeated grades previous to high school are highly at risk of dropping out. Those students who are prematurely making the transition to adult roles either through work, marriage, or parenting are also more likely to leave school. And, finally, research on the effect of family background finds that youths from poor families, those from single parent families, and those whose parents did not graduate from high school face an increased risk of experiencing difficulty in school and of dropping out.

Qualitative research on school dropouts, moreover, provides a framework with which to understand why those who are at risk of early school leaving in high school would decide to leave school rather than to continue on to graduate in the bottom of their class. Specifically, Tinto's theory of school withdrawal helps us to understand the interactive process whereby poor educational outcomes, as well as social and economic disadvantage, influence school membership and lead to the decision to withdraw. Empirical research has also found that the degree to which high schools operate as communities, and thus promote membership, has an important influence on educational outcomes for at-risk youths.

What the current literature cannot tell us, however, is how dropouts and graduates arrived at such disparate points in their level of school performance and engagement in school. One reading of this literature is that the manner by which school systems respond to a student's poor school performance and disengagement may have an important influence on his or her chances of dropping out. To what extent do school systems' discipline policies in middle schools and high schools, grade retention policies, or reliance on tracking contribute to academic failure or inhibit school attachment? Does moving to larger high school settings have negative effects on youths at risk of becoming high school dropouts? As discussed previously, these questions have been largely unaddressed because of the lack of data on the school experiences of dropouts and graduates prior to the tenth grade. It is to these questions that we now turn.

Chapter 3

Examining the Relationship Between School Experiences and School Dropout: The Fall River Study

Previous research has clearly shown that the school experiences of dropouts reflect an array of poor educational outcomes. By the tenth grade, youths who will later drop out of school are, on average, doing poorly in school, are more likely than graduates to report having discipline problems and lower attendance, and are more likely than graduates to have repeated grades previous to high school. For policymakers, these comparisons raise several questions: What role did a youth's school experiences play in the development of this poor performance and disengagement from school? Are the differences between dropouts and graduates that we observe at the tenth grade reflected throughout their school careers? Are there critical points during which the school career paths of dropouts and graduates diverge? And, how do grade retention policies, curriculum tracking, or aspects of the organization of schools influence the chances that a youth will drop out? The purpose of the Fall River study is to address these questions through an analysis of the school experiences of one cohort of youths. This chapter describes the Fall River data set and the general methodological and statistical approach that will be used in the chapters that follow.

The next three chapters present the findings with regard to overall trends in school career paths of dropouts and graduates; the impact of a youth's experiences following the school transitions to middle school and to high school on later school outcomes; and the association between grade retention and early school leaving. More broadly, we want to explore the degree of evidence for three alternative policy perspectives regarding school-based dropout prevention efforts. This chapter begins with a discussion of these three perspectives and what they predict we would find when the relationship between school experiences and dropping out is examined.

EXAMINING THE RELATIONSHIP BETWEEN SCHOOL EXPERIENCES AND EARLY SCHOOL LEAVING: THREE PERSPECTIVES

How should we think about the relationship between school experiences and dropping out? The findings presented in the previous chapter can be interpreted in several different ways. One reading is that youths do poorly in school and drop out largely because of what happens at home and not because of what happens at school. The focus of this first perspective, explained most eloquently by Chester Finn, is that dropping out may be school-related but not school-caused. Finn poses the question:

Are we sure that the primary forces leading young people to drop out are rooted in the school or school system rather than in the young people themselves, in their personal environment, or in trends and developments in the larger society? Do we know how to alter those forces? . . . To the degree that dropping out is caused by factors beyond the school's control, the symptom is not likely to be eradicated by school based remedies. Insofar as it is a manifestation of linked social pathologies and inherited characteristics, it is more like 'going on welfare' or 'committing a crime' than like the commonplace problems of school effectiveness. (Finn, 1987, pp. 14–15)

To advocates of this perspective, the path to dropping out begins when students from educationally disadvantaged families enter school. These youths do poorly in school and are more likely to fail grades early in their school careers. In adolescence, dropouts begin to get in trouble both in and out of school and, without the necessary support and guidance from home, end up withdrawing. Indeed, the results of the Baltimore study presented in the previous chapter could easily be taken as evidence that schools are doing their job for poor children. This first perspective, then, would argue that dropout prevention efforts that aim to change the in-school experiences of youths would do little to affect the likelihood that a student will drop out. Improving poor children's chances of school success may require expanding the scope of school involvement rather than reforming current practices.

A second perspective on the relationship between school experiences and dropping out would argue that the lack of educational motivation and support that at-risk youths receive in school has as much of an influence on their educational outcomes as their educationally disadvantaged position at home. As we saw in the previous chapter, the literature on school dropout provides some evidence that the manner in which school systems respond to the problems faced by at-risk youths may have an important influence on their later outcomes. A second interpretation, then, is that a student's propensity to leave school is influenced by family background, by cumulative and persistent school failure, and by the inattention and unresponsiveness of school systems to the complex array of problems faced by disadvantaged youths. In this framework, the act of dropping out is the manifestation of a nest of problems including poor school experiences. For example, Dale Mann argues:

The singular outcome—not finishing high school—is in fact a nest of problems. Most students quit because of the compounded impact of, for example, being poor, growing up in a broken home, having been held back in the fourth grade, and finally having slugged 'Mr. Fairlee,' the school's legendary vice-principal for enforcement. These young people need a range of things, just as any system's at-risk population will need services that fit their hurts. If the problem is complex, so will be the solution. (Mann, 1986, p. 7)

Mann's quote illustrates a common theme in the literature on school dropout. Dropping out is most often portrayed as a cumulative process whereby persistent and escalating school failure leads to disengagement and to the decision to drop out. There has been little empirical investigation of whether the path to dropping out takes the form of a slow and steady deterioration in academic performance or whether there are critical points during which the academic processes that lead to dropping out initiate or accelerate. This second perspective would portray the path to dropping out as an individualized phenomenon based on the progression and interplay of school failure, a youth's individual circumstances, and a youth's interaction with the school environment, the timing and nature of which will vary from youth to youth. One student may drop out because of difficulty adjusting to the school system as an immigrant, often staying at home to translate for parents, and the greater rewards of an after school job. Another student may drop out because balancing the competing roles of student and parent in a school with no day care facility is difficult.

A third perspective on the relationship between school experiences and school dropout focuses on the degree to which the individual manifestations of a student's disengagement and the academic processes that lead to school withdrawal can be linked to, and are influenced by, the structure, organization, and policies of schools. Simply put, the cumulative nature of poor school experiences may not be solely individualized. Rather, there may be critical points during which students are more likely to encounter academic difficulties or during which the various manifestations of disengagement from school are most likely to develop. According to this view, while a youth's propensity to leave school may be largely influenced by background characteristics and individual circumstance, specific school policies or the current institutional design of schools may directly exacerbate the academic and engagement problems of at-risk youths. Recent research in adolescent development has focused on the middle school years as a critical period in the formation of attachment to school. Many educators in this field argue that the current structure of middle schools and junior high schools does not meet the developmental needs of at-risk youths (Carnegie Council on Adolescent Development, 1990). Similarly, opponents of school systems' grade retention policies argue that this school experience negatively influences a student's later school performance and/or school engagement.

These three interpretations of the literature on early school leaving do not offer mutually exclusive answers to the question: What is the relationship between school experiences and early school leaving? Large, bureaucratic high schools may be less able to deal with a youth's individual circumstances. Being retained in grade may increase the chances that a youth will drop out, even if most of the variation in early school leaving could be attributed to family background characteristics. And, making schools more responsive to the needs of adolescents may mean compensating for the lack of guidance and support for education received at home. Different interpretations of the role school experiences play in determining a youth's school outcomes, however, imply quite different policy directions. Each of these interpretations would also predict very different relationships between progressive school experiences and school dropout.

For example, advocates of the first perspective would argue that a student's poor school performance and whether a reaction to that poor school performance is to act out and decide to leave has very little to do with school policy or what happens in school. If this portrayal accurately portrays the path to dropping out then we would expect that knowledge of that student's family characteristics, ability, and motivation to complete school would tell us as much about his or her chances of dropping out, as would knowledge of how that poor school performance developed as she or he moved through the school system. On the other hand, if school experiences do matter, then whether students are recommended for retention or for participation in a remedial program, whether they are called when absent, or whether there is day care available in the school will play an important role in determining the chances of them staying in school.

An important question, however, is to what extent dropouts' poor school experiences can be linked to aspects of the organization and policy of schools. As discussed above, advocates of the second perspective emphasize that the path to dropping out is different for every youth.

The common element in dropouts' school experiences is not a particular event but a cumulative history of poor school performance, exacerbated by unresponsive institutional policies. If dropping out is solely an individualized phenomenon, we would expect to find a lot of variance in the school antecedents to dropping out. We would also not expect that any single event would emerge as more predictive than any other.

Advocates of the third perspective would argue that a youth's disengagement from school and the academic processes that lead to dropping out can be linked to aspects of school structure and policy. This perspective would predict that, when controlling for background characteristics, specific school experiences would have an independent impact on the chances that a youth would drop out. For example, if the size of a school has an important influence on the school performance and attachment of at-risk youths, then we would expect that dropouts would experience an increase in academic and adjustment difficulties when they moved to the larger and more complex institutions of middle schools and high schools. Similarly, if grade retention policies harm students' chances of graduation, then we would expect to find that nonpromoted students face an increase in the risk of dropping out even when controlling for differences in the school performance of retained and promoted youths.

We can begin to test the degree of evidence for these three perspectives by asking two general questions. First, what do trends in the school career paths of dropouts and graduates tell us about how school performance and disengagement develop over the course of a youth's school career? And, second, is there evidence that elements of school organization or practices have an independent impact on the chances that a youth will drop out? A partial list of such institutional variables that have been associated with either dropping out directly or with having disproportionate impact on youths academically at risk would include school policies, such as those regarding grade retention, discipline, and attendance; aspects of school organization, such as curriculum tracking; and institutional characteristics, such as school transitions and high school size (Barro and Kolstad, 1987; Becker, 1987; Bryck and Driscoll, 1988; Felner et al., 1981; Fine, 1991; Garbarino, 1980; Pittman and Haughwort, 1987; Massachusetts Advocacy Center, 1986, 1988). The Fall River data set allows us to examine how two of these school experiences—grade retention and the stress of the school moves to middle school and to high school—influence the likelihood that a youth will drop out.

Grade retention is one of the strongest correlates of early school leaving. This association has often been taken as evidence that a school system's policies of retaining students places them at a higher risk of dropping out. The Fall River data set, described in the next

section, affords a unique opportunity to explore the association between grade retention and school dropout. It provides detailed data
on the timing and incidence of retention throughout students' school
careers. I examine how much of the association between grade retention and school dropout can be explained by differences in the pre-
and postretention performance of retained and promoted youths, and
the extent to which the impact of retention may differ by the number
of times a student is retained, or by the grade in which she or he is
retained. I also investigate how much of the association between
grade retention and school dropout can be explained by an effect of
being overage for grade.

Previous empirical research on school dropout has primarily concen-
trated on identifying school and personal characteristics that predict poor
school performance and poor school outcomes. There has been little
empirical research, however, on identifying the intermediate processes
whereby a student's attributes interact with the institutional climate and
organization of schools to produce these different outcomes. As we
found in the previous chapter, Bryk and Thum's empirical findings on
the organizational characteristics of high schools suggest that how high
schools are organized may make it easier or harder for lower performing
students and those from disadvantaged backgrounds. Similarly, the
qualitative literature on school dropouts suggests that an important element in the process by which poor school performance translates into
school withdrawal is the extent to which students who are performing
poorly in school, and particularly those from disadvantaged backgrounds, experience isolation and disengagement from school.

The moves from elementary schools to middle and junior high schools
and from these middle level schools to high school are central and important events in a youth's school career. At each of these transitions,
students move to larger and more complex environments where they
encounter a new social structure and face new academic demands. Research in adolescent development has focused on these transitions as
periods where students encounter academic and adjustment difficulties.
In the context of qualitative research on school dropouts, the ability of
youths to successfully maneuver these school transitions may also have
an important impact on their chances of graduating.

The Fall River data set allows us to trace the school career paths of
dropouts and graduates both between and during the transitions to
middle school and high school. In addition, I examine how a student's
performance following a normative school change is associated with the
likelihood of early school leaving. Before discussing the general methodological approach and measures that will be used to examine the
impact of both school transitions and grade retention, the next section
describes the Fall River data set.

THE DATA SET

Data for this study were collected from school transcript information on students who comprised the Fall River, Massachusetts, public school's seventh-grade class of 1980–1981. The cohort was initially identified from seventh-grade home room registers. Detailed transcript data were collected for each youth from fourth grade to dropout, transfer, or graduation. Yearly transcript data included school in attendance, courses, course grades, grade retentions, and, if reported, attendance. A limited number of family background characteristics and grade failures previous to the fourth grade were also recorded. Attendance and background data were not available for the majority of students who dropped out prior to the ninth grade.

Data were collected on 757 students, approximately 90 percent of dropouts and 95 percent of graduates in the initial cohort. Thirty-five percent of the initial cohort dropped out of school before receiving a high school diploma, while 38 percent graduated and 22 percent transferred to another school system. The remainder of this section describes the Fall River public school system, the Fall River data set, and the cohort and sample composition in greater detail.

School System Characteristics and Organization

Fall River, Massachusetts, is a small, urban city of slightly over ninety thousand residents. In the 1980 census, Fall River had the lowest median educational level (8.8 years) and the lowest per capita income in Massachusetts. In 1980, only 35.5 percent of Fall River residents over 25 had high school diplomas, compared to a state average of 72.7 percent. These low levels of educational attainment are partially due to the large influx of Portuguese immigrants to the Southeastern Massachusetts area since the mid–1960s, the third such wave of Portuguese migration to the area. In 1980, 14.8 percent of Fall River's families lived below the poverty line; 44.1 percent of families had incomes below $10,000.

The Fall River public school system is comprised of twenty-eight grammar schools, four middle schools serving grades 6 to 8, and one comprehensive high school. Most students in this study made the transition to middle school in the sixth grade and the transition to high school in the ninth grade. Youths from eight grammar schools, or approximately 20 percent of the sample, remained in their grammar school in the sixth grade and made the transition to middle school in the seventh grade. Fall River adopted two different grading arrangements in response to parental concern that some students lived too far away from the new middle schools and should be one year older before making this school move.[1]

The Fall River school system serves approximately 12,000 students, 60 percent of whom are identified by the school system as low income. One-third of students in the Fall River public schools are ethnic or racial minorities, 72 percent of whom are Portuguese immigrants or students whose first language is Portuguese.

Cohort Definition and Cohort Outcomes

The cohort, identified through home room registers, was defined as all students who were enrolled in the seventh grade in one of Fall River's four middle schools at the beginning of the 1980–1981 school year.[2] Students enrolled in special education, nongraded classrooms, were excluded.

One thousand and fifty-two youths were enrolled in the seventh-grade class at the beginning of the 1980–1981 school year. Students were coded as dropouts, transfers, or graduates based on the information recorded on their permanent record.[3]

Table 3.1 shows outcome measures for the initial cohort and for the sample of students for whom school transcript data were collected. Approximately 35 percent of the initial cohort dropped out of school before receiving a high school diploma, while 38 percent graduated and 22 percent transferred to another school system.[4] Outcomes were not determined for 5 percent of the initial cohort.[5] Slightly over 20 percent of dropouts left school in the seventh or eighth grade while an additional 12.5 percent dropped out in the transition to or during the first year of high school. Early school leavers were then relatively evenly disbursed among tenth-, eleventh-, and twelfth-grade dropouts (see Table 3.1).

Data Collection

Detailed transcript data were recorded for each youth from the fourth grade to dropout, graduation, or transfer. The Fall River public school system maintained two transcript cards for each youth: a middle school card and a life card. The life card, or the permanent school transcript, recorded information on the data of entry into the school system, school in attendance, grades, and courses for each year. The middle schools maintained a second transcript card. This middle school card recorded life card data, attendance, and some family background information. Whenever possible, I recorded information from the middle school card. This transcript information included place of birth, parents' places of birth, parents' occupations, number of siblings, date of entry into the school system, and a youth's incidence of retention from kindergarten to third grade. Transcript data for each year included school, courses, course grades, grade retentions, and, if reported, attendance. Dropout and transfer codes, class rank, and year of graduation, school leaving,

Table 3.1
Cohort and Sample Composition: Fall River Data Set

	COHORT N	%	SAMPLE N	%	% of Cohort Entered
TOTAL	1052		757		71.96%
Total Non-Transfers Nonmissing	767		716		93.35%
Dropouts	368	34.98%	329	43.46%	89.40%
Middle school drops	86	8.17%	75	9.91%	87.21%
High school drops	282	26.81%	254	33.55%	90.07%
Graduates	399	37.93%	378	49.93%	94.74%
Transfers	230	21.86%	51	6.74%	22.17%
Local high schools	133	12.64%	19	2.51%	14.28%
Other school systems	97	9.22%	32	4.23%	32.29%
Missing Outcomes	55	5.23%	0	0	0

Distribution of Dropouts by Grade of Withdrawal

	Percent of Dropouts
Seventh and Eighth	22.56%
Ninth	12.50
Tenth	22.26
Eleventh	23.48
Twelfth	19.21

or transfer were recorded for each youth. IQ and achievement test data were rarely reported on a student's transcript. Data on disciplinary infractions and ability grouping in the middle schools were also not reported.

If the middle school card was unavailable, transcript data were obtained from the life card.[6] Middle school cards were not available for middle school dropouts, students who transferred prior to the ninth grade, and some high school dropouts and graduates. Specifically, attendance and background data were unavailable for middle school dropouts and were missing for slightly over 20 percent of high school dropouts and graduates.[7]

EXAMINING TRENDS IN THE SCHOOL PERFORMANCE AND ENGAGEMENT OF DROPOUTS AND GRADUATES: MEASURES

The Fall River data set provides an important opportunity to enrich our understanding of the nature and dynamics of school dropout by providing previously unavailable data on the middle school and early high school antecedents to early school leaving. A first step is to compare the school careers of dropouts and graduates. The next chapter describes trends in the school performance of dropouts and graduates on the basis of four summary measures of school performance: (1) mean academic grades, (2) mean social grades, (3) attendance, and (4) the incidence of grade retention.

The qualitative literature on school dropout distinguishes between academic performance and school engagement. A grade point average is the most commonly used measure of how well a student does in school. Attendance is the most obvious measure of school participation and engagement. In this study, I have disaggregated a youth's grade point average into two measures of school performance: mean academic grades and mean social grades. A mean academic grade is defined as the average grade a youth received each year in reading, math, geography or history, science, English, and foreign language, if taken, measured on a 0 to 4.0 scale. These mean academic grades are intended to measure a youth's academic performance.

A youth's grades in courses such as physical education or art may measure something quite different than academic ability and performance, particularly during the grammar school and middle school years. Grades in these courses may measure a student's attitude, level of cooperation, engagement, and effort in school. In elementary and middle school, in particular, the grade a child receives in courses such as art most likely reflects a teacher's assessment of his or her attitude in class. Good performance in these courses could reflect an attachment to a particular teacher or subject, while poor performance may reflect discipline problems or an overall level of disengagement. Thus, grades in nonacademic courses provide another measure of school engagement and of the messages a student received from teachers regarding school performance irrespective of academic competence.

The mean social grade was defined as the average grade a youth received in art, music, health, physical education, spelling, handwriting, and shop during the elementary and middle grades. At the high school level, the mean social grade was defined as the average grade a youth received in nonacademic courses such as elective, vocational, or business courses.

EXAMINING THE RELATIONSHIP BETWEEN SCHOOL EXPERIENCES AND EARLY SCHOOL LEAVING: MEASURES AND METHODOLOGY

Statistical Techniques

Chapters 5 and 6 will use multivariate analysis to examine the extent to which a youth's experience following school transitions and in being retained in grade are associated with the likelihood of dropping out, when controlling for differences in the school performance and measured background characteristics of youths. Chapter 5 asks the question: Is there evidence that school transitions are critical points in the academic careers of early school leavers? Chapter 6 explores how the experience of being retained in grade may influence the chances that students will drop out. Throughout this analysis, I primarily focus on the association between these two school experiences and whether a youth dropped out versus graduated or transferred to another school system.[8] The likelihood of dropping out was estimated using a logit technique for analyzing dichotomous dependent variables. To those familiar with these statistical methods, it would appear that event history or duration analysis, which looked both at whether and when a youth dropped out, would best maximize the information contained in this longitudinal data set (Willett and Singer, 1991). Duration analysis was not used to model the grade in which a youth dropped out because of my focus on grade retention.

Youths enter the risk period for dropping out at age 16. In order to drop out previous to the spring of their sophomore year in high school, a student must have repeated a grade. Therefore, the probability of dropping out prior to the spring of the tenth grade is close to zero for those who were never retained in grade, making duration analysis an inappropriate approach. For consistency, then, I present the results of estimating the relationship between progressive school experiences and school dropout using a logit analysis of the likelihood of dropping out for the entire sample and for subgroups in the sample in both my analysis of the impact of school transitions and the impact of grade retention.

In Chapter 6, I also use a discrete time hazard model to examine the degree to which being overage for grade influences the age of withdrawal. One interpretation of the strong association between grade retention and early school leaving is that grade retention might increase the chances that a youth would drop out through an impact of being overage for grade. Youths who are one or more years overage for grade become eligible to drop out when they are still in middle school or are making the transition to high school. If grade retention had a large discouragement effect, we may expect that being older than classmates would have a greater effect on the likelihood of dropping out at 16 than at older age ranges. Event history analysis is particularly suited to address this question.

Presentation of Results

Logit coefficients are not directly interpretable. By setting independent variables at specific values, however, we can calculate the change in the likelihood of dropping out for a change in the value of an independent variable. For each equation, I present the results of the logit analysis using the calculation of the derivative of the logistic probability function when all variables included in the equation are set at their mean. Thus, one can interpret the values reported for each equation as the change in the probability of dropping out for a change in the independent variable when all values are set at their mean.[9] In each table, I report the t-statistics associated with the logistic regression coefficients. The logit coefficients associated with each equation are reported in the appendixes to each chapter. I also report the computed chi-square value from the likelihood ratio test statistic on the joint hypothesis that all coefficients except the intercept are zero and, in several cases, McFadden's pseudo-R^2 measure based on the likelihood ratio.[10]

Because the logit model is nonlinear, estimates of the effect of a parameter on the likelihood of dropping out will vary depending upon the values of the independent variables. In several cases, I present the predicted effect of a change in the independent variable on the probability of dropping out for two sample cases. In the first case, estimates of the effect of a one-unit change in the parameter of interest is presented for a student whom we would consider highly at risk of dropping out. This youth is a male, whose father worked in an unskilled occupation, who is native born with two siblings, who changed schools twice, and who is from an average census tract.[11] The second case is a youth moderately at risk of dropping out. This youth has a similar background, but has mean academic grades and attendance one-half of a standard deviation below the mean for each year.

Measures

Table 3.2 presents the variables that will be used throughout the multivariate analyses in Chapters 4, 5, and 6.

Father's Occupation. The Fall River school system recorded parents' occupations at the time the student entered the school system. Parental occupation was the only socioeconomic background variable reported on the school transcript. There is a long tradition in research of using parents' occupations as proxies for socioeconomic background, largely because occupation is often available in public documents.

Parents' occupations were coded according to the Census Bureau's Occupational Classification Codes for Detailed Occupational Categories. Parental occupation was then recoded into one of three occupational categories—professional, skilled, and unskilled—according to the Census' Major Occupation Group Recodes. In addition, parents who were unemployed or who were not in the home at the time a student entered the school system were placed in a fourth occupational category of "other." Clearly, this category cannot be interpreted as measuring the

Table 3.2
Definition of Census Tract, Demographic, and Background and School Performance Variables

School Performance

# Retentions	Number of times a youths was retained in grade (grades k-8).
Mean Academic Grades:	Mean grade (0 to 4.0) youth received in English, language, math, history/geography, science and foreign language, if taken.
Attendance	Days in attendance in each grade.

Personal and Family Characteristics

Female	1 if female, 0 if male.
Siblings	Number of siblings as reported on school transcript.
Father's Occupation	
Father professional	Dummy variables representing father's occupation.
Father unskilled	Father professional is excluded. Based on father's
Father skilled	occupation reported on school transcript. Coded
Father other	according to the Occupational Classification Codes for detailed Occupational Categories.
Nativity	
Native/parents native	Dummy variables representing youth's nativity based on
2nd-Generation	parents' and youth's place of birth reported on school
Immigrant pre-k	transcript. Excluded variable, native/parents native
Immigrant k+	born.

Census Tract Characteristics

% High School	Percentage of adults in census tract who have completed four or more years of high school based on 1980 census data.
% Public Assistance	Percentage of households in census tract with public assistance income based on 1980 census data.
% O/F/L	Percentage of employed adults in census tract working as Operators, fabricators or laborers based on 1980 census data.

School Characteristics

School Quality	A qualitative variable measuring the quality of the grammar school youth attended in the fourth grade (1=excellent, 7=poor).
# School Changes	Number of times a youth changed schools (4-8).
MISSING VALUES	In addition to above, each equation contained dummy variables for missing values for: census tract characteristics, number of siblings, father's occupation, nativity, mean academic grades in each yea,r and attendance in each year.[a]

[a] See Maddalla (1977) for a discussion of this approach as well as alternative approaches to estimation with missing observations.

effect of occupation, as much as it may measure the effect of living in a single parent home.

Father's occupation was used as the measure of socioeconomic background because information on a mother's occupation at the time of entry into the school system may be unreliable. At the time students entered the school system, 60 percent of mothers for whom occupation was recorded reported that they were not employed. Since most students entered the school system in kindergarten, we would expect that many of these women would later work, and that the occupational distribution of a mother's employment obtained from the transcript would not accurately reflect the later occupational distribution of mothers in the cohort. As a result, a father's occupation was used as the measure of a youth's socioeconomic background.

The distribution of fathers' occupations reflected the low levels of education attainment in Fall River. Only 3.5 percent of students in the sample for whom information on their father's occupation was available had fathers who were employed as professionals. Thirty-five percent of the sample had a father who was coded as working in a skilled occupation, while 41 percent of students' fathers were employed in unskilled occupations. For 20 percent of the nonmissing sample, father's occupation was recorded on the school transcript as either unemployed or not in the home (see Appendix 3-A).

Nativity. When youths enrolled in school, the school system recorded the place of birth of the student and his or her parents. Using this information, I constructed dummy variables to measure: (1) whether a youth entered the school system as an immigrant; (2) whether a youth was an immigrant but entered the school system in kindergarten; (3) whether a youth was a second-generation American; and (4) whether both the student and his or her parent(s) were born in the United States (see Table 3.2). Of students in the sample whose nativity was determined, approximately 14 percent were second-generation Americans. Nine percent of students whose nativity was identified immigrated to the United States before kindergarten, 15 percent immigrated after kindergarten.

Census Tract Variables. As seen in Table 3.2, three census tract characteristics were included in the analysis to control for neighborhood and community influences on educational outcomes, and as a proxy for socioeconomic status. Each youth was assigned the average 1980 characteristics of the census tract or tracts that were associated with the grammar school she or he attended in the fourth grade. For most grammar schools, youths assigned to the school were drawn from one census tract. In several cases, students from two or three census tracts attended one grammar school. For these grammar schools, I used the average characteristics of the tracts associated with that school. Given this method, we would expect that there is measurement error in the assignment of tract characteristics to youths, and, thus, that the coefficients on the census tract variables would be biased toward zero.

Three out of nine potential census tract characteristics were chosen as a control for a general neighborhood effect.[12] Census tract characteristics are highly correlated with each other. The percentage of adults employed as operators, fabricators, or laborers, the percentage of families in the census tract receiving public assistance income, and the percentage of adults who had graduated from high school were chosen because they were highly correlated with the remaining five excluded tract measures, such as per capita income. As a result, the included variables should not be interpreted as the influence of a particular neighborhood characteristic, but as a more general neighborhood parameter.

School Quality. The school quality variable is a measure of the quality of the grammar school a youth attended in the fourth grade. This variable was constructed through an interview with a former teacher and current city counselor, and a school administrator and former middle school vice-principal, both of whom were involved in a city-wide reading program during the time the cohort was attending grammar school.

In constructing this index, I asked the educators to rate each of the grammar schools on the basis of the quality of the teaching staff, the quality of the principal, and the overall school climate. Forty-five percent of the schools received ratings of either good or average, 16 percent received overall ratings of excellent, and 25 percent received ratings of very poor or more. The correlation between the school quality index and the census tract variables is .4.

School Changes. Most youths in the Fall River public school system changed schools twice—once in the transition to middle school and once in the transition to high school. Students also changed schools because of residential mobility. Previous research on both school and residential mobility has found that youths who have high rates of school mobility have greater difficulties in school and are more likely to drop out (Felner et al., 1981; Goldstein, 1991). In the Fall River cohort, dropouts, when compared to graduates, had statistically significantly higher rates of school mobility. From the fourth to the eighth grade, for example, the average number of school changes for dropouts was 1.74 compared to an average number of school changes for graduates of 1.37.

SUMMARY

Over the past decade, almost every major literature review on early school leaving has issued a call for longitudinal research to identify the various paths to dropping out and the degree to which school policies or specific school experiences may influence a youth's school performance and engagement (Catterall, 1986; Rumberger, 1987; Willett and Singer, 1991). Answering this call for research is not, however, an easy task. It requires following a group of students through their school careers—a source of information that is currently unavailable in any large longitudinal survey of youths. The Fall River study represents an ambitious attempt to begin exploring the school antecedents to school leaving by examining the paths to dropping out among one cohort of youths. This data set improves upon previous studies by providing information on the extent to which dropping out occurs in the middle school years and the extent to which these early dropouts differ from late grade dropouts and graduates. The longitudinal nature of the data set will allow me to trace how the school career paths of dropouts and graduates differ by grade of dropout and graduating class rank. And, perhaps most important, this data set allows us to move beyond simple comparisons of the extent to which dropouts and graduates differ late in their school careers, to a more systematic analysis of the influence of school experiences on school outcomes.

Each of the chapters that follow discusses in more detail the methodological approach and statistical and interpretative limitations of my findings. Before proceeding, however, let me briefly point out several of the most important limitations of this study.

This study is limited to one school system. I cannot, as a result, determine whether these findings are generalizable across school systems with different promotion policies, grade and classroom organization, school populations, and school structures and sizes. While limiting this study to one school system does not impede my ability to adequately describe the school correlates of early school leaving among this cohort, it does limit my ability to draw broader conclusions about the population of dropouts in other school systems. To what extent would my findings on school transitions differ if I had chosen a school system with a small high school or a school system with different middle school policies? To what extent would these findings differ if the school system was organized according to a k–8, 9–12 grade arrangement rather than according to k–5, 6–8, 9–12 schools?

Relying on school transcript information raises a second set of problems. The Fall River data set does not include detailed information on a youth's family background and home environment, early measures of ability, measures of expectations and motivation, or detailed data on school policy. This lack of information constrains my ability to fully identify the causal relationships between specific school experiences and the likelihood of school dropout. For example, if retained students are more likely to drop out even after controlling for differences in the grades and attendance of promoted and nonpromoted youths, is this because grade retention raises the likelihood of early school leaving or is it because retained and promoted youths differ in ways that are not reflected in their grades and attendance?

The lack of detailed information on a student's background also meant that I could not follow up on some of the more interesting questions raised in this analysis. For example, the Fall River data set allows us to examine whether academic difficulties youths encounter following school transitions affect their chances of dropping out but does not allow me to ask: What characteristics of a student's background are associated with greater difficulties during school transitions? In the chapters that follow, I have tried to steer away from the academic pitfall of calling for more research or placing numerous caveats in front of any findings that may seem persuasive or conclusive. At the same time, one of the contributions of the Fall River study, as a first attempt at examining the middle school and early high school antecedents to early school leaving, is that my findings raise an array of new questions and possible new directions for research. So, while avoiding calls for new research as a way to evade thinking hard about the potential policy implications of my findings, I have included discussion of what new research and policy questions are raised through this analysis.

NOTES

1. This district policy was formulated when Fall River moved to a largely k–5, 6–8 grading arrangement in the 1970s, and was based on concerns regarding the geographic proximity of youths to the middle schools. All of the schools that retained their sixth-grade classrooms were in the South End of Fall River and were schools that were not in close proximity to one of the middle schools. According to Margaret Condon, Superintendent of Curriculum and Instruction in the Fall River public schools, parents from the schools that were not in geographic proximity to the middle schools voiced opposition to the middle school system because their children would be too young to travel alone to the middle schools. As a compromise, these schools retained their sixth-grade classes and students moved to the middle schools in the seventh grade. The district-wide policy of grammar (k–5) and middle schools (6–8) was instituted in the 1978–1979 school year. Thus, the youths in the Fall River sample—the graduating class of 1985–1986—were the second cohort to make the transition to middle school in the sixth grade.

2. In Massachusetts, students become eligible to drop out of school at age 16. Youths who have repeated more than two grades will turn 16 in the seventh grade. The seventh grade was chosen as the year to identify the cohort in order to include these early dropouts.

3. Students were coded as having dropped out if they were coded as withdrawing, rather than transferring from school, on their permanent record. Dropout codes that were used by the school system included "over 16," "married," or "left for work." Students were coded as having graduated if they were recorded as having graduated from high school on their permanent records and

high school transcripts. Finally, students were coded as transfers if they were identified on their transcripts as having transferred to another school system. In most cases, the receiving school system or school was also identified.

4. Slightly over 20 percent of the cohort transferred out of the Fall River public school system after the seventh grade. The majority transferred to one of two local technical high schools. Both of these institutions are regional public technical high schools that accept youths through a competitive application process. In addition, 15 percent of local transfers were to local Catholic high schools. Dropout rates in both of these institutions are low. The average school characteristics of transfers were similar to those of later graduates. For example, the average fourth-grade mean academic grade of students who transferred was not very different from those of later graduates (see Table 4.1).

5. Outcome data were not obtained for approximately 5 percent of the cases. Because the cohort was identified through handwritten home room registers, many of these missing outcomes could be misspellings. Other missing outcomes are youths who registered in the Fall River school system for the seventh grade but never attended.

6. The middle school card was sent from the middle school to the high school in the ninth grade for use by the high school guidance department. If a youth dropped out in middle school, the school discarded the middle school card. In addition, the middle school card was sent to the receiving school system or school when a student transferred. Thus, middle school cards, which were kept at the high school, were not available for middle school dropouts or transfers previous to ninth grade. In addition, some of the middle school cards were discarded by the high school guidance office by mistake. A youth's middle school card could also be missing if the student was supposed to transfer to a school system but did not leave, or if the middle school card was never forwarded by the middle school.

7. For example, sixth-grade mean academic grades were recorded for 96 percent of high school dropouts and 97 percent of graduates. In comparison, sixth-grade attendance was recorded for only 74 percent of high school dropouts and 80.7 percent of graduates. Attendance and background data could also be missing for students if this information was not recorded on the middle school card at entry into the school system.

8. Students in the Fall River cohort either graduated, transferred, or dropped out of school. The average mean academic grade of transfers in the fourth grade was not statistically significantly different than that of graduates. As I noted, most transfers were students who transferred to one of the technical high schools in the area or to one of the Catholic high schools, which have very low dropout rates (see note 4). If we assume that students who were not happy with their education in the school system could choose to leave and participate in another school system, then we would assume that students were choosing between dropping out and transferring or graduating. One method of modeling this process would be to use a multinomial logit that estimated separately the likelihood of transferring, graduating, or dropping out. As I noted, data were obtained for only a small sample of transfers. Therefore, I estimated the likelihood of dropping out versus transferring or graduating. Each equation was also estimated for the likelihood of dropping out versus graduating, excluding trans-

fers. The results of my analysis were virtually identical for either method. I have, therefore, reported the results of the analysis when information on all youths was included in the equation.

9. The formula for the cumulative logistic probability is: $P(Y) = 1/(1 + e^{-x\beta})$. The derivative of this function with respect to X is $\beta P(1 - P)$ for given values of the independent variables.

10. McFadden's pseudo-R^2 is computed as $R^2 = 1 - (\text{Log } L_\theta/\text{Log}_\Omega)$, where Log L_θ is the log of the maximum likelihood function when all parameters are included and Log_Ω is the log of the maximum likelihood function when maximized with respect to the intercept solely (Maddala, 1986, p. 40). Jan Kmenta also refers to this pseudo-R^2 measure as the *likelihood ratio index* (Kmenta, 1986, p. 556).

11. Each sample youth is from an average census tract where the school he attended has a quality index of 4 and where 32.3 percent of adults were high school graduates, 22.4 percent of families received public assistance, and 31.2 percent of adults were employed as operators, fabricators, and laborers.

12. These nine census tract characteristics included: the percentage of children living in non-English speaking homes; per capita income; median family income; the child poverty rate; the unemployment rate; the percentage of families headed by women; the percentage of the families receiving public assistance income; the percentage of workers employed as operators, fabricators, or laborers; and the percentage of adults living in the census tract who had graduated from high school.

## Chapter 4

What Do the School Careers of Dropouts and Graduates Look Like?

This chapter will focus on three questions. To what extent do dropouts and graduates in the Fall River cohort differ in terms of their early school performance? What do trends in the grades, attendance, and incidence of grade retention tell us about the path or paths to dropping out? And, how well could we have predicted a youth's later school outcomes on the basis of a pupil's fourth-grade characteristics?

The educational attainment of youths in the Fall River cohort reflected a continuum of outcomes. Some students in this cohort dropped out as early as the seventh grade. Others stayed in school until twelfth grade, but still did not graduate. Some graduates would go on to college, while others ended formal education with their high school diploma. Comparing all dropouts to all graduates may mask important differences in these students' school careers, differences that may hold keys to the determinants of school dropout. The Fall River data set does not contain information on post-high school educational participation. We can, however, examine differences in the school performance of graduates by their graduating class rank. In this chapter, I will discuss trends in the school performance of early grade dropouts (seventh-, eighth-, and ninth-grade dropouts); late grade dropouts (tenth-, eleventh-, and twelfth-grade dropouts); the bottom third of the graduating class; and the middle and top thirds of the graduating class.[1] These groups differ in terms of both their average characteristics as of the fourth grade and in their school experiences after the fourth grade.

The first section of this chapter compares the grades and attendance of these different groups of youths in the fourth grade. I then trace the school career paths of students by grade of dropout and graduating class rank on the basis of four summary measures of school performance: mean academic grades; attendance; mean social grades; and grade retention. This second section examines trends in the school performance of all youths by whether a student moved to a middle school in the sixth grade. Finally, this chapter presents a multivariate analysis of the likelihood of early school leaving on the basis of a youth's fourth-grade grades and attendance, early grade retentions, and available background characteristics. This chapter presents a broad overview of trends in the school career paths of these different groups of youths, the major findings of which will be explored in more detail in the chapters that follow.

TRENDS IN MEAN ACADEMIC GRADES, ATTENDANCE, AND MEAN SOCIAL GRADES

Early Grades and Relative Standing of Dropouts and Graduates

Table 4.1 compares the average fourth-grade mean academic grades, mean social grades, and mean attendance of dropouts and graduates by grade of dropout and class rank. To restate, a youth's mean academic grade in each year is the average grade received in reading, math, geography/history, science, and foreign language, if taken, measured on a 0 to 4.0 scale. A youth's mean social grade is the average grade received in nonacademic courses including music, art, physical education, and health. The last column of Table 4.1 converts fourth-grade mean academic and social grades into a percentile rank. The percentile rank was calculated by sorting youths, first, by their mean academic grades and, second, by their mean social grades. A youth with a percentile rank of 1.0 had the highest mean academic and mean social grade in the fourth grade.

As early as the fourth grade, the average relative standings of dropouts and graduates reflected their later school outcomes. Seventh-, eighth-, and ninth-grade dropouts, who will be called early grade dropouts, had average percentile ranks that placed them in the bottom quarter of the fourth-grade class. These youths represent 35 percent of dropouts and slightly over 16 percent of nontransfers in this study. The average fourth-grade mean academic grade of these early dropouts of 1.76 was slightly above a C $-$. This average grade was significantly lower than those of both late grade dropouts and graduates (see Table 4.2).

At the other extreme, youths who later graduated in the top two-thirds of the graduating class were also, on average, in the top of their fourth-grade class. The average fourth-grade mean academic grade of the top two-thirds of graduates of 3.06 was significantly higher than

Table 4.1
Average Fourth-Grade Mean Academic Grades, Mean Social Grades, Attendance, and Percentile Rank by Grade of Dropout and Graduating Class Rank

	Mean Academic Grades	Mean Social Grades	Attendance	Percentile Rank
Seventh-grade dropouts n = 23	1.71	2.58	—	.24
Eighth-grade dropouts n = 34	1.73	2.94	—	.24
Ninth-grade dropouts n = 33 / 27	1.82	2.88	162.26	.27
Tenth-grade dropouts n = 64 / 51	2.17	2.91	161.73	.38
Eleventh-grade dropouts n = 69 / 51	2.25	2.91	164.71	.42
Twelfth-grade dropouts n = 57 / 41	2.33	2.91	168.24	.43
Bottom 1/3 graduates n = 95 / 77	2.28	2.94	164.29	.42
Middle 1/3 graduates n = 119 /102	2.69	2.95	164.13	.55
Top 1/3 graduates n = 136 /112	3.38	2.99	167.88	.78
Transfers n = 42/37	2.77	2.95	165.70	.58

Note: n = Sample size for grades/ sample size for attendance: Sample size for grades = number of youths for whom fourth-grade mean academic grades and attendance were available. As discussed in Chapter 3, attendance data were available for a smaller number of dropouts and graduates.

either those of late grade dropouts or youths who later went on to graduate in the bottom third of their class.

Late grade dropouts and the bottom third of the graduating class fall in between these two extremes. Together these two groups comprised 44.5 percent of nontransfers in this study. In contrast to early dropouts, the average fourth-grade mean academic grade of late grade dropouts (tenth- to twelfth-grade dropouts) was not substantially different from the average grade of students who later graduated in the bottom third of their class (2.27). The average percentile ranks of tenth-, eleventh-, and twelfth-grade dropouts, and the bottom third of the graduating class, clustered around the fortieth percentile of the class.

Table 4.2
A Comparison of the Fourth-Grade Performance of Early Dropouts, Late
Grade Dropouts, and Graduates by Class Rank

	Mean Academic Grades	Mean Social Grades	Attendance	Percentile Rank
Early drops (7th-9th)	1.76	2.82	—	.254
Late drops (10th-12th)	2.26	2.92	—	.411
t diff	(5.40)	(2.33)		(5.69)
Late Drops	2.26	2.92	164.02	.411
Bottom 1/3 grads	2.27	2.95	164.29	.417
t diff	(.10)	(1.66)	(.18)	(.19)
Bottom 1/3 grads	2.27	2.95	164.29	.417
Mid 1/3 grads	2.69	2.95	164.13	.554
t diff	(4.02)	(.00)	(.09)	(3.98)
Mid 1/3 grads	2.69	2.95	164.13	.554
Top 1/3 grads	3.38	2.99	167.88	.777
t diff	(7.99)	(1.69)	(2.69)	(7.75)

Note: See Appendix 4-A for means, standard deviations, and sample sizes for values reported in this
         table.

Trends in Mean Academic Grades

What are the school experiences of these different groups of dropouts
and graduates? Figures 4.1, 4.2, and 4.3 show trends in the mean academic grades of dropouts and graduates by the grade in which a youth
dropped out and by a youth's graduating class rank beginning in the
fourth grade and continuing until dropout or graduation.

Figure 4.1 shows trends in the mean academic grades of seventh-,
eighth-, and ninth-grade dropouts. As we saw in the previous section,
these early grade dropouts started substantially below their counterparts. The school performance of early dropouts, moreover, deteriorated
quite rapidly after the fourth grade. For example, the average mean
academic grade of ninth-grade dropouts declined from 1.82 in the fourth
grade to 1.25 in the eighth grade, a 30 percent decline.

Figures 4.2 and 4.3 document trends in the mean academic grades of
late grade dropouts and graduates by class rank. Perhaps the most striking fact that emerges is that the average mean academic grades of ninth-
and later grade dropouts, as well as those of the bottom third of the
graduating class, declined precipitously following the transition to high
school. From the eighth to the ninth grade, the average mean academic
grade of tenth- and later grade dropouts declined by almost 47 percent.
Youths who later graduated in the bottom third of their class also ex-

Figure 4.1
Trends in Mean Academic Grades; Early Dropouts and All Graduates

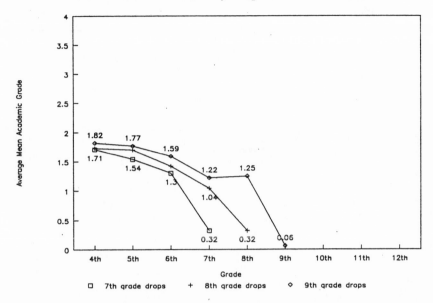

perienced more than a 30 percent decline in their average grades from the eighth to the ninth grade (see Table 4.3).

Importantly, the average mean academic grade of the late grade dropouts also declined more dramatically than those of graduates from the fifth to the sixth grade, when most youths were making the transition to middle school. Table 4.3 shows trends in the mean academic grade of both late grade dropouts and graduates by class rank. Clearly, students' moves to both middle school and to high school are accompanied by declines in their average grades. The degree to which a youth's grades declined following these school moves was also correlated with later school outcomes. From the fifth to the sixth grade, the average mean academic grades of late grade dropouts declined by 11 percent compared to a decline of 4 percent in the average mean academic grades of graduates.

Trends in the average grades of late grade dropouts and graduates did not look dramatically different during middle school. From the sixth to eighth grade, the average grades of both late grade dropouts and graduates declined moderately. Dropouts, however, did not recover from the losses incurred following the school changes to middle school and to high school. Thus, the academic difficulties experienced by dropouts following these school moves translated into permanent shifts in their academic status.

Figure 4.2
Trends in Mean Academic Grades; Late Grade Dropouts and Bottom One-
Third Graduates

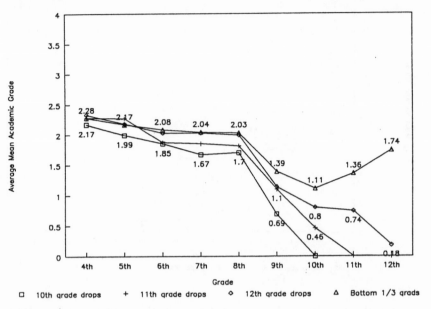

It was in the transition to high school that many late grade dropouts
fell into serious academic difficulty. One measure of academic difficulty
is course failures. During middle school, late grade dropouts were much
more likely than graduates to have course failures. However, the majority of late grade dropouts were not in serious academic difficulty
during middle school. This was not true after the transition to high
school. For example, from the eighth to the ninth grade, the percentage
of tenth- to twelfth-grade dropouts who failed 25 percent or more of
their credits increased from 5.3 to 60.7 percent compared to an average
increase for graduates from 2.6 to 8.3 percent. Figure 4.4 describes these
failure rates in more detail by grade of dropout and class rank.

Declines in grades during the transition to middle school and to high
school may reflect changes in academic performance. Declines in grades
may also reflect differences in grading procedures among elementary,
middle level, and high school teachers. The extent to which grade declines associated with school transitions are the result of very real
changes in performance, or are due to the fact that middle school and
high school teachers grade more severely, is an unresolved question
(Eccles and Midgley, 1989; Epstein and Peterson, 1991). Some researchers have found that grade declines associated with these school moves

Figure 4.3
Trends in Mean Academic Grades; Middle and Top Two-Thirds of Graduating Class

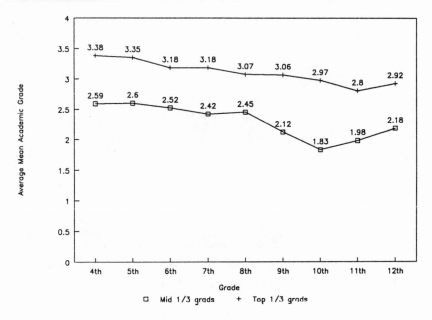

Table 4.3
Trends in Mean Academic Grades, Middle School and Ninth-Grade Drops, High School Drops, and Graduates, 4th–9th Grade

	4th	4th-5th	5th-6th	6th-8th	Transition to High School
		Percentage Change			
7th-9th grade Drops	1.76	-4.55%	-14.29%*		
10th-12th Drops and Graduates	2.65	-3.40%	-6.64%*	-3.35%	-20.35%*
10th-12th Grade Drops	2.26	-5.31%	-10.75%*	-4.71%	-46.70%*
Bottom Third Graduates	2.27	-4.41%	- 4.15%	-2.88%	-31.19%*
Mid/Top Third Graduates	3.06	-1.96%	-4.67%*	-3.15%	- 5.42%*

Note: * = Average change in mean academic grade statistically significant at the .05 level.

Figure 4.4
**A Comparison of the Percentage of Youths Who Received F's in 25 Percent
or More of Their Credits in Eighth and Ninth Grades**

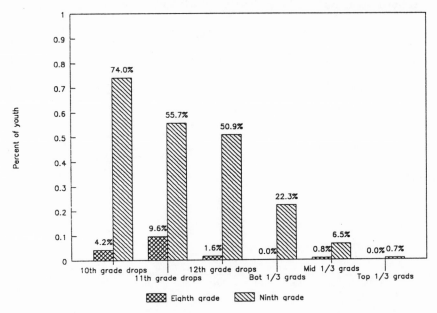

are not accompanied by a decline in students' achievement test scores
(Eccles and Midgley, 1989). The implications of each interpretation will
be discussed in greater detail in the next chapter. Regardless of the cause
of the decline, the differential changes that dropouts and graduates
experienced following these school moves are critical points of divergence in these youths' school careers.

Trends in Attendance and Mean Social Grades

Figure 4.5 and Table 4.4 show trends in the attendance of late grade
dropouts and graduates beginning in the fourth grade. As seen in Figure
4.5, attendance in the fifth grade did not equal 180. Fifth-grade attendance was, as a result, excluded from the analysis of changes in performance between grades in Table 4.4.

Trends in the average attendance of late grade dropouts and graduates
follow a quite different pattern than trends in mean academic grades.
During middle school, we found that the average grades of late grade
dropouts and graduates declined moderately. In sharp comparison, the
average attendance of both late grade dropouts and graduates declined
significantly from the sixth to the eighth grade. Changes in attendance,

Figure 4.5
Trends in Attendance: Late Grade Dropouts and Graduates

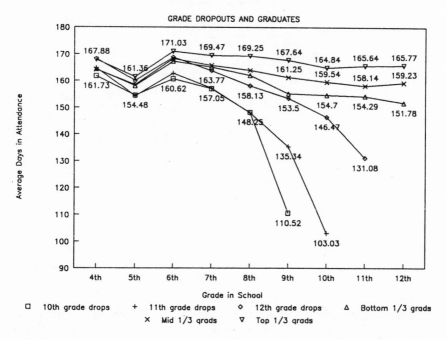

GRADE DROPOUTS AND GRADUATES

Table 4.4
Trends in Attendance: High School Drops and Graduates, 4th–9th Grade

	4th	4th-5th	6th-8th	Transition to High School
			Percentage Change	
10th-12th Drops and Graduates	165.14	1.28%	-6.60%*	-8.79%*
10th-12th Grade Drops	164.02	-.32%	-7.94%*	-12.96%*
Bottom Third Graduates	164.29	-1.78%	-3.12%*	-4.32%
Mid/Top Third Graduates	166.09	+2.41%*	-2.35%*	-1.20%

Note: * = Average change in attendance statistically significant at the .05 level.

Figure 4.6
Trends in the Mean Social Grades of Late Grade Dropouts and Graduates

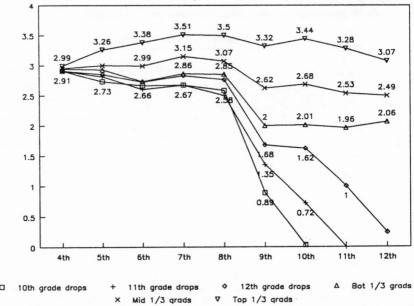

moreover, differed dramatically across groups. From the sixth to the eighth grade, the average attendance of students declined by 1.78 days, on average, for those who would later graduate in the top third of the graduating class; 4.35 days for the middle third of graduates; 5.26 days for the bottom third of graduates; and 13 days for late grade dropouts.

Patterns in the average mean social grades of these groups also suggest that the school attachment of late grade dropouts and graduates diverged significantly during middle school (Figure 4.6 and Table 4.5). It is interesting to note that trends in the average mean social grades of these groups reflect both the grade declines associated with school transitions, and increasing dispersion on measures of engagement during middle school. Looking at Table 4.5, we find that the average mean social grades of dropouts, like that of mean academic grades, declined much more dramatically than those of graduates from the fifth to the sixth grade and following the transition to high school. Differences in the mean social grades of dropouts and graduates, however, became even more pronounced during middle school.

As discussed in Chapter 3, a student's mean social grade, or grades received in courses such as music, art, and physical education, may reflect his or her level of cooperation, attitudes toward, and engagement in school. When examining trends in the average mean social grade of

Table 4.5
Trends in Mean Social Grades, Middle School and Ninth-Grade Drops, High School Drops, and Graduates, 4th–9th Grade

	4th	4th-5th	5th-6th	6th-8th	Transition to High School
		Percentage Change			
7th-9th Grade Drops	2.82	-6.74%*	-9.88%*		
10th-12th Drops and Graduates	2.95	-.34%	-1.01%	+1.37%	-25.25%*
10th-12th Grade Drops	2.92	-4.63%*	-4.60%*	-1.85%	-50.67%*
Bottom Third Graduates	2.95	-1.69%	-5.86%*	+4.40%*	-30.53%*
Mid/Top Third Graduates	2.97	+5.72%*	+1.59%	+3.13%*	- 8.81%*

Note: * = Average change in mean social grade statistically significant at the .05 level.

graduates, we find that from both the fourth to the fifth grade and from the sixth to the eighth grade, the average mean social grade of graduates increased. Thus, throughout this period, graduates received increasingly positive feedback from teachers in the form of nonacademic grades. The average mean social grade of dropouts, however, declined throughout middle school.

How much of the declines in students' grades from the fifth to the sixth grade and the increasing variance in attendance can be linked to the transition to middle school? We can examine this question by comparing patterns in the average grades and attendance of students in the Fall River cohort by whether a youth moved to a middle school, or remained in a grammar school, in the sixth grade.

TRENDS IN MEAN ACADEMIC GRADES AND ATTENDANCE BY THE TIMING OF THE TRANSITION TO MIDDLE SCHOOL

Most students in the Fall River public school system made the transition to middle school in the sixth grade. As discussed in Chapter 3, youths from eight of the twenty-eight grammar schools, or approximately 20 percent of the sample, remained in their grammar school in the sixth grade and made the transition to high school in the seventh grade. Thus, declines in the average grades of all youths from the fifth to the sixth grade would underestimate the average decline in grades associated with the normative school transition to middle school.

Table 4.6 shows trends in the average mean academic grades of youths by whether or not they changed schools in the sixth grade. These results clearly show that the significant decline in the average grades of students in the Fall River cohort from the fifth to the sixth grade is ascribable to changes in grades associated with school transitions. From the fifth to the sixth grade, the average mean academic grades of those who made the transition to middle school in that year declined by approximately 8 percent. In sharp contrast, the average grades of those who did not change schools in the sixth grade showed no discernable decline.

Late grade dropouts who moved to the middle school in the sixth grade experienced much larger declines in their average grades than graduates. Among youths who made the transition to middle school in the sixth grade, the average mean academic grade of late grade dropouts declined by approximately 14 percent compared to a decline of approximately 4 percent in the average grades of youths who later graduated in the bottom third of their graduating class. In addition, dropouts, regardless of the timing of the transition to middle school, experienced much more dramatic declines in their average grades following the transition to high school.

Notice that the average mean academic grades of youths who made the transition to middle school in the seventh grade did not decline in that year. Previous research on school transitions has generally found that grades decline following a school transition regardless of the grade in which youths changed schools (Blyth et al., 1983; Crockett et al., 1989). This finding, that average grades did not decline for youths in the Fall River public school system who made the transition to middle school in the seventh grade, may not, however, contradict the findings of previous research. Students in the Fall River school system who changed schools in the seventh grade may have experienced less stress during this school move than if the entire cohort had changed schools in that grade. Students who changed schools in the seventh grade were not a new cohort. Rather, they moved to the new school after their peer group had had a chance to adjust and become established in their new environment. These students, then, may have had the experience of being new members of the class rather than being new students among an entirely new class of students—a single school experience that has not been shown to have a substantial impact on school performance (Felner et al., 1981).

Table 4.7 shows trends in attendance by the timing of the transition to middle school. Perhaps the most important finding in Table 4.7 is that trends in attendance did not differ dramatically by whether or not a youth experienced a school change in the sixth grade. From the fourth

Table 4.6
Trends in the Mean Academic Grades of Youths by Whether or Not Student Moved to the Middle School in the Sixth Grade

	4th	4th-5th	5th-6th	6th-7th	7th-8th	8th-9th	n
				Percentage Change			
Middle School 6th[a]	2.66	-3.0%	-8.1%◆	-2.6%	-2.2%	-18.0%◆	456[b]
Grammar School 6th	2.57	-4.3%	0.0%	-1.2%	+1.6%	-26.0%◆	106
MIDDLE SCHOOL 6TH							
10th-12th Grade Drops	2.30	-4.3%	-14.1%◆	-4.2%	-2.2%	-47.4%◆	152
Bottom 1/3 Grads	2.27	-4.8%	-4.0%	-2.0%	-1.5%	-31.3%◆	87
Mid/Top 1/3 Grads	3.0	-2.0%	-5.6%◆	-2.0%	-3.0%	-7.0%◆	217
GRAMMAR SCHOOL 6TH							
10th-12th Grade Drops	2.11	-5.0%	0.0%	-.5%	+1.0%	-42.8%◆	48
Bottom 1/3 Grads[c]	2.26						10
Mid/Top 1/3 Grads	3.09	-3.0%	+1.0%	-1.7%	+2.3%	-12.5%◆	48

a. Trends in grades of 10th-12th grade drops and all graduates. Excludes youth who transferred, and youths who attended a school other than a middle school or one of the eight grammar schools in the sixth grade (e.g., youths who attended Catholic schools).
b: Sample size reported as of sixth grade.
c: Sample size too small

Notes: ◆ = change in grade significant at the .01 level; ▲ = change in grade significant at .05; * = change in grade significant at .10.

Table 4.7
Trends in the Attendance of Youths by Whether or Not Student Moved to the Middle School in the Sixth Grade

	4th	Percentage Change				n
		4th-6th	6th-7th	7th-8th	8th-9th	
10th-12th Grade Drops	164.03	-0.29%	-2.68%◆	-4.76%◆	-6.65%◆	156[b]
Graduates	166.00	1.81%◆	-1.20%◆	-.96%	-2.0%◆	301
Middle School 6th[a]	164.74	+1.1%◆	-1.3%◆	-1.5%◆	-9.1%◆	367
Grammar School 6th	167.00	+1.6%◆	-3.2%◆	-2.5%◆	-11.49%◆	90
MIDDLE SCHOOL 6TH						
10th-12th Grade Drops	163.04	-0.5%	-1.9%*	-4.7%◆	-15.1%◆	116
Graduates	165.47	+1.8%◆	-1.0%*	-1.0%*	-1.7%◆	251
GRAMMAR SCHOOL 6TH						
10th-12th Grade Drops	166.68	+0.6%	-4.8%◆	-4.3%◆	-11.0%◆	40
Graduates	166.64	+2.8%◆	-2.0%*	-0.8%	-3.30%◆	50

a: Trends in grades of tenth-twelfth grade drops and all graduates. Excludes youths who transferred and youths who attended a school other than a middle school or one of the eight grammar schools in the sixth grade (e.g., youths who attended Catholic schools).

b: Sample size reported as of sixth grade.

Notes: *Yearly attendance was available for approximately 78 percent of youths who attended middle school in the sixth grade and approximately 85 percent of youths who attended grammar schools in the sixth grade. Because of these smaller samples, I have not reported trends in attendance by graduating class rank (see note 4).*

◆ = change in grade significant at the .01 level; ▲ = change in grade significant at .05; * = change in grade significant at .10.

to the sixth grade, the average attendance of both dropouts who attended a grammar school and those who attended a middle school remained relatively constant. Beginning in the sixth grade, the average attendance of dropouts declined significantly in each successive year regardless of the timing of the transition to middle school.

One interpretation of these differences between patterns in dropouts' and graduates' attendance and pattern in their grades is that the decline in dropouts' attendance during middle school and the precipitous decline in their mean academic grades following the transition to high school are linked. Simply stated, for those youths who are showing signs of disengagement during middle school, the difficult transition to high school may deal a blow from which they cannot recover. A second interpretation is that late grade dropouts are a heterogeneous group made up of two distinct groups of youths: those whose path to dropping out is a slow process of disengagement beginning in middle school and those who have a difficult transition to high school. In essence, this second interpretation would suggest that these average trends are really two trends rather than one. In an analysis not presented here, I compared changes in grades following the transition to high school for both late grade dropouts who had large declines in their attendance during middle school (15 or more days) and those who did not. I found that dropouts experienced dramatic declines in their average mean academic grades following the school change to high school regardless of whether their attendance had declined substantially during middle school.[2]

This section has focused on comparing trends in the school performance of late grade dropouts to that of youths who graduated in the bottom, middle, and top two-thirds of the graduating class. Before proceeding, let me briefly summarize the main findings of this analysis. By the tenth grade, similar to the findings of previous research, late grade dropouts in the Fall River study looked dramatically different from graduates in terms of their grades and attendance (see Figures 4.2, 4.3, and 4.4). This is not the entire story, for the average grades and attendance of late grade dropouts and the bottom third of the graduating class did not differ early on in their school careers.

I have identified two important differences in the school careers of late grade dropouts and graduates that produced these disparate school outcomes. First, late grade dropouts experienced much more dramatic declines in their average grades than graduates following the school change to both middle school and to high school. From eighth to ninth grade, the average mean academic grades of late grade dropouts declined by almost 47 percent following the transition to high school compared to an average decline in the mean academic grades of graduates of 11 percent. Similarly, the percentage change in late grade dropouts' grades following the transition to middle school was nearly three times as large

Table 4.8
Percentage of Youths with at Least One Grade Failure Previous to the Fourth and Ninth Grade, by Grade of Dropout and Class Rank

| | % at Least One Grade Failure | | |
Grade of Drop/ Class Rank	k-3	k-8th	Difference
7th-grade drops	30.4%	96.8%	66.4%
8th-grade drops	52.9%	97.6%	44.7%
9th-grade drops	60.0%	93.9%	33.9%
10th-grade drops	50.0%	73.5%	23.5%
11th-grade drops	23.2%	33.3%	10.1%
12th-grade drops	28.1	36.8	8.7%
Bottom 1/3 grads	14.7	23.2	8.5%
Middle 1/3 grads	16.0	18.5	2.5%
Top 1/3 grads	4.4	4.4	0.0

as that experienced by graduates. These youths do not recover from grade losses incurred following school transitions. As a result, data from the Fall River study suggest that it is during normative school transitions that the average academic grades of late grade dropouts diverge from those of graduates.

Second, the average attendance of late grade dropouts began to decline in the sixth grade—a level of disengagement that accelerated in late middle school and in the transition to high school. Trends in students' attendance were quite different from trends in grades in that changes in attendance could not be linked to the stress of school transitions. The average attendance of late grade dropouts began to decline in the sixth grade among both youths who changed school in the sixth grade and those who remained in their grammar school.

TRENDS IN GRADE RETENTION

The Fall River public school system officially retained youths from kindergarten to eighth grade. Table 4.7 shows the proportion of dropouts and graduates who were retained in at least one grade early and late in their school career. Because youths must be 16 in order to be eligible to drop out of school, early grade dropouts, by definition, must be overage for grade by the time they leave school. Students who enter school at their modal grade level and who never fail a grade become eligible to drop out of school sometime during the spring of their sophomore and the fall of their junior year. As documented in Table 4.8, almost all of early grade dropouts and a high proportion of tenth-grade dropouts had experienced a grade retention by the time they dropped out.

The incidence of grade retention among early dropouts largely confirms what we found when we looked at trends in these youths' grades.

Table 4.9

Comparison of the Average Fourth-Grade Mean Academic Grade of Students Who Did and Did Not Repeat at Least One Grade from Kindergarten to Third Grade, by Grade of Dropout and Class Rank

| | Average Fourth-Grade Mean Academic Grade | | | |
| | Repeated a grade k-3 | | Did not repeat k-3 | |
	Ac 4th	n	Ac 4th	n
Early grade dropouts	1.66	45	1.86	45
Late grade dropouts	1.97	64	2.40	126
Bottom 1/3 graduates	1.98	14	2.32	81
Mid/Top 2/3 graduates	2.35	25	3.14	230
Transfers	2.02	8	2.96	34
% Drop	70.0%		33.2%	

Note: Sample sizes reported are for those who were enrolled in the school system in the fourth grade.

Reflecting their difficulties early on in school, over one-half of early grade dropouts (seventh- to ninth-grade dropouts) experienced at least one grade retention from kindergarten to third grade. By late middle school, almost all of early dropouts repeated at least one grade.

A surprising finding is that, on average, late grade dropouts were more than twice as likely as youths who graduated in the bottom third of their class to have experienced a grade retention early on in their school careers despite similar grades and attendance. Table 4.9 compares the average mean academic grades of dropouts and graduates by whether or not a youth repeated a grade early in his or her school career.

Table 4.9 is striking in the degree to which it confirms the findings in the previous section. First, we find that among students who repeated early grades and among students who did not, early grade dropouts had lower grades than either late grade dropouts or graduates. Second, we find that the average grades of late grade dropouts and the bottom third of the class were similar among youths who repeated grades and among those who did not repeat grades from kindergarten to third grade.

The higher incidence of both early and late grade retention among dropouts, regardless of the grade in which they dropped out, however, identifies another important correlate of school leaving. Chapter 6 will review previous research on grade retention. A common belief among teachers is that early grade retentions are beneficial and often reduce the chances of both later grade retentions and school failure (Smith and Shepard, 1987; Tompchin and Impara, 1992). This practice of early retentions, primarily on the basis of a teacher's assessment of a student's "readiness," was prevalent in the Fall River school system. Over one-quarter of students in this cohort repeated a grade from kindergarten to the third grade; 11 percent of students were retained in either kindergarten or first grade. And, as we see in Table 4.9, those students who repeated early grades dropped out at more than three times the rate of their counterparts who had not experienced an early grade retention.

Indeed, the extremely high dropout rates among those who experienced an early grade retention adds yet another dimension to the question of whether grade retention, as a policy, may raise the likelihood that a student will drop out of school. Is the experience of being retained in grade something that youths will carry with them throughout their school career regardless of how they do in school? Or, can we explain the higher dropout rates among retained youths by their lower school performance? These questions will be explored in more detail in Chapter 6.

PREDICTING THE LIKELIHOOD OF DROPPING OUT ON THE BASIS OF FOURTH-GRADE SCHOOL PERFORMANCE

This chapter has compared the school career paths of early grade dropouts (seventh- to ninth-grade dropouts), late grade dropouts (tenth- to twelfth-grade dropouts), and graduates by class rank. Previous studies that examined the early school predictors of school leaving have generally compared dropouts, as a group, to all graduates. For example, Norman Lloyd, in an oft-quoted study, found that approximately 68 percent of the later school outcomes of dropouts and over three-quarters of the later school outcomes of graduates could be predicted on the basis of third-grade grades, attendance, achievement, and IQ scores as well as information on a parent's occupation and educational attainment, family size, and composition (Lloyd, 1978).

These broad aggregations, however, mask important differences in the population of dropouts and graduates in school systems with high dropout rates. If we had simply compared the average fourth-grade characteristics of all dropouts in the Fall River study to those of all graduates, we would have concluded that these two groups looked significantly different. The average fourth-grade mean academic grade of dropouts, when not distinguishing between the grade in which students left school, was 2.10. The average fourth-grade mean academic grade of graduates was 2.85—a difference from dropouts that is statistically significant. Much of this difference, however, is driven by the much lower grades of early grade dropouts and the much higher grades of the top two-thirds of graduates. For, as we found in the first section of this chapter, the majority of dropouts in this study did not look dramatically different in the fourth grade in terms of their grades and attendance from youths who would later go on to graduate in the bottom third of their graduating class, suggesting that we would not have been able to identify these students as being at risk of early school leaving. We can address the predictive power of early school performance more directly by asking: How well could we have predicted a youth's later school outcomes on the basis of fourth-grade characteristics?

Table 4.10 presents the results of predicting the likelihood of dropping out on the basis of a youth's demographic and fourth-grade school characteristics, early grade retentions, and fourth-grade mean academic grades. As discussed in Chapter 3, background characteristics and yearly attendance were not available for middle school dropouts. This information was available for high school dropouts and graduates. For prediction purposes, I estimated the likelihood of dropping out on the basis of fourth-grade mean academic grades, mean social grades, early grade retentions, fourth-grade school quality, the census tract characteristics associated with the school attended in the fourth grade, and a youth's gender for the entire sample. I then included information on the father's occupation, nativity, and family size, as well as fourth-grade attendance when predicting the likelihood of dropping out for the sample of youths who participated in the ninth grade. The logistic regression coefficients associated with this equation are reported in Appendix 4-C.

As seen in Table 4.10, a youth's fourth-grade mean academic grade is strongly associated with the likelihood of school dropout. The results of Equation 4.1, reported in Table 4.10, would predict that, at the mean, a 1.0 increase in fourth-grade mean academic grades is associated with a .208 decrease in the likelihood of dropping out when controlling for mean social grades, previous grade failures, gender, and fourth-grade school characteristics. Even after controlling for fourth-grade school performance and a youth's demographic and school characteristics, youths who repeated grades previous to the fourth grade were more likely to drop out of school than those who had never repeated a grade.

The results of Equation 4.1 provide a useful way of summarizing the findings of this chapter. The bottom of this table shows the predicted probability of dropping out and the percent of each group correctly predicted. A dropout was classified as "correctly predicted" if his or her predicted probability of dropping out was above .5. Graduates were coded as "correctly predicted" if their predicted probability of dropping out was below .5. Slightly over three-quarters of early dropouts and approximately 85 percent of youths who later graduated in the middle and top two-thirds of the graduating class could be correctly identified as drop-

Table 4.10
Logit Analysis Results of Equation Predicting the Likelihood of Dropping Out on the Basis of Fourth-Grade School Performance and Demographic Characteristics

	Equation 4.1		Equation 4.1	
	Change P(Drop)		Change P(Drop 9th or later)	
4th-grade performance				
Mean academic grades	-.208[a]	(7.20)[b]	-.154	(5.52)
Mean social grades	-.231	(1.89)	-.236	(1.82)
Attendance			-.000	(.10)
# of retentions (k-3)	.199	(4.24)	.174	(3.74)
School quality	.036	(2.90)	.022	(1.77)
Census Tract				
% HS grads	-.366	(.93)	-.439	(1.11)
% Public Ass.	1.860	(2.75)	-1.726	(2.58)
% O/F/L	-.861	(2.07)	-.976	(2.41)
Female	-.111	(2.66)	-.084	(2.00)
# of siblings			.025	(2.09)
Father skilled			.216	(2.11)
Father unskilled			.185	(1.74)
Father other			.255	(2.27)
Immigrant k+			1.72	(1.39)
Immigrant pre-k			.33	(.03)
2nd-generation			.64	(.64)
Chi-square	191.30		160.16	
Pseudo-R²	.1846		.1775	

	Predicted Probability	% Correctly Predicted	Predicted Probability	% Correctly Predicted
Total		68.2		71.7
7th-grade drops	.648	75.0		
8th-grade drops	.675	81.6		
9th-grade drops	.661	72.8	.60	69.5
10th-grade drops	.556	56.4	.543	62.5
11th-grade drops	.485	44.1	.416	35.6
12th-grade drops	.475	48.1	.364	29.7
Bottom 1/3 grads	.432	60.2	.354	79.4
Mid 1/3 grads	.349	74.1	.297	81.0
Top 1/3 grads	.149	97.0	.152	98.0

a. Partial derivative evaluated at the mean values of the independent variables including missing values.
b. t-statistics in parentheses
Note: The equation also contained parameters for missing observations (see Appendix 4-C).

outs or graduates simply on the basis of their fourth-grade school performance, early grade retentions, and fourth-grade school characteristics. In comparison, late grade dropouts' predicted probability of school leaving, which were slightly higher than those of the bottom third of graduates, means that we would not have correctly predicted these students' outcomes on the basis of their fourth-grade characteristics.

SUMMARY

The purpose of the Fall River study was to enrich our understanding of the nature and dynamics of school dropout by providing previously unavailable data on the middle school and early high school antecedents of school dropout. Previous research on school dropout, discussed in Chapter 2, has provided a detailed picture of the characteristics that distinguish dropouts from graduates at or around the time of dropping out. In Chapter 3, I outlined several perspectives on the relationship between early school leaving and school experiences that could be drawn from research on the social, academic, and personal correlates of school dropout.

The findings presented in this chapter challenge two of the most common portrayals of the relationship between school experiences and school dropout. While early grade dropouts could be distinguished early on in their school career by their poor performance in school, the average grades and attendance of late grade dropouts did not look dramatically different from those of youths who graduated in the bottom third of their class as of the fourth grade.

I found that there were three important differences in the school careers of these late grade dropouts and graduates. First, late grade dropouts experienced much larger declines in their average grades following the school transition to both middle school in the sixth grade and to high school in the ninth grade. Second, dropouts, regardless of the grade in which they dropped out of school, were much more likely than graduates to have repeated grades both previous to and after the fourth grade. And, third, late grade dropouts, regardless of the grade in which they dropped out of school, began to show signs of disengagement from school as early as the sixth grade, a level of disengagement that accelerated in late middle school and in high school. Clearly, then, trends in the school career paths of late grade dropouts and graduates, and particularly the degree to which differences in the performance of students following school transitions represented critical points of divergence, lead us away from the hypothesis that the path to dropping out operates independently of school performance.

Indeed, the degree to which the school career paths of late grade dropouts follow such distinct patterns as they move through middle school and into high school also challenges the assumption that dropping out is largely an individualized phenomenon. As described in Chapter 2, a second perspective on the relationship between school experiences and school dropout portrays the path to dropping out as an individualized phenomenon, arising from a complex nest of problems. As Whelage and his fellow authors assert in their study of alternative schools, "at risk students arrive at their disengagement, failure, and decision to drop out via many different routes" (Whelage et al., 1989, p. 75). Averages may mask substantial variance in the individual manifestations of school dropout. Nevertheless, if the path to dropping out could be best characterized as one that is different for every youth, we would have observed patterns that differed by the grade in which students dropped out of school or we would not have observed any clear patterns at all in trends in late grade dropouts' school performance.

The failure of these conventional portrayals of the path to dropping out to adequately describe trends in the school career paths of late grade dropouts challenges us to develop a third conception of the relationship between a youth's school experiences and school outcome. As discussed in Chapter 3, a third perspective on the relationship between school experiences and school dropout focuses on the degree to which the individual manifestations of school dropout could be linked to and are influenced by aspects of the structure, organization, and policies of school. In this chapter, I found that both grade declines following school transitions and grade retention are strongly associated with the likelihood that a student would drop out.

In order to develop a framework to understand the findings presented in this chapter, we need to understand not only whether these school experiences increased the chances that a youth would drop out of school, but both how and why difficulty during school transitions and the experience of being retained in grade may influence a youth's educational trajectory. An important theme in qualitative research on school dropout is that school membership is a critical ingredient in determining whether a student who is having difficulty in school will decide to leave or persist. To restate, dropping out, as described in this literature, is an act of rejecting membership in a community in which youths feel marginal, gain little self-esteem, perceive few rewards, and which they also experience as rejecting them. To what extent did the difficulties that students encountered following school transitions and the experience of repeating a grade pose barriers to school membership and weaken a student's attachment to school? The next two chapters will attempt to address this question through analyses of the association between the likelihood of school dropout and both of these school experiences.

NOTES

1. There were 661 youths who graduated in the Fall River public school's graduating class of 1985–1986. A youth was coded as graduating in the top third of the class if his or her graduating class rank was between 1 and 220. Similarly, youths were coded as being in the middle third of their graduating class if their graduating class rank was between 219 and 440. Youths who graduated a year late, in their thirteenth year of high school, were coded according to their class rank for the graduating class of 1985–1986. Because students transferred into the Fall River public school system after the seventh grade, the graduating class of 1985–1986 was comprised of youths in this cohort who graduated and transfers into the school system who also graduated. Youths who transferred into the school system were more likely to graduate in the middle and bottom third of the graduating class. Thus, a higher proportion of this cohort are coded as having graduated in the top third of the graduating class, than in the middle and bottom two-thirds.

2. If late grade dropouts were a heterogeneous group made up of students whose path to dropping out was precipitated by declines in attendance and a group who had a difficult transition to high school, we would not expect to find a substantial decline in the average mean academic grades of dropouts who had large declines in attendance from the eighth to the ninth grade. I find, however, that dropouts experienced dramatic declines in their average mean academic grades during the transition to high school regardless of changes in their attendance from the sixth to the eighth grade. For example, among the sample of youths who completed the tenth grade, youths who had large declines in their attendance from the sixth to the eighth grade (15 or more days) experienced a 41 percent decline in their average mean academic grades following the transition to high school. In comparison, the average mean academic grade of late grade dropouts who did not have a large decline in attendance from the sixth to the eighth grade declined by 36.4 percent following the transition to high school.

Chapter 5

School Transitions and School Dropout: A Model for Investigating the Impact of School Transitions

When students make the school change from grammar school to middle school and from middle school to high school, they move to larger, more anonymous environments where they encounter new social structures and face new academic demands. Previous research on these school moves, often called normative school transitions, have found that they are difficult periods for youths.[1] On average, grades decline following a school move, particularly following the transition to high school. For example, the average grades of students in the Fall River study declined by 8 percent following the move to middle school in the sixth grade and by 18 percent following the transition to high school.

When we looked at trends in the average grades of dropouts and graduates in the Fall River study, we found that it was largely following these school transitions that trends in the academic grades of late grade dropouts diverged from those of graduates. For example, from the eighth to the ninth grade, the percentage of tenth- to twelfth-grade dropouts who failed 25 percent or more of their credits increased from 5.3 to 60.7 percent compared to an increase for graduates from 2.6 to 8.3 percent.

Why would grade changes associated with school transitions as early as the sixth grade raise the chances that a youth would drop out? One answer is that whenever students do more poorly in school, they are more likely to drop out. In addition, students' academic and adjustment difficulties during the first year of middle school and high school may pose significant barriers to their ability to form positive attachments and become integrated into these larger and more complex environments—

an integration that qualitative research on early school leaving argues is critical for persistence. In this chapter, I explore both whether and how a student's performance during the first year of middle school influences his or her chances of dropping out. I begin with a discussion of previous research on school transitions. I then examine the extent to which dropout rates differed by changes in a student's grades following the school move to middle school in the sixth grade and to high school in the ninth grade. Drawing upon Tinto's research on the importance of adjustment difficulties in determining college persistence, I then develop a model with which to examine whether a student's adjustment difficulties during the first year of middle school had an independent impact on the likelihood of dropping out when controlling for later school performance.

PREVIOUS RESEARCH ON SCHOOL TRANSITIONS

Why Are School Transitions Difficult for Youths?

Any school transition is stressful. Youths must sever personal ties and leave comfortable physical settings and routines to form new personal bonds and adjust to a new physical environment. The transitions to middle schools, junior high schools, and high schools are distinguished from other kinds of school moves because they also involve changes in the size and complexity of the physical environment, changes in role, and changes in the academic demands and organization of classrooms.[2]

The first major change involves size. In the Fall River school system, twenty-eight grammar schools feed into four middle schools, which feed into one comprehensive high school. Larger schools mean more anonymity, complexity, and freedom.

The second major change is that youths move to a more heterogeneous social structure where their status changes from being the oldest to the youngest peer group in the school. A student's peers are also trying to adapt to the new physical environment (Felner et al., 1982). In this social setting, in sharp contrast to a move to an established classroom, it may be more difficult for students to adapt since they cannot easily understand the routines of the new environment, or find a niche in an established social structure.

Finally, these transitions also involve changes in pedagogy, skill demands, the structure of classrooms, and academic schedules. At each of these transitions, tracking and departmentalization increase. Students experience changes in the organization of classrooms and the kind of work they are expected to produce. In middle school and junior high school, adolescents are less likely to be in self-contained classrooms and are more likely to be tracked by ability than they are in elementary schools (Becker, 1987; Eccles et al., 1991). Middle school and junior high school classrooms are also characterized by less personal and more disciplined student/teacher relationships, and by greater use of whole class instruction (Eccles et al., 1991). Indeed, Eccles and Midgley argue that it is largely these differences between the educational demands, attitudes of teachers, and classroom organization of elementary and middle schools that account for the academic difficulties encountered following school transitions (Eccles et al., 1991; Eccles and Midgley, 1989; Midgley et al., 1989).

The Impact of School Transitions on School Performance

In summation, during normative school transitions, a youth's peer and academic relationships are in a state of flux at the same time that he or she is trying to adapt to a new, larger, and more complex physical environment. It is not surprising that youths experience some difficulties in adjusting to these new environments. The most consistent finding in the literature on the effect of school transitions is that students' average grades decline significantly following these school moves—declines that are observed regardless of the grade in which youths change schools (Blyth and Simmons, 1987; Blyth et al., 1983; Crockett et al., 1989; Felner et al., 1981; Schulenberg et al., 1984).[3] Students are also likely to experience some short-term adjustment difficulties. For example, students who are in their first year of middle school, junior high school, or high school are less likely to participate in extracurricular activities and are more likely to report feelings of anonymity than their peers in the same grade who had not changed schools (Blyth and Simmons, 1987; Blyth et al., 1983; Crockett et al., 1989; Neilsen and Gerber, 1979).

In the previous chapter, I noted that there is an ongoing debate as to whether declines in grades following normative school moves can be attributed to changes in academic performance, or to differences in grading procedures among elementary schools, middle schools, and high schools. Some researchers have found that grade declines associated with these school moves are not accompanied by declines in students' achievement test scores, suggesting that teachers simply grade harder in middle schools and in high schools (Eccles and Midgley, 1989). If all students experienced similar declines in their average grades following a school transition, then students may simply adjust to this new grading schema. But, as we found in the previous chapter, grade declines varied widely from student to student. Some students experienced very moderate grade declines, while other students saw dramatic changes in their average grades. Whether these changes are due to academic difficulty, or are due to a youth knowing as much, working as hard, and yet still getting worse grades, is an important question. Both the experience of having difficulty in school and the experience of being graded harder for the same quality of work would, however, be perceived by students as very real difficulties, especially if there is a great deal of variance in grade changes across youths.

Unfortunately, there has been little research on the extent to which grade declines following school transitions vary from student to student. Harriet Feldlaufer, Jacquelynne Eccles, and Carol Midgley did find that differences in classroom practices between elementary and junior high school produced the greatest academic difficulty for lower performing students (Midgley et al., 1989). Several studies have also found that black students experience larger grade declines than whites following the move to both junior high school and high school (Felner et al., 1981; Simmons et al., 1991). The Fall River data set allows us to investigate the extent to which students' grades changed following the move to middle school and to high school, as well as the association between these grade declines and later school outcomes.

DROPOUT RATES BY CHANGES IN GRADES FOLLOWING SCHOOL TRANSITIONS

Table 5.1 documents the extent to which grade declines following the move to the middle school in the sixth and the transition to high school in the ninth grade varied across students in the Fall River cohort. Mean academic grades were coded on a 0 to 4.0 scale. A student who had a B average in the fifth grade and a B− average in the sixth grade would have a −.33 decline in his or her average mean academic grades from the fifth to the sixth grade.

As seen in Table 5.1, the average grades of students who moved to the middle schools in the sixth grade declined moderately from grade 5 to 6. Grade changes following the school move to high school were much larger. From the eighth to the ninth grade, the average grade of students who moved to the high school and did not drop out in the ninth grade declined by .48. Table 5.1 also documents the extent to which dropout rates varied by the degree of academic difficulty students encountered following each school change. In particular, we find that students who experienced an average grade decline of two-thirds of a grade level (−.67 or greater) or more following both the transition to the middle school and to the high school were more likely to drop out than those who experienced more moderate declines in their average grades.

SCHOOL TRANSITIONS AND SCHOOL DROPOUT: A MODEL

Why would the extent to which a student's grades decline following a school move influence one's chances of graduating from high school?

Table 5.1
Dropout Rates by Changes in a Youth's Mean Academic Grades Following the Transition to Middle School in the Sixth Grade and the Transition to High School in the Ninth Grade

	Changes in Mean Academic Grades, 5th-6th[a]	
Change in Grade Average = -.24[b]	Proportion Dropped Out	Percent of Students with Change
< = - 1.68	.58	2.1%
-1.34 to -1.67	.76	3.0%
-1.01 to -1.33	.62	6.5%
-.68 to -1.0	.46	9.9%
-.34 to -.67	.35	20.9%
.1 to -.33	.32	25.6%
0 to .33	.35	15.5%
.34 to .67	.40	9.9%
.68 or more	.40	6.4%

	Changes in Mean Academic Grades, 8th-9th[c]	
Change in Grade Average change = -.48	Proportion Dropped 10th or later	Percent of Student with Change
<= - 2.01	.67	3.7%
1.68 to -2.0	.60	7.2%
-1.32 to -1.67	.58	8.9%
-1.01 to -1.33	.52	13.2%
-.68 to -1.0	.44	14.5%
-.34 to -.67	.27	20.9%
.1 to -.33	.21	13.8%
0 to .33	.09	10.9%
.34 to .67	.18	6.8%

a. Changes in grades were calculated only for students who attended one of Fall River's four middle schools in the sixth grade.
b. Average change in grade from fifth to sixth were calculated using a youth's fifth-grade grades in the second year for those who repeated fifth grade.
c. Grade changes calculated for students who attended but did not drop out during the ninth grade.

A simple answer is that whenever students do more poorly in school, they are more likely to drop out. If students do not recover from the grade losses incurred during school transitions, these grade declines would represent a permanent increase in their risk of school leaving.

A second explanation is that academic and adjustment difficulties in a new school would raise the chances of early school leaving by posing barriers to school membership and engagement. During school transitions, students must adapt and form positive attachments in larger and more complex institutions. Qualitative research on school dropout argues that the extent to which a student is engaged in school and has formed attachments to both the institution and to the goals of schooling are critical determinants of persistence. A student's academic difficulty following these school moves may pose significant barriers to, and may reflect a failure to become, integrated into these new school communities. A theory of school membership would suggest, then, that difficulty in the first year of middle school and high school means more to a student's persistence than would academic difficulty in nontransition years. Grade declines following these school moves may provide an index of both academic difficulty and the degree to which a student experienced difficulty in adjustment. If the extent to which a student is able to become engaged in middle school and high school is an important determinant of continued persistence, then one would expect that a student's performance during the first year of middle school and high school would have an independent impact on the likelihood of school dropout even when controlling for posttransition performance. Indeed, examining the relationship between performance following school transitions and the likelihood of school dropout provides an empirical test of the hypothesis that a student's school membership is an important factor in determining whether a poorly performing student will decide to remain in school.

Tinto's Theory of School Withdrawal and School Adjustment

In Chapter 2, I argued that Tinto's theory of withdrawal from college provided a framework with which to understand why youths who were doing poorly in school, and particularly those from disadvantaged backgrounds, would leave high school rather than continue on to graduate in the bottom third of their graduating class. To restate, Tinto posits that the likelihood that a student will withdraw from school is a function of the extent to which the individual develops an attachment to school and becomes integrated into the life of the school community (Tinto, 1987). In Tinto's research, a student's experiences during the first term and ability to successfully make the transition to college are of particular importance. Most students will experience some adjustment difficulties separating themselves from past associations, adjusting to the new academic demands of college, and creating new attachments. For others, however, adjustment difficulties may pose significant barriers to their incorporation into the social and intellectual life of the community, an incorporation that is necessary for persistence.

Indeed, Tinto argues that a youth's experiences during the first term of college take on special meaning. Students who encounter significant academic difficulty early on may be more likely to conclude that they do not fit into the social and intellectual life of the community. For example, Tinto notes that students who perceive too great a decrease in their academic performance in the first term of college are more likely to withdraw. Doing poorly in a course during the first term of college may have a greater impact on school attachment than would difficulty in a course in the second or third term, when students could draw upon positive past experiences or rely on an established support system to cope with this academic stress (Tinto, 1987). Similarly, social and personal experiences during the first term take on special meaning. As Tinto notes: "one is led to the notion that contact among students and faculty may be more appropriate earlier in the student's career than later after intellectual and social membership has been established" (Tinto, 1987, p. 69).

The transition to college is different in many respects from the school moves to middle school and to high school. When students move to these middle level and secondary schools, they are not required to leave their families and friends. They are not likely to be balancing jobs, families, and school. Nor can difficulties in adjustment, particularly in the transition to middle school, result in immediate withdrawal for most students. For adolescents, however, the stresses of these school moves may be as challenging as those facing young adults in the transition to college. Many of the same barriers to school membership that are encountered by college students during their first term may be encountered by adolescents as they move into middle school and high school. As Tinto notes:

Institutions of higher education are not unlike other human communities. The process of educational departure is not substantially different from the other processes of leaving which occur among human communities generally. In both instances, departure mirrors the absence of social and intellectual integration into the mainstream of community life and the social support such integration provides. (Tinto, 1987, p. 180)

A Model for Investigation of the Impact of Normative School Transition on the Likelihood of School Dropout

Is there evidence that a student's academic difficulty following school transitions would have long-term implications for school membership and persistence in school? We can investigate this question by estimating the relationship between progressive school performance and school leaving. Equation 1 presents a model for estimating the effect of a student's mean academic grades in the fourth through eighth grades on the chances of that student dropping out. In this equation, the effect of a student's grades in the sixth grade is considered separately for youths who did and did not make the transition to middle school in the sixth grade through the use of an interaction term (Ac_{6th}*Middle).

$$P(DROP \text{ after } ninth) = \alpha + \beta_1 Ac_{4th} + \beta_2 Ac_{5th} + \beta_3 Ac_{6th} + \beta_4 Ac_{6th}\text{*}Middle + \beta_5 Ac_{7th} + \beta_6 Ac_{8th}$$

where:

Ac Middle		= student's mean academic grade in each year
		= 1 if a student attended a middle school in the sixth grade, 0 if not
P(Drop after ninth)		= probability student drops out after the ninth grade given that he or she did not drop out prior to the ninth grade

The coefficient on the interaction term in the sixth grade allows us to test the hypothesis that performance in the year following the normative school transition to middle school has an independent impact on the likelihood of dropping out when controlling for posttransition performance. To restate, students who encountered academic difficulty following school transitions may be more likely to drop out because these grade declines represented permanent shifts in their academic status. If this was the only effect of school transitions, one would not expect to find that a student's performance following a normative school move would have an independent effect on the likelihood of school dropout when controlling for posttransition performance. Simply put, the relationship between progressive school performance and school dropout should be cumulative. For example, if I estimate the likelihood of dropping out solely as a function of a youth's fourth-grade grades, I would expect that the coefficient on fourth-grade performance would be large and statistically significant. In an equation that estimated the likelihood of dropping out as a function of both fourth- and fifth-grade performance, however, the coefficient on fourth-grade performance should be reduced in both size and significance since fifth-grade performance is determined both by current experience and by how well a youth did in the fourth grade. If the relationship between progressive school experiences and school dropout is simply cumulative, then a youth's performance in the highest grade included in the equation would have a large and statistically significant association with dropping out and no previous year of school performance would predict dropping out better than any other.

Tinto's theory of school withdrawal suggests that the extent to which students encounter academic and adjustment difficulties following the school transitions to middle school and to high school may impose significant barriers to their integration into these school communities. The failure of a student both academically, and perhaps socially, in these new environments may then initiate or accelerate a process of disengagement from school, and a conflict between the youth and the school as an institution. To restate, this interpretation would suggest that grades in the year following a normative school move would measure both a youth's academic experiences and the degree to which a youth successfully adapted to the new school environment. If this level of adaptation had an important influence on dropping out, a youth's grades in transition years would have an independent impact on the likelihood of dropping out even when controlling for posttransition performance. In Equation 1, the interaction term $(Ac_{6th}*Middle)$ tests this hypothesis.

Equation 1 expresses the relationship between the likelihood of dropping out on the basis of fourth- to eighth-grade mean academic grades for the sample of students who did not drop out prior to the ninth grade. In order to examine the impact of performance in transition years controlling for posttransition performance, I need to restrict the analysis to those youths who participated in, and did not drop out during, the last year included in the equation. For example, in order to examine the impact of a youth's performance during the first year of high school (9th grade), we need to estimate Equation 1 for the sample of students who did not drop out prior to or during the ninth grade.

This model provides a direct method of examining the effect of performance in the first year of middle school. It relies on the fact that grades in each successive year are correlated with grades in previous years. The high degree of multicollinearity among the included parameters will, however, result in large standard errors. One approach to dealing with this problem would be to omit several intermediate grade levels (e.g., using a youth's mean academic grades in the fourth, sixth, and eighth grade). This approach was not, however, necessary. In this analysis, performance in school is measured by mean academic grades in each year. Mean social grades are not included in the equation in order to reduce multicollinearity.

Finally, Equation 1 includes information on a student's school performance prior to and after the transition to middle school, but does not include information on differences in students' prior engagement or measured background characteristics. A third potential explanation for the association between transition performance and school dropout is that the large grade declines associated with school transitions are reflections of a student's poor school performance and disengagement from school rather than experiences that increased chances of leaving school. In order to control for other factors that may increase the chances of dropping out, I estimated a second series of equations that included information on fourth- to eighth-grade attendance, the number of times a student repeated or failed a grade prior to the eighth grade, and the measured demographic and family background characteristics.

RESULTS

The Effect of School Performance Following the Transition to Middle School in the Sixth Grade

Table 5.2 presents the results of estimating the relationship between the conditional likelihood of dropping out and single grade mean academic grades. The first equation estimated the conditional likelihood of dropping out given ninth-grade participation on the basis of mean academic grades from the fourth to the eighth grade. The second and third columns of Table 5.2 present the results of estimating the conditional likelihood of dropping out on the basis of fourth- to ninth-grade characteristics for the sample of tenth-grade persisters, and from fourth- to tenth-grade characteristics for those who attended the eleventh grade. Each equation also included dummy variables for missing observations in each year. The logit coefficients associated with each equation are reported in Appendix 5-A.

Looking at Table 5.2, we find that the estimated impact of mean academic grade in the last two years included in each equation is large and statistically significant. This finding is consistent with the hypothesis that the impact of school performance is cumulative. Once we have controlled for later performance, a youth's performance in the fourth, fifth, and seventh grades does not provide any further information, nor do grades in the sixth grade for those who did not attend a middle school in that year. The interaction term measuring the additional impact of sixth-grade mean academic grades for those who made the transition to middle school in that year is significantly related to the conditional likelihood of dropping out, even when controlling for school performance

Table 5.2
Effect of Single Grade Mean Academic Grades on the Conditional Likelihood of Dropping Out Given Persistence to the Ninth, Tenth, and Eleventh Grades

WITH INTERACTION TERM SIXTH GRADE

	P(Drop 9th or later)		P(Drop 10th or later		P(Drop 11th of later)	
ACADEMIC GRADE						
Fourth	-.007 [a]	(.19) [b]	.015	(.43)	.011	(.54)
Fifth	.003	(.08)	.027	(.69)	.023	(1.01)
Sixth	-.044	(.95)	-.029	(.64)	.001	(.02)
Sixth*Middle [c]	-.091	(4.00)	-.076	(3.56)	-.048	(3.66)
Seventh	-.094	(2.43)	-.008	(.20)	-.001	(.03)
Eighth	-.236	(5.94)	-.121	(3.0)	-.032	(1.29)
Ninth			-.217	(7.68)	-.049	(2.76)
Tenth					-.150	(7.25)
N	683		642		569	
Actual freq. [d]	.3734		.3333		.2478	

a. Partial derivative evaluated at the mean values of the independent variables including missing values.
b. t-statistics in parentheses.
c. Sixth*Middle is an interaction term taking on the value 1*Sixth for youths who made the transition to middle school in sixth grade and 0 otherwise.
d. Actual frequency = observed frequency of dropping out in that grade or later grades given persistence to grade.

Note: The equation also contained parameters for missing observations and an interaction term for youths who were neither in one of the eight grammar schools or in the middle schools in the fourth grade. See Appendix 5-A.

after the transition to high school. Thus, a youth's academic performance following the normative school transition to middle school appears to have an important influence on the likelihood of dropping out independent of its impact on later school performance.

The Effect of School Performance Following the Transition to Middle School in the Sixth Grade Controlling for Differences in Background and Attendance

Table 5.3 presents the results of estimating the relationship between single grade school performance and the conditional likelihood of dropping out controlling for differences in the background and census tract characteristics available in the Fall River data set, the incidence of retention, the cumulative number of times a youth changed schools, and attendance from the fourth to the eighth grade.

As seen in Table 5.3, including information on differences in the mea-

Table 5.3
Effect of Single Grade Mean Academic Grades, Attendance (4–8), and Background Variables on the Conditional Likelihood of Dropping Out Given Persistence to the Ninth, Tenth, and Eleventh Grades

WITH INTERACTION TERM SIXTH GRADE

	P(Drop 9th or later)		P(Drop 10th or later		P(Drop 11th or later)	
ACADEMIC GRADE						
Fourth	.021	(.46)	.046	(1.13)	.016	(.86)
Fifth	.019	(.41)	.037	(.89)	.017	(.85)
Sixth	-.038	(.67)	-.036	(.69)	-.002	(.09)
Sixth*Middle	-.091	(2.93)	-.078	(2.81)	-.042	(2.96)
Seventh	-.067	(1.50)	.003	(.04)	.010	(.45)
Eighth	-.185	(3.95)	-.084	(1.91)	-.019	(.82)
Ninth			-.202	(6.51)	-.041	(2.56)
Tenth					-.122	(3.61)
ATTENDANCE						
Fourth	.006	(2.06)	.007	(2.46)	.007	(3.51)
Fifth	-.003	(.98)	-.003	(1.10)	-.002	(.97)
Sixth	.003	(.78)	.001	(.46)	.000	(.16)
Seven	.001	(.29)	.003	(.98)	.000	(.16)
Eighth	-.012	(4.93)	-.009	(4.09)	-.004	(3.09)
# Retentions	.163	(3.61)	.131	(3.19)	.012	(.52)
# School changes	.080	(2.31)	.073	(2.28)	.023	(1.47)
School quality	.010	(.71)	.006	(.47)	.005	(.83)
Census Tract						
% HS grads	.168	(.34)	.314	(.71)	.148	(.65)
% Public ass.	1.798	(2.44)	1.428	(2.20)	.441	(1.32)
% O/F/L	-.685	(1.30)	-.472	(.98)	-.182	(.75)
Female	-.074	(1.58)	-.050	(1.16)	-.021	(.92)
# of Siblings	.008	(.63)	.010	(.82)	.002	(.35)
Father skilled	.058	(.51)	.056	(.54)	.003	(.06)
Father unskilled	.063	(.55)	.076	(.74)	.017	(.34)
Father other	.120	(.97)	.118	(1.06)	.055	(1.01)
Immigrant k+	.107	(1.17)	.060	(.70)	.009	(.18)
Immigrant pre-k	.015	(.15)	.001	(.01)	-.075	(1.43)
2nd-generation	.070	(.77)	.005	(.08)	.009	(.26)
N	683		642		569	
Actual freq.	.3734		.3333		.2478	

Note: See notes to Table 5.2.

sured background and census tract characteristics, the incidence of re-tentions, school moves, and fourth- to eighth-grade attendance have a negligible effect on the estimated impact of grades during the first year of middle school. At the mean of the independent variables, this equation predicts that an increase in a student's sixth-grade mean academic grade for those who attended the middle school in that year is associated with a decrease in the conditional likelihood of dropping out given ninth-grade persistence of .091 compared to an estimated decrease of .096 when not controlling for attendance and background characteristics.

The Impact of School Performance During the Normative Transition to Middle School: An Illustration

The importance of a youth's academic experiences during the first year of middle school is most clearly illustrated by examining the predicted change in the conditional probability of dropping out for a sample youth. Table 5.4 compares the result of a 1.0 grade increase in a student's mean academic grades in various years for a youth who persisted to the tenth grade. This sample youth is a male whose father worked in a skilled occupation, who is native born with three siblings, and who changed schools twice. He is from a census tract in the south end of Fall River where the school he attended had a quality index of 4 and where 32.2 percent of adults were high school graduates, 22.41 percent of families received public assistance, and 31.24 percent of employed adults were operators, fabricators, or laborers. In addition, this sample youth had never failed a grade.

The first column of Table 5.4 shows the predicted impact of a change in mean academic grades in each year for a youth with these sample background characteristics who had mean academic grades and attendance one standard deviation below the mean in each year. For a student with these characteristics—a youth who performed poorly throughout his school career—the predicted probability of dropping out is .673. The second column of Table 5.4 shows the predicted impact of a change in mean academic grades in each year for a youth whom we would consider moderately at risk of dropping out. This sample youth had similar background characteristics but had mean academic grades and attendance one-half of a standard deviation below the mean for each year. Finally, the third column of this table shows the predicted probability of dropping out given tenth-grade persistence for a youth with these sample characteristics who had average mean academic grades and attendance in each year.

Consistent with the hypothesis that the impact of school performance is cumulative, we would predict that better performance in the eighth and ninth grades would substantially decrease the likelihood of dropping out regardless of previous school performance. Given eighth- and ninth-

Table 5.4

Comparison of Effect of Changes in Single Year Mean Academic Grades on the Conditional Likelihood of Dropping Out in Tenth Grade or Later for a Sample Youth

	Youth, High Risk	Youth, Moderate Risk	Youth, Average Risk
Predicted P(Drop/10th)	.673	.473	.219
	Change in Probability Drop for a 1.0 Increase In Mean Academic Grade In		
Fourth grade	+.044	+.052	+.038
Fifth grade	+.042	+.049	+.038
Sixth grade	-.051	-.055	-.036
Sixth grade/middle	-.135	-.136	-.082
Seventh grade	+.001	+.001	+.000
Eighth grade	-.126	-.128	-.077
Ninth grade	-.207	-.198	-.13

Notes: Sample youth is a male whose father worked in an unskilled occupation, who is native born with three siblings, who changed schools twice and who is from a census tract in the south end of Fall River where the school he attended has a quality index of 4, and where 32.2 percent of adults were high school graduates, 22.4 percent of families received public assistance, and 31.2 percent of adults were operators, fabricators, or laborers.

In addition: **high-risk youth** = mean academic grades and attendance 4th-9th one standard deviation below the mean for youth in each year; **moderately at-risk youth** = mean academic grades and attendance one-half of a standard deviation below the mean in each year; **average risk** = mean academic grades and attendance at the mean for each year.

grade performance, these results suggest that better performance in non-transition years would have a small impact on the conditional likelihood of dropping out. In comparison, even when including information on a student's performance in the ninth grade, we would predict that better performance during the transition to middle school would substantially reduce the likelihood of dropping out. Notice also that the predicted impact of changes in a youth's mean academic performance during the transition to middle school is larger for high and moderately at-risk youth than for a youth with average mean academic grades and attendance. These results suggest that, for students at the margin, better performance in transition years would improve their chances of dropping out.

Findings on the Impact of Performance During the Transition to High School

This analysis of the relationship between single grade performance and the likelihood of school dropout has focused on examining the impact of the normative school transition to middle school. Theoretically, if grades in the year after a normative school change measure whether a youth successfully adapted to the new school environment, then we would also expect to find that grades in the ninth grade, after the transition to high school, would have a large and independent impact on the likelihood of dropping out when controlling for posttransition performance.

We can examine the impact of the transition to high school controlling for later school performance for the sample of youths who attended the eleventh grade. As seen in Table 5.3, the estimated impact of mean academic grades in the ninth grade, when controlling for differences in the background, school experiences, and attendance from the fourth to the eighth grade, is statistically significantly associated with the likelihood of dropping out even when controlling for tenth-grade performance. It is more difficult, however, to interpret the results for ninth-grade mean academic grades.

As documented throughout this analysis, when estimating the conditional likelihood of dropping out based on progressive school experiences, the most recent grade included in each equation captures a student's cumulative academic experience and has a large and statistically significant association with the likelihood of dropping out. The next to last year included in each equation also appears to be associated with dropping out. For example, both eighth- and ninth-grade mean academic grades are significantly associated with the conditional likelihood of dropping out given tenth-grade persistence. Thus, it is unclear whether the statistical significance of mean academic grades in the ninth grade should lead one to conclude that performance in the transition to high school has an independent impact on the likelihood of school dropout or that the next to last grade included in the equation will measure part of the cumulative impact of academic performance.

Findings on the Impact of Attendance

In the previous chapter, I found that late grade dropouts also experienced much larger declines in their average attendance throughout middle school. Regardless of the timing of the transition to middle school, I found that the average attendance of late grade dropouts began to decline in the sixth grade—a level of disengagement that accelerated in late middle school and in the transition to high school. In the analysis presented in Table 5.3, a youth's attendance in eighth grade emerges as an important predictor of early school leaving.[4] Thus, it appears that a student's pre-high school level of engagement in school has an important influence on the likelihood he or she will drop out, independent of its effect on performance in the ninth and tenth grade.

The importance of eighth-grade attendance once again raises the question: To what extent are the dramatic declines in the grades of dropouts during the transition to high school a reflection of pre-high school levels of engagement? As we will see in Chapter 7, recent attention has been drawn to the middle school years as a critical period in the formation of attachment to school. This analysis, as well as the results presented in the previous chapter, provide empirical evidence that this period may also play an important role in the path by which youth become disengaged and drop out of school. The extent to which a student's disengagement in middle school influences his or her ability to cope with the stresses of adjustment to high school is an important question. Such a link would lead policy away from a sole focus on intervening during normative school transitions, and toward a focus on engagement both previous to and after normative school changes. Thus, further attempts at disentangling the progression and interplay of school-related experiences that precede the decision to drop out are critical for the formation of policy regarding school transitions.

Finally, in these equations, fourth-grade attendance has a positive and statistically significant association with dropping out when controlling for later attendance and school performance. There is, to my knowledge, no reason to expect that students who had higher attendance in the fourth grade, when controlling for later experiences, would be more likely to drop out than students with similar characteristics who had lower fourth-grade attendance. A check of attendance in fourth grade showed no signs that these results were driven by outliers. This anomalous result is, therefore, confusing, and one for which I have no explanation.

SUMMARY

This chapter addressed the question: Is the ability of students to successfully maneuver the school transition to middle school and to high school an important contributor to the likelihood that they will drop out of school? I began by examining how dropout rates differed by the extent of students' grade declines following school transitions. Most students in the Fall River school system experienced moderate declines in their average grades when they moved to middle school and to high school. Average grades declined by no more than one-third of a grade level, on average, during the first year of middle school. Average grades declined by .48 grade levels following the transition to high school.

Students who had large declines in their average grades when they moved to middle school in the sixth grade were more likely to drop out of school than those who experienced less academic difficulty following these school moves. For example, students whose average mean academic grades declined by between one and one and one-third grade levels from the fifth to the sixth grade were 30 percent more likely to drop out than those whose average mean academic grades declined by no more than one-third of a grade level. In order to identify the causes of school leaving, we need to understand not only whether grade declines following school transitions make youths more likely to drop out, but how these experiences affected students' career paths. Part of the higher dropout rate among students who experienced large declines in their average grades following the transition to middle school can be attributed to the fact that whenever students have lower grades, they are more likely to drop out. Part of the higher dropout rate among those who experienced large declines in their grades following the transition to middle school is that these grade declines provide an overall index of their ability to successfully adapt to the new academic and social environments of middle school and high school.

Multivariate analysis allows us to examine how much of the higher dropout rate among students who experienced large grade declines during the first year of middle school can be attributed to permanent declines in their academic performance and how much may be attributed to an independent effect of the extent to which a student is integrated into the life of the school. I found that a student's performance during the first year of middle school had an important impact on the chances that he or she would drop out of school. Students who had difficulty during the first year of middle school were more likely to drop out even after including information on their school performance through the transition to high school. The findings presented in this and the preceding chapter, then, provide strong evidence that school transitions are critical periods in the academic careers of early school leavers. Before discussing the policy and research implications of these findings, the next chapter will conduct a similar analysis of the association between grade retention and school dropout.

NOTES

1. Felner et al. (1981) refer to normal grade progression that requires a move to a new school such as the transition from elementary to middle school as a "normative" school transition. These normative transitions are distinguished from school transitions due to school transfer.

2. This discussion is based on conversations with Richard Weissbourd, research associate at the Malcolm Weiner Center for Social Policy, Harvard University, and on my reading of the discussion of the nature of normative school transitions in Felner et al. (1981, 1982, 1988), Blyth and Simmons (1987), and Eccles, Lord, and Midgley (1991).

3. There is some evidence that the impact of the transition to high school is less disruptive for youths who attend kindergarten to eighth-grade elementary

schools versus an elementary, middle level school, high school grade structure (Blyth et al., 1983). The less disruptive effect of the high school transfer for those in a kindergarten to eighth-grade system may be due to the timing of the school transition or it may be due to the fact that two transitions are more stressful than one (Crockett et al., 1989).

4. In an analysis not presented here, I find that when estimating the conditional likelihood of dropping out on the basis of mean academic grades and attendance from fourth to ninth grade for the sample of tenth-grade persisters and from fourth to tenth grade for the sample of eleventh-grade persisters, eighth-grade attendance has a statistically significant association with the conditional likelihood of dropping out even when controlling for later attendance.

Chapter 6

Grade Retention and School Dropout: Investigating the Association

One of the most consistent findings in the literature on early school leaving is that dropouts are much more likely to be overage for grade by the time they drop out. The strength of the association between grade retention and school dropout, widely cited in the literature, is impressive. Fully 77 percent of youths in the Fall River cohort who repeated at least one grade dropped out of school, compared to only 25 percent who had never failed a grade.

High dropout rates among retained youths are often used as evidence that grade retention is harmful. The problem with such comparisons is that it is unclear to what extent higher dropout rates among retained youths reflect the fact that school systems retain students because they are doing poorly in school and, thus, are already likely to drop out. In this chapter, I examine how much of the higher dropout rates among retained youths can be attributed to an independent impact of grade retention, and how much may be due to the simple fact that those students who are most likely to drop out due to poor educational performance may also be those most likely to experience a grade retention. I also examine the effect of grade retention by the number of times a student was retained, and by whether the retention was prior to or after the fourth grade.

Students who experience a retention may face an increased risk of school leaving because they do more poorly in school or have lower self-esteem as a result of that retention. Students who are retained in grade may also be at a higher risk of dropping out because a grade retention makes them overage for grade. Youths who are older than their classmates may feel different than their peers, particularly during adolescence. In addition, being overage for grade may increase the risk of school dropout because these students become eligible to leave school (turn 16) while they are still in middle school or are making the difficult transition to high school.

Because Fall River is an immigrant community, there were youths in the school system who were overage for grade but who had never been retained in grade. The data set includes information on the timing and incidence of retention as well as a youth's age in grade and grade of entry into the school system. This aspect of the data set presents an unique opportunity to examine whether there is an effect of being overage for grade that operates independently of the effect of retention and how being overage for grade influences the timing of school withdrawal. In particular, in the last section of this chapter, I employ a hazard model to address the question: Are overage youths at a greater risk of dropping out because they are still in middle school or are in their first year of high school when they become eligible to leave school?

PREVIOUS RESEARCH ON THE EFFECTS OF GRADE RETENTION

The Impact of Retention on School Performance

The question of whether grade retention is an effective tool to remediate poor school performance has been widely studied. This literature almost unanimously concludes that retention is not as effective as promotion in improving student performance.[1] Metaanalyses conducted by Gregg Jackson (1975), Thomas Holmes (1983), Holmes and Kenneth Matthews (1984), and, more recently, Holmes (1989), examined research findings on the effect of grade retention using studies that had matched retained and promoted pupils prior to retention. The general conclusion of these reviews is that promoted students perform better than non-promoted students in the next year on measures of academic achievement, personal adjustment, self-concept, and attitudes toward school. In addition, Holmes (1983) found that studies that followed youths for as much as five years after retention most often established that the academic achievement of retained pupils continued to lag behind that of promoted students in the years following retention.

Research findings on the effect of retention differ by whether retained or promoted youths are compared on the basis of their academic achievement at the same age or after completion of the same grade. Holmes (1989) concluded that studies that used same age comparisons generally found large negative effects of retention. Studies that used same grade comparisons did not find negative effects of retention when retained youths were compared to promoted youths after completion of the same grade. While this question needs to be further investigated, neither comparison shows long-term academic benefits of retention. In addition, the consensus in the literature is that the questionable academic benefits of retention are accompanied by negative effects on self-esteem and attitudes toward school.

The Association Between Grade Retention and Early School Leaving: Previous Research

As we found in Chapter 2, one of the most consistent findings in research on school dropout is that high school students who drop out are more likely than graduates to be overage for grade or to have failed grades. A widely quoted finding from the Youth in Transition Study is that one grade retention increases the risk of dropping out by 40 to 50 percent, and more than one by 90 percent (Bachman et al., 1971). A similar association between grade retention and early school leaving is found in the more recent High School and Beyond Survey. In this survey, sophomores who reported that they repeated at least one previous grade dropped out at more than twice the rate of youths who reported that they had never repeated a grade (Barro and Kolstad, 1987).

Despite the strength of the association between grade retention and early school leaving, there have been few attempts to identify how much of this association can be attributed to an independent impact of grade retention, to the impact of grade retention on later school performance, or to the simple fact that youths who perform poorly could be both more likely to drop out and to be retained in grade. Several analyses of data from individual school systems, including Chicago and Austin, have found that youths who are overage for grade drop out at higher rates even when controlling for differences in their achievement test scores (Grissom and Shepard, 1989). These studies, however, often imputed retentions from age in grade, had few controls for actual school performance such as grades and attendance, and had primarily controlled for postretention rather than preretention performance.

A DESCRIPTION OF THE INCIDENCE OF GRADE RETENTION AND ITS ASSOCIATION WITH EARLY SCHOOL LEAVING AMONG THE FALL RIVER COHORT

The Fall River data set allows for analysis of the association between grade retention and early school leaving for grade retentions that occurred between kindergarten and eighth grade. Fully 36 percent of youths in the Fall River sample repeated at least one grade during this grade span; 21 percent in the cohort repeated only one grade, while an additional 16 percent were retained in grade more than once. Youths

Figure 6.1
Distribution of Retentions by Grade in Which Retained

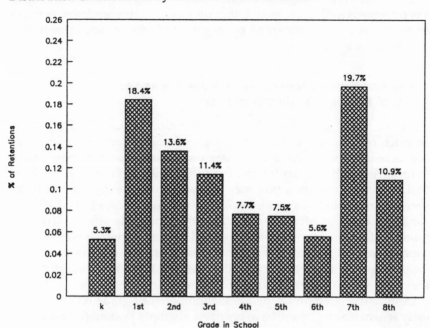

who were retained were most likely to have repeated the first or the seventh grade (see Figure 6.1).

Consistent with the findings of previous research, youths who repeated grades were much more likely to drop out than those who were never retained. In the Fall River sample, fully 77 percent of youths who were retained at least one grade left school before graduating or transferring compared to approximately 27 percent of those who never repeated a grade. Youths who repeated one grade were highly likely to drop out. Students who had repeated two or more grades were almost exclusively dropouts (see Table 6.1).

EXAMINING THE ASSOCIATION BETWEEN GRADE RETENTION AND EARLY SCHOOL LEAVING

Methodology and Measures

To restate, students in this study who repeated a grade from kindergarten to eighth grade were nearly three times more likely to drop out of school as those who had never experienced a grade retention. The question this chapter addresses is: Does repeating a grade actually in-

Table 6.1
Distribution of Retentions and Dropout Rates by Number of Retentions

	Percentage of Youths Retained, k-8	Probability Drop Given Retained
None	63.51%	27.39%
One	20.65%	69.18%
Two or more	15.84%	93.75%
One or more	36.49%	76.87%

crease the likelihood that students will drop out or do youths who are retained have characteristics that would have made them more likely to drop out regardless of whether they had experienced that retention? This analysis examines the extent to which the estimated association between grade retention and school dropout can be explained by differences in the pre- and postretention school performance of promoted and retained youths and by the impact of being overage for grade, independent of whether or not a student was retained. In addition, I examine how the estimated impact of a grade retention differs by the number of times a youth was retained, and by the grade that a youth repeated. The background measures—census tract variables and demographic, family background, and school characteristics—used in this analysis are those described in Chapter 3. A youth's mean academic grade will be used as the measure of a youth's school performance.

Failing a grade, second to dropping out, is perhaps the most dramatic indicator of serious difficulty in school. The fact that both grade retention and school dropout are evidence of school failure raises two important problems when trying to identify whether grade retention, as a policy, hurts youth's chances of graduating. The first problem is that students who have given up on school while they are still in middle school and who are showing signs of dropping out will very likely repeat the seventh or eighth grade. By late middle school (8th grade), nearly all of middle school dropouts had experienced a retention. Indeed, fully 84 percent of middle school dropouts were not promoted in either the seventh or the eighth grade as compared to 13.7 percent of later dropouts and only 1.6 percent of graduates (see Table 6.1). Because students must turn 16 before dropping out, these seventh- and eighth-grade retentions among middle school dropouts may reflect the fact that these students had dropped out, albeit not legally. Thus, repeating a grade in late middle school and formally leaving school within the next year or so may be the same outcome. In analyzing the relationship between grade retention and early school leaving, one must be careful to distinguish between retentions that precede dropping out, and thus may contribute to the decision to leave school, and retentions that may reflect the decision to drop out.

A simple approach to dealing with these questionable grade retentions is to exclude either late grade retentions (seventh- and eighth-grade retentions) or early grade dropouts (seventh- to ninth-grade dropouts) from the analysis. In this chapter, I estimate the likelihood of dropping out on the basis of retentions that occurred from kindergarten to sixth grade for the entire sample. I also estimated the effect of grade retentions that occurred in kindergarten through eighth grade for the sample of youths who completed the 9th grade (tenth-grade persisters).

A second important problem that arises when estimating the relationship between grade retention and the likelihood of school dropout is that grade retention can be considered an endogenous variable, determined by many of the same characteristics that would predict school dropout. Consider the relationship between early grade retentions— grade retentions in kindergarten to fourth grade—and dropping out. We may expect that those characteristics that would predict poor early school outcomes, such as grade retention, would also predict later poor school outcomes, such as dropping out. These characteristics include family background, personal and school performance characteristics, as well as unmeasured factors such as motivation, attachment to school, and underlying ability.

When examining the association between grade retention and early school leaving in the Fall River data set, I can control for measured differences among youths, such as grades, which might lead a student to be more likely to be retained in grade and to drop out. The problem, however, is that I cannot control for unmeasured differences, such as motivation. This is also true in the case of underlying ability, which could be measured through early IQ scores or achievement tests, but which were not available in the Fall River data set. In its simplest form, the estimated impact of retention is comprised of both the true effect of a grade retention on the likelihood of dropping out, and the degree to which promoted and retained youths differ in terms of these unmeasured characteristics. In this example, the amount of bias would be determined by: (1) the degree to which both early grade failure and dropping out are manifestations of the same underlying problems youths face in successfully progressing through school; and (2) the degree to which these differences between retained and promoted youths, as well as between dropouts and graduates, are not reflected in school performance, as measured by grades and attendance.[2] In general, then, one would expect that the endogeneity of grade retention would result in overestimates of its impact; a bias that should be considered when interpreting these results.

The Association Between Grade Retention and Dropping Out Not Controlling for School Performance

Table 6.2 presents the results of estimating the relationship between grade retention and the likelihood of dropping out for the entire sample and for the sample of youths who completed the ninth grade, controlling for a youth's measured background characteristics, fourth-grade school quality, and number of school changes. Equation 1 provides an estimate of the association between the cumulative incidence of grade retention and early school leaving, not controlling for school performance.

The results of Equation 1 illustrate the substantial association between the likelihood of dropping out and the number of times youths repeated a grade. For the entire sample, repeating a grade was associated with a .29 increase in the likelihood of dropping out at the mean when controlling for a youth's background, fourth-grade school quality, and the number of times he or she changed schools. For the sample of tenth-grade persisters, grade retention was associated with an increase of .24 in the likelihood of dropping out, controlling for background and neighborhood characteristics.

The Association Between Grade Retention and Dropping Out Controlling for School Performance

How much of the association between the cumulative incidence of grade retention and the likelihood of dropping out can be explained by differences in the school performance of promoted and retained youths? Table 6.3 compares the results of five equations estimating the likelihood of dropping out for the entire sample. Equation 2 estimates the effect of retention when fourth-grade mean academic grades—a measure of academic performance—is included in the equation. Equation 3 includes information on a student's mean academic grades and attendance from the fourth to the sixth grade. And, finally, Equations 4 and 5 examine the effect of retention by the number of times a student repeated a grade and by the timing of retention.

As seen in Table 6.3, fourth-grade mean academic grades (Equation 2) and mean academic grades and attendance after fourth grade (Equation 3) explain some but not all of the association between the incidence of grade retention and dropping out. For the entire sample, the estimated impact of the incidence of grade retention falls by approximately one-third when controlling for difference in the grades and attendance of youths. Even after controlling for school performance, however, youths who repeated grades were more likely to drop out than those who never repeated grades.

Table 6.2
Effect of Grade Retention Controlling for Background

P(DROP) and P(DROP Tenth Grade or later)

	Equation 1 Change P(Drop)		Equation 1 Change P(Drop 10th or later)	
# of retentions	.289[a]	(7.48)[b]	.240	(6.38)
School quality	.020	(1.70)	.012	(1.01)
# School changes	.102	(3.04)	.092	(3.17)
CENSUS TRACT				
% HS grads	-.077	(.20)	-.378	(.99)
% Public Ass.	1.440	(2.30)	1.092	(1.72)
% O/F/L	-.739	(1.86)	-.763	(1.93)
Female	-.121	(3.01)	-.080	(1.99)
# of siblings	.027	(2.30)	.027	(2.36)
Father skilled	.193	(1.91)	.182	(1.76)
Father unskilled	.197	(1.91)	.215	(2.15)
Father other	.277	(2.50)	.242	(3.09)
Immigrant k+	.110	(1.46)	-.011	(.13)
Immigrant pre-k	-.021	(.25)	-.044	(.55)
2nd generation	-.035	(.50)	-.012	(.19)
Effect of Grade Retention				
Youth high risk	.299		.175	
Youth moderate risk	.299		.198	

[a] Partial derivative evaluated at the mean values of the independent variables including missing values.

[b] t-statistics in parentheses.

Note: The equation also contained parameters for missing observations (see Appendix 6-A).
P(Dropped 10th or later) = Probability dropped out in tenth, eleventh, or twelfth grade given participated in tenth grade.

Table 6.3
Effect of Grade Retention Controlling for Fourth-Grade Mean Academic Grades, Fourth- to Sixth-Grade Mean Academic Grades and Attendance, Demographic, and Background Characteristics

By Number of Retentions and Grade Retained

	Equation 1	Equation 2	Equation 3	Equation 4	Equation 5
# of retentions	.289[a] (7.48)[b]	.200 (4.99)	.193 (4.18)		
Retentions = 1				.196 (3.50)	
Retentions > 1				.348 (2.97)	
Retentions k-3					.193 (3.77)
Retention 4-6					.192 (2.07)
Mean Academic Grade					
Fourth		-.161 (5.79)	-.021 (.49)	-.022 (.51)	-.021 (.49)
Fifth			-.036 (.76)	-.033 (.74)	-.036 (.76)
Sixth			-.256 (5.65)	-.246 (5.65)	-.256 (5.64)
Attendance					
Fourth			.005 (1.47)	.004 (1.45)	.005 (1.47)
Fifth			-.006 (1.76)	-.005 (1.74)	-.006 (1.76)
Sixth			-.005 (1.62)	-.005 (1.64)	-.005 (1.62)
Effects of Grade Retentions on High and Moderately At-Risk Youth					
Youth High Risk	.299	.175	.110		
Retentions = 1				.136	
Retentions > 1				.198	
Retentions k-3					.108
Retentions 4-6					.108
Youth Moderate Risk	.299	.198	.167		
Retentions = 1				.187	
Retentions > 1				.289	

111

Table 6.3 (continued)

By Number of Retentions and Grade Retained

	Equation 1	Equation 2	Equation 3	Equation 4	Equation 5
Youth Moderate Risk					
Retentions k-3					.159
Retentions 4-6					.159

[a] Calculation of derivative of logistic probability function with all values (including missing values) set at their mean.

[b] t-statistics in parentheses.

Notes: Control variables not reported in this table but included in each equation include those reported in Table 3.2. These are school quality, number of school changes, census tract characteristics, gender, number of siblings, father's occupation, and nativity. Each equation also contained parameters for missing observations. See Appendix 6-A.

In addition, both a single grade retention and more than one retention were associated with statistically significant increases in the likelihood of dropping out, controlling for a youth's school performance (Equation 4). For the entire sample, one grade retention was associated with a .196 increase in the probability of dropping out, at the mean, when controlling for the measured background and school performance variables. Repeating more than one grade was associated with a quite substantial (.348) increase in the likelihood of dropping out.

Table 6.4 shows the results of Equations 1 through 5 when estimated for the sample of youths who completed the ninth grade (tenth-grade persisters). The results are quite similar to those found for the entire sample. For the sample of tenth-grade persisters, the estimated impact of grade retention falls by approximately one-half when controlling for mean academic grades and attendance from the fourth to the ninth grade, from .240 to .131. Even when controlling for school performance in the first year of high school, however, students who completed the ninth grade, and who repeated grades, were statistically significantly more likely to drop out than their counterparts who had never repeated a grade.

The Association Between Grade Retention and Dropping Out by Grade Repeated

This analysis has treated all retentions as similar events; being retained in kindergarten in this analysis is comparable to being retained in the sixth grade. Many teachers believe that early grade retentions are beneficial to youths while retentions that occur in later grades are more harmful (Smith and Shepard, 1987; Tompchin and Impara, 1992). This perspective would predict that later grade retentions would have a larger impact on the probability of dropping out than retentions that occur in earlier grades.

Equation 5 examines how the estimated impact of grade retention differs by whether or not a youth failed grades previous to or after the fourth grade. Looking both at the results for the entire sample and for the sample of youths who did not drop out prior to the tenth grade (Tables 6.3 and 6.4), I find that the estimated impact of early and late grade retentions are quite similar.[3] These results, then, suggest that there may be an effect of repeating a grade that operates independently of school performance and of the grade in which a youth was retained.

What then can we conclude from this analysis? First, pre- and post-retention school performance and differences in students' personal characteristics account for some, but not all, of the association between grade retention and early school leaving. When controlling for a youth's mean academic grades and attendance beginning in the fourth grade, the es-

Table 6.4

Effect of Grade Retention on the Likelihood of Dropping Out During or After the Tenth Grade Controlling for Fourth-Grade Mean Academic Grades, Fourth- to Eighth-Grade Mean Academic Grades and Attendance, Demographic, and Background Characteristics

By Number of Retentions and Grade Retained

	Equation 1	Equation 2	Equation 3	Equation 4	Equation 5
# of retentions	.240[a] (6.38)[b]	.183 (4.48)	.131 (2.60)		
Retentions = 1				.127 (2.28)	
Retentions > 1				.204 (1.84)	
Retention k-3					.114 (2.34)
Retention 4-8					.115 (1.41)
Mean Academic Grade					
Fourth			.038 (.78)	.032 (.76)	.033 (.78)
Fifth			.033 (.65)	.029 (.65)	.029 (.65)
Sixth			-.119 (2.04)	-.103 (2.02)	-.103 (2.03)
Seventh			.000 (.00)	.001 (.02)	.000 (.01)
Eighth			-.094 (1.74)	-.082 (1.76)	-.082 (1.74)
Ninth			-.178 (4.32)	-.155 (4.32)	-.155 (4.30)
Attendance					
Fourth			.010 (2.84)	.009 (2.81)	.009 (2.84)
Fifth			-.004 (1.01)	-.003 (1.00)	-.003 (.99)
Sixth			.004 (1.02)	.003 (.98)	.003 (1.02)
Seventh			.003 (1.00)	.003 (1.02)	.003 (1.00)
Eighth			-.008 (2.88)	-.007 (2.88)	-.007 (2.88)
Ninth			-.005 (3.05)	-.004 (3.05)	-.004 (3.05)
Effects of Grade Retentions on High and Moderately At-Risk Youth					
Youth High Risk	.276	.200	.096		
Retentions = 1				.110	
Retentions > 1				.154	

Youth High Risk
Retentions k-3   .093
Retentions 4-6   .092

Youth Moderate Risk
Retentions = 1   .276   .210   .141   .152
Retentions > 1   .228

Retentions k-3   .114
Retentions 4-6   .115

---

[a] Calculation of derivative of logistic probability function with all values (including missing values) set at their mean.

[b] t-statistics in parentheses.

Notes: Control variables not reported in this table but included in each equation include those reported in Table 3.2. These are school quality, number of school changes, census tract characteristics, gender, number of siblings, father's occupation, and nativity. Each equation also contained parameters for missing observations. See Appendix 6-A.

timated impact of a grade retention, at the mean, fell by approximately one-third for the entire sample and by close to one-half for the sample of tenth-grade participants. Even after controlling for grades and attendance, however, retained youths were substantially more likely to drop out than students who were never retained. For example, the results of Equation 3 for the sample of tenth-grade participants would predict that a youth who had failed a grade previous to high school would be 58 percent more likely to drop out of school than a youth who had never failed a grade even if these two students had similar background characteristics and had the same grades and attendance in middle school and in the ninth grade.[4] The effect of retention, moreover, does not seem to vary by whether youths were retained previous to or after the fourth grade.

One possible explanation for these results is that youths who are retained have unobserved characteristics that distinguish them from those who never repeated a grade. As discussed previously, one may argue that the remaining association between grade retention and school dropout could be measuring the effect of differences in the underlying ability and school attachment of retained and promoted youths, differences not reflected in a student's mean academic grades and attendance.

Another hypothesis is that the experience of repeating a grade has an impact on self-esteem and attitudes toward school that operates independently of school performance. Holmes and Matthews, in their review of the literature, found that youths who were retained had lower self-esteem and attitudes toward school than comparable youths who were promoted (Holmes and Matthews, 1984). Deborah Byrnes, in a qualitative study of the impact of first-, third-, and sixth-grade retentions, documented that youths perceived their retention as a punishment and a stigma. For example, when nonpromoted children were asked what was the worst thing about not passing, the most common responses were: "being laughed at and teased," "being punished," "being sad," "getting bad grades," and "being embarrassed" (Byrnes, 1989). These research findings suggest that repeating a grade has a negative impact on self-esteem and attitudes toward school that may increase student disengagement and the likelihood of school dropout.

A third, and related explanation, is that being overage for grade, regardless of whether or not a youth was retained, raises the likelihood of school dropout, particularly during adolescence. Being older than one's peers may lead students to feel like failures and/or to feel negatively self-conscious. Teachers may treat youths who are older differently regardless of their academic performance. The similarity in the estimated impact of grade retentions that occurred both previous to and after the fourth grade would support the notion that being overage for grade, no matter when a youth was retained, has an impact on an individual's attitudes toward and experiences in school that may not be reflected in grades or attendance. This line of argument would suggest that the association between grade retention and early school leaving that is not explained by differences in the background and school performance of youths could be explained by being overage for grade.

The Impact of Grade Retention Controlling for Age

A student may be overage for grade because of a grade retention. Students may also be older than their classmates if they were immigrants to the school system and were placed below their modal grade level, or if they entered school overage for grade. In the Fall River data set, sixty-one youths, or approximately 8 percent of the sample, had never repeated a grade but were overage for grade as of the seventh grade. In addition, eight youths who had repeated a grade were not overage for grade by the seventh grade. These cases allow us to estimate whether there is an effect of a youth's age on the probability of dropping out and whether, after controlling for age, there is an effect of repeating a grade over and above the impact of being overage for grade.

Table 6.5 compares two equations estimating the relationship between the incidence of retention and dropping out, controlling and not controlling for age.[5] A youth's age in seventh grade was introduced as a continuous variable measured as age in months. In the seventh grade, youths were at their modal grade level if they were between 11 years and 9 months, and 12 years and 8 months, at the beginning of the seventh grade. Age was included as a continuous variable because we would expect the effect of being one month overage for grade would be much less than the effect of being nine months older.

As seen in Table 6.5 (Equation 6), age is positively and statistically significantly associated with the likelihood of early school leaving. Being overage for grade explains almost all of the remaining effect of grade retention on the likelihood of dropping out. Controlling for age, school performance, attendance, and background characteristics, there is no statistically significant association between the cumulative incidence of grade retention and school dropout. Thus, the results of Equation 6 suggest that the association between grade retention and the probability of dropping out that is not explained by school performance can be explained by the effect of being overage for grade.

This finding is best demonstrated in a comparison of the predicted probabilities of dropping out presented in the bottom of Table 6.5. As this comparison shows, Equation 6 predicts that, at the mean of the remaining independent variables, a youth who is 13 years old in seventh grade would be approximately 19.6 percentage points more likely to drop out than a youth who is 12 years old even if they had similar

Table 6.5
Effect of Grade Retention Controlling for Fourth- to Sixth-Grade Mean Academic Grades and Attendance, Demographic, and Background Characteristics

By Number of Grade Retentions and Age Seventh Grade

	Equation 4		Equation 6	
Age in 7th (mnths)			.0165	(3.64)
Retentions==1	.196[a]	(3.50)[b]	.032	(.45)
Retentions>1	.348	(2.97)	.001	(.00)
Mean Academic Grade				
Fourth	-.022	(.51)	-.023	(.53)
Fifth	-.033	(.74)	-.034	(.74)
Sixth	-.246	(5.65)	-.243	(5.55)
Attendance				
Fourth	.004	(1.25)	.005	(1.81)
Fifth	-.005	(1.74)	-.005	(1.76)
Sixth	-.005	(1.80)	-.005	(1.62)

Predicted Probability Drop At Mean Values of Independent Variables
Equation 6

Youth Age 12, no retentions	.271
Youth Age 13, no retentions	.467
Youth Age 13, one retention	.502
Youth Age 12, one retention	.299

[a] Calculation of derivative of logistic probability function with all values (including missing values) set at their mean.

[b] t-statistics in parentheses.

Notes: Control variables not reported in this table but included in each equation are school quality, number of school changes, census tract characteristics, gender, number of siblings, father's occupation and nativity. Each equation also contained parameters for missing observations.

backgrounds and school performance. In comparison, this equation predicts that a youth who is 13 and had repeated a grade would be only 3.5 percentage points more likely to drop out than a youth with comparable characteristics who is 13 but had never repeated a grade. Thus, estimating Equation 6 for the entire sample suggests that being overage for grade substantially increases the chances of dropping out. On the other hand, a grade retention, when controlling for a youth's age, is associated with a small and statistically nonsignificant increase in the probability of early school leaving. This finding does not suggest that grade retention has no effect on the chances that a student will drop out. It does suggest, however, that a large proportion of the impact of grade retention may operate through an effect of being overage for grade.

Why is it important to distinguish the effect of age versus the effect of grade retention? Distinguishing the effect of age from that of grade retention has several important policy implications. First, as noted previously, teachers and school administrators commonly believe that retaining children in early grades is not harmful while retaining students in later grades is. If, however, there is an impact of being overage for grade regardless of whether or not a student repeated a grade, then there would be no basis to the argument that early retentions are not harmful, even if they were effective in remediating poor performance. And, indeed, this finding on the impact of being overage for grade is consistent with my finding that both early and late grade retentions were associated with significant increases in the likelihood of school dropout. Second, if there is an effect of being overage for grade, then policies of retaining youths with remediation will not mitigate the impact of that retention. These policy implications will be discussed in more detail in Chapter 8.

Understanding how much of the higher dropout rates among retained youths can be explained by an effect of being overage has important implications for policy. The results presented here, however, cannot be considered conclusive. First, the estimated impact of being overage for grade that operates independently of retention is based on a small number of cases and, while suggestive, needs to be further investigated. Second, this analysis does not resolve the question: Why do youths who are overage for grade have higher probabilities of dropping out when controlling for grade retentions, academic performance, attendance, and background? This is perhaps the most important question that this analysis raises. Are youths who are overage for grade treated differently by their peers, classmates, and teachers? If overage students are treated differently, is this because they are assumed to have repeated grades? Or, is there an independent effect of being overage that influences a student's interactions with classmates, teachers, and the school environment? For example, in one survey, 74 percent of teachers stated that overage children cause more behavior problems than other students in the fourth to seventh grades. In comparison, only 44 percent of teachers stated that overage children cause more behavior problems in kindergarten to third grade (Tompchin and Impara, 1992). A final question, then, is: Does the negative impact of being overage for grade largely occur or accelerate during the middle school years or during adolescence?

Examining the Hazard of School Leaving by Age

Students who are two or more years below their modal grade level turn 16 while they are still in middle school (seventh or eighth grade). Youths who are one year overage for their grade, moreover, are making the difficult transition to high school during the year they become eligible to leave school. In the previous chapters, I found that both late middle school and the transition to high school are difficult times for youths. These periods may be particularly critical for students who are overage for grade because they coincide with their eligibility to leave school. At the high school level, youths who are overage for grade may feel less discouraged or conspicuous. This perspective would predict that being overage for grade has the greatest impact on the likelihood of dropping out at age 16. In this section, I use an event history analysis to explore the extent to which being overage for grade influences the timing of school withdrawal.

Table 6.6 describes dropout rates by age and grade for students who were in the school system—had not dropped out or graduated—during each age range. These conditional probabilities, called hazard rates, are defined as the likelihood that a youth will drop out in each age range given that he or she did not drop out or graduate in the previous age interval. For example, during the year in which youths turned 16, approximately 25.5 percent dropped out of school. Among those who did not drop out at 16, 15.6 percent dropped out the following year, at age 17.

As seen in Table 6.6, at each age range there was a marked difference between dropout rates among youths who were behind in grade and those who were enrolled at or above their modal grade level. For example, over 30 percent of the ninety-eight youths who turned 16 in the ninth grade, and thus who were one year overage for grade, dropped out. In comparison, 15 percent of youths who were enrolled in the tenth grade during the year in which they turned 16 dropped out.

The descriptive statistics reported in Table 6.6 do not support the notion that being overage for grade had a greater effect on the likelihood of dropping out at age 16. Indeed, it is striking how similar the hazard

Table 6.6
Proportion of Youths Who Dropped Out at 16, 17, 18, and 19

Age / Modal Grade Level		Hazard Rate by Grade					
		7th	8th	9th	10th	11th	12th
Sixteen / 10th[a]	25.5	1.00	68.3	32.7	15.5	12.7	---
n	(706)	(31)	(63)	(98)	(309)	(205)	--
Seventeen / 11th	15.6	-	-	45.0	30.3	14.1	8.9
n	(527)			(20)	(66)	(262)	(179)
Eighteen / 12th	18.2	-	-	-	50.0	23.9	15.4
n	(286)				(12)	(46)	(228)
Nineteen / 12th	30.6	-	-	-	-	50.0	27.0
	(49)					(6)	(43)

a. **Modal grade level**: sixteen=10th, seventeen=11th, eighteen=12th. Youths who were enrolled in school at age 19 were, by definition, one year overage for grade.

Notes: Youths began to graduate at age 17. Thus, beginning at age 17, youths left the school system either because they dropped out or because they graduated. Hazard rates reported are the proportion who dropped at during each risk period. Transfers were excluded from the analysis.

rate for groups is across time periods. At seventeen, twenty of the sixty-six youths who were behind one grade level and had not dropped out at age 16 left school. This 30 percent hazard rate for youths who were enrolled more than one year below their modal was again twice as high as the rate for youths who were enrolled at their modal grade level (eleventh grade) during the next year, when they turned 17. The hazard rate for youths enrolled one year below their modal grade was also substantially higher at age 18. A similar trend is found when examining the hazard rate for youths who, at 16, were enrolled two years below their modal grade level. At age 16, almost 70 percent of youths who were enrolled in the eighth grade dropped out of school. The hazard rate for this group, however, remained at close to 50 percent for the duration of their school careers.

Table 6.7 describes how being overage for grade affects the logit-hazard of dropping out when controlling for school performance. The logit-hazard of dropping out was estimated using a discrete-time hazard model that estimated the hazard of dropping out at ages 16 to 19. The equation also controlled for the number of times a youth changed schools and the timing of immigration into the school system. Variables that were statistically insignificant, including fourth-grade mean academic grades and attendance, school quality, census tract variables, father's occupation, and nativity were excluded from the final model. Graduates as well as youths who had not dropped out or graduated by age 19 are censored observations. The logit coefficients and equations used to es-

Table 6.7
Coefficient Estimates for Logit-Hazard of Dropping Out by Risk Period and Being Behind in Grade

	Equation 7 Controlling for 6th-grade grades and attendance		Equation 8 Controlling for 6th-and 8th-grade grades and attendance	
	coefficient	(t-stat)	coefficient	(t-stat)
one	1.9525		-.6082	
age 17	-.1273	(.63)	6.4146	(2.51)
age 18/19	.1621	(.70)	6.7769	(2.64)
below 1	.5365	(2.01)	.6176	(2.29)
below 2+	2.1119	(6.83)	2.1741	(6.60)
below 1 * age 17	.1174	(.23)	- .2427	(.55)
below 2 * age 17	-1.1523	(1.99)	-2.1521	(3.37)
below 1 * age 18/19	-.2016	(.49)	-.4415	(1.01)
below 2 * age 18/19	-1.1527	(1.88)	-1.9065	(2.91)

Predicted Increase in the Odds of Dropping Out for Youths at or Below Modal Grade Level, By Risk Period

	At Modal Grade Level	Enrolled Below Modal Grade Level Below one Grade	Below Two or more grades
Actual Hazard			
Sixteen	.146	.327	.785
Seventeen	.120	.303	.450
Eighteen or Nineteen	.153	.258	.500

Increase in Odds of Dropping Out from those at Modal Grade Level

Sixteen		2.24	5.38
Seventeen		2.52	3.75
Eighteen or Nineteen		1.68	3.27

PREDICTED INCREASE IN ODDS

Controlling for 6th grade mean academic grades and attendance

Sixteen		1.71	8.26
Seventeen		1.92	2.61
Eighteen and Nineteen		1.40	2.61

Controlling for 6th and 8th grade mean academic grades and attendance

Seventeen		1.45	1.19
Eighteen and Nineteen		1.02	1.31

timate the effect of being overage for grade on the hazard of dropping out by age are reported in Appendix 6-B.

The first section of Table 6.7 shows the estimated logit coefficients and t-statistics on the variables distinguishing the hazard by risk period and by being overage for grade. The first equation controlled for school changes, the timing of immigration, and a youth's grades and attendance in the sixth grade. During the year in which youths in the Fall River sample turned 16, students were enrolled in the seventh to the eleventh grades. In the next year, the grade span for youths who did not drop out at age 16 ranged from the ninth to the twelfth grade. Equation 8 estimated the impact of being overage for grade when information on a youth's eighth-grade school performance was included in the equation for those who did not drop out at age 16 through the use of an interaction term (see Appendix 6-B).

The results of both equations show that being enrolled below modal grade level was associated with a statistically significant increase in the logit-hazard of dropping out when controlling for grades and attendance. The t-statistics on the interaction terms of grade by risk period (e.g., below 1*age 17) test the null hypothesis that there is no difference in the hazard rate between that time period and age 16. These results confirm that there was not a statistically significant difference in the impact of being enrolled one year below modal grade level across risk periods. The increase in the hazard rate associated with being two or more years behind grade level was statistically significantly higher at age 16 than at ages 17 and 18. As we saw in the descriptive statistics, the hazard rate for youths who were enrolled two years or more below grade level when they turned 16 (seventh and eighth grade) was substantially higher than the hazard rate for these youths in later periods. Indeed, all of youths who were enrolled in the seventh grade when they turned 16 dropped out. It would be inappropriate to interpret the high dropout rate among students who were in the seventh or eighth grade when they turned 16 as evidence that being in middle school leads a youth to leave school. Many of those who dropped out in middle school, as discussed previously, became one or two years overage for grade because they failed the seventh or eighth grade. Thus, both the higher dropout rates and the incidence of seventh- and eighth-grade retentions among this group may reflect the decision to withdraw from school.

Both the uncontrolled hazard rates and the results of Equations 7 and 8 would lead us to reject the hypothesis that being overage for grade places youths at greater risk of dropping out at age 16 than in other periods. Youths who are in middle school or who are making the difficult transition to high school when they become eligible to drop out are very likely to make the decision to leave school. However, these youths continue to be at a higher risk of early school leaving throughout their school career.

Table 6.7 also shows the predicted increase in the relative odds of dropping out at ages 16, 17, and 18–19 when controlling for differences in school performance in sixth and eighth grade. Students who were one grade below their modal grade level when they turned 16 were more than twice as likely (odds = 2.24) to drop out of school at 16 as those enrolled at or above their modal grade. When controlling for differences in the measured background characteristics and sixth-grade grades and attendance, the predicted increase in the relative odds of dropping out at age 16 associated with being one year over age for grade falls to 1.71— still over seventy percent more likely.

The results of Equation 8 suggest that a large proportion of the increase in the odds of dropping out associated with being overage for grade during the risk periods 17 and 18–19 can be explained by school performance at the end of middle school (eighth-grade grades and attendance). Thus, overage youths who make the decision not to drop out at age 16 continue to be at a greater risk of dropping out in part because of the difficulties they continue to encounter in school.

SUMMARY

In the 1980s, opponents of grade retention cited the strong association between grade retention and dropping out as evidence that school systems' policies were placing youths at risk of early school leaving. In this study, fully 77 percent of youths who had repeated at least one grade dropped out of school compared to only 25 percent of youths who had never failed a grade. This simple comparison of the dropout rates of retained and nonretained youths has been interpreted by policymakers, researchers, and advocates to suggest that retaining youths increases their chances of dropping out. In the context of the overall literature on grade retention, this conclusion is understandable. It is, however, misguided. As Bachman and his fellow researchers cautioned in their 1971 study:

It would be tempting to argue from this that no one should ever fail a grade in school, lest he become a dropout. That conclusion may in the end prove to have some validity, but the present data are not sufficient to make the case . . . whether it is an important cause in its own right, or merely a very revealing symptom, remains to be demonstrated. (Bachman et al., 1971, p. 54)

A central premise of this book is that if research is to inform school policy, researchers must move beyond descriptive statistics to more rigorous analyses of how and why school experiences, such as grade retention, influence school outcomes for youths. This chapter focused on the question: How much of the association between grade retention and school dropout can be explained by differences in the pre- and postretention grades and attendance of students and by the incidence and timing of grade retention?

To briefly summarize, I find that approximately one-third of the association between grade retention and school dropout can be explained by differences in the school performance of youths as measured by grades and attendance. Even after controlling for a youth's background and school performance, however, youths who have repeated grades are substantially more likely to drop out than those who have never experienced a grade retention. This finding holds true regardless of whether grade retention occurred early or late in a youth's school career.

This chapter also presented an exploratory analysis of whether being overage for grade increased the chances of dropping out and whether the impact of being overage for grade could explain the higher dropout rates among retained youths. In this study, estimates of how much of the effect of being overage for grade operated independently of school performance were based on a small number of cases. My findings do suggest that being overage for grade may increase the likelihood of school dropout and that this effect may explain a large proportion of the association between grade retention and early school leaving. In addition, I find that youths who were overage for grade were at a higher risk of dropping out throughout their school careers. Youths who were in middle school, or who were making the transition to high school at the time they turned 16, were very likely to make the decision to leave school. At the same time, many who were overage for grade made the decision to stay in school after they turned 16. Based on an analysis of the impact of being overage for grade on the hazard of dropping out by age, I found that overage youths who decided to stay in school after age 16 remained at a higher risk of early school leaving primarily because of their poor school performance in eighth grade.

Identifying both how and why grade retention influences a youth's chances of graduating has important implications for policy. As we will see in Chapter 8, rates of grade retention have risen dramatically in the past two decades. In 1990, as many as one-third of youths were overage for grade by the time they reached high school. Previous research on grade retention has questioned the validity of this policy as a tool for improving students' short-term academic performance and school adjustment. The findings presented in this study lend further evidence to the conclusion that such policies have long-term negative impacts on a student's chances of graduating. Given our current high rates of grade retention, these findings suggest that efforts to reduce the incidence of grade repetition both early and late in students' school careers may be an important means of dropout prevention. At the same time, my analysis of the impact of grade retention raises several important questions for further research.

The chances that a student who is doing poorly in school will be retained in grade varies widely across school districts, schools, and often, teachers within the same school. Retention rates depend largely upon school system policies and teachers' and principals' attitudes toward the benefits of retention. This important element of grade retention may provide a means for disentangling the causal relationships between grade retention and school dropout. A first step is to replicate this analysis in longitudinal studies that include more adequate information on individual teacher and school policies concerning retention, and measures of youths' educational expectations, motivation, and ability.

Qualitative research could also play a critical role in sorting out the lines of causality between grade retention and school dropout. Most qualitative research on grade retention has focused on the impact of early grade retentions on teachers' and students' attitudes following nonpromotion. This research has provided key insights into how grade retention is experienced by teachers and students. A similar line of research is needed if we are to identify how being overage for grade and grade retention affect a youth's experience in school during adolescence, middle school, and early high school. For example, does early grade retention affect a youth's performance and attitudes toward school throughout his or her school career, or does the impact of being overage for grade largely occur or accelerate during adolescence? Addressing these questions will allow us to better identify whether grade retention increases a student's chances of dropping out and will allow us to better design alternatives.

In this and the preceeding chapter, we have focused on understanding both whether and how grade retention and student difficulties following the school transition to middle school and high school influence the chances of dropping out. In both cases, we find some evidence that both of these school experiences may create barriers to school membership and school attachment. Before discussing the policy implications of my findings regarding both school transitions and grade retention, the next chapter discusses how we can use these findings to develop a better understanding of the nature of school dropout.

NOTES

1. This section summarizes the literature reviews of Jackson (1975), Holmes and Matthews (1984), and Holmes (1983, 1989). While these are the most comprehensive and widely cited reviews of the literature on the effect of school retention, they are not the only such reviews. For other excellent reviews of the

literature, see Karweit (1991), Niklason (1984), Overman (1986), and Rose et al. (1983).

2. One method of addressing this problem would be to remove the correlation between the grade retention variable and the error term in the equation through the use of an instrumental variable. An instrumental variable is a variable that is correlated with grade retention but would not be correlated with school dropout. The difficulties of finding such an instrument are obvious. The central role that a school's retention policies play in the decision to retain youths suggests that differences in school policy could be used as an instrumental variable. In the Fall River data set, there was a wide variance in the rates of retention across grammar schools both because of differences in school policy regarding retention and because of differences in the characteristics of youths attending the schools. Unfortunately, while there was a statistically significant difference in retention rates across individual schools when controlling for differences in students' attributes, the F-statistic on grammar school rates of retention predicting the individual likelihood of being retained was not statistically significant. Thus, there was not a strong enough correlation between grammar school rates of retention (as measured by the grammar school youths attended in the fourth grade) and individual student outcomes to justify its use as an instrumental variable. Measurement error in the policy variable—caused by ascribing all of students' grammar school retentions to their fourth grade school as well as using school as a proxy for policy—may have accounted for this result. This approach has promise and may, in the future, allow for more adequate investigation of the relationship between grade retention and school dropout.

3. As seen in Table 6.4, the coefficient on fourth- to eighth-grade retentions for tenth-grade participants was not statistically significant. The coefficient on grade retentions from grades four to eight may not have reached traditional levels of statistical significance because there were a fewer number of late grade retentions in this smaller sample. Only nine percent of the tenth-grade participants repeated grades after the fourth grade. In comparison, 17 percent of the tenth-grade sample failed at least one grade early on in their school career (kindergarten to fourth grade). Nevertheless, the direction of the findings for the tenth-grade persisters is quite similar to those found for the entire sample.

4. Among the sample of high school participants, the predicted probability of dropping out for a youth with no grade retentions is .211 at the mean of the independent variables including grades and attendance from fourth to the ninth grade. The predicted probability of dropping out for a youth with a grade retention is .3326.

5. I have not presented the results of estimating Equation 6 for the sample of youths who completed the ninth grade. In the entire sample, approximately sixty-nine youths had either not repeated a grade but were overage for grade or had repeated a grade but were not overage for grade. When excluding seventh- to ninth-grade dropouts, only forty-five youths fell into one of these two categories. Thus, it is more difficult to distinguish the effects of being overage from the effect of a grade retention in this smaller sample.

## Chapter 7

The Two Dropout Problems: A Framework for Dropout Prevention Policy

In the last several chapters I have assembled a set of facts that describe and distinguish the school career paths of dropouts and graduates in the Fall River data set. I found that students' ability to maneuver school transitions and the experience of being retained in grade had important impacts on their chances of graduating. The question that remains is: What can these findings tell us about the nature of dropping out in school systems with high dropout rates and potential directions for dropout prevention policy?

One of the most important findings of this study is that there are two quite different stories to be told about the path to dropping out among students in the Fall River public schools. The first story is that of early grade dropouts (seventh- to ninth-grade dropouts). These students fit the stereotype of the dropout as a student who encounters substantial difficulty early on in his or her school career and whose path to dropping out is marked by persistent and deteriorating levels of school performance.

Conventional portrayals of the path to dropping out have largely failed to describe the school career paths of late grade dropouts and graduates in this study. In particular, students who dropped out after the ninth grade did not appear to be a distinct population for whom the path to dropping out operated independently of school experiences. The average fourth-grade grades and attendance of late grade dropouts were quite similar to those of youths who later graduated in the bottom third of their class. In addition, the school performance of these two groups followed quite similar patterns as they moved through middle school and into high school.

Trends in the school career paths of late grade dropouts also lead us away from a focus on the individual manifestations of poor school performance and disengagement, as well as from portrayals of the path to dropping out as a varied, complex, and largely individualized phenomenon. Trends in the average grades and attendance of late grade dropouts previous to the tenth grade did not differ dramatically by the grade in which they left school. In particular, I could identify distinct junctures at which the grades and attendance of tenth- to twelfth-grade dropouts diverged from those of graduates. First, late grade dropouts experienced much larger declines than graduates in their average grades following the school transition to both middle school in the sixth grade and to high school in the ninth grade. Second, the average attendance of late grade dropouts declined significantly from the sixth to the eighth grade regardless of when they dropped out. For example, from grades 6 to 8, the average attendance of tenth- and eleventh-grade dropouts declined by twelve and fourteen days, respectively. Even students who dropped out as late as the twelfth grade had an average decline in their attendance of ten days from grades 6 to 8. In comparison, the average attendance of students who graduated in the bottom third of their class declined by five days, on average, during this period.

Why would we find such distinct trends in the school performance of late grade dropouts and graduates? And, why is it during middle school that the school career paths of dropouts and graduates begin to diverge? In 1990, the Carnegie Corporation labeled the period of early adolescence "Turning Points" (Carnegie Council on Adolescent Development, 1990). This phrase reflects an emerging consensus in research that the period of adolescence, from roughly ages 10 to 15, is characterized by dramatic growth and change in a youth's physical, emotional, cognitive, and social development. Until relatively recently, education and human service professionals predominately believed that the preschool and early childhood years were the most important formative periods for children, and that adolescence was primarily characterized by pubertal development (Petersen and Epstein, 1991). New advances in the field of development are now leading many to conclude that development does not end at age 6, nor is the direction of a student's school career firmly set in early childhood (Elliot and Feldman, 1990). Rather, early adolescence has emerged as another formative period. During adolescence, students begin to define themselves, their roles, their aspirations, and their group membership. This identity formation is strongly influenced by a student's early school performance and experience. But, as youths move through adolescence and experience increasing independence, the decisions they make regarding their education, the associations they form, and the degree to which they form a positive sense of themselves, their aspirations, and their abilities will have long-term important implications for their life course.

In this chapter, I will argue that research in adolescent development provides a final piece of the puzzle for understanding the path to dropping out among late grade dropouts. Recent research on the nature of development changes that occur during adolescence provides important insights into why it is during middle school, rather than earlier or later in their school career, that the paths of dropouts and graduates become more defined. In addition, research on the influence of students' social context in determining the direction of their school careers allows us to develop a better understanding of the manner in which students' school experiences influence their school membership during adolescence.

The first section of this chapter presents a brief discussion of the findings of the Fall River study in the context of research on the nature of developmental changes that occur during adolescence and the influence that school policies have on a student's development. In the second section of this chapter, I discuss how we can draw upon the findings of this and the previous chapters to develop a new conception of the nature of school dropout in school systems with high dropout rates.

THE PATH TO DROPPING OUT: A DEVELOPMENTAL PERSPECTIVE

As this cohort of dropouts and graduates moved through the Fall River school system they faced a succession of developmental tasks and academic challenges. We began this story in grade 4, when most youths were 9 years old. Within the next several years, these early adolescents would enter one of the most important periods in their cognitive, emotional, physical, and personal development.[1] Biologically, adolescents enter puberty and undergo a multitude of physical and psychological changes. Cognitively, early adolescents show an increased capacity for abstract thinking. And, socially, young adolescents begin to expand their networks beyond the family and begin to experience greater independence. A student's peer group takes on new meaning as students become increasingly aware of their social context and relative status among their peers.

The confluence of these dramatic changes in a youth's development means that during adolescence students enter an important period in their identify formation during which they will begin to define their roles, capacities, goals, and aspirations in relation to their social environment. For example, Marcia Linn and Nancy Songer argue that during adolescence social context has a greater effect on cognitive development and educational attainment than at earlier ages (Linn and Songer, 1991). These authors note:

Adolescents are constructing a view of themselves and a view of the group to which they belong that fundamentally influences their progress and their accomplishments. This process is particularly powerful during adolescence because students at the same time develop greater awareness of sex-role stereotypes and status differences and are more responsive to the view of their peers. (Linn and Songer, 1991, pp. 406–7)

Adolescence has long been portrayed as a very difficult, contentious, and stress-filled time in a child's life. Newer research, however, has questioned the long held assumption that adolescence is inherently difficult and full of "storm and stress" (Brooks-Gunn, 1991; Hauser and Bowlds, 1990; Smetana et al., 1991). Indeed, there is an emerging consensus that this period of identify formation is marked by not one, but several developmental paths. As students begin to define their roles, the different paths become reflected in an increased sorting among groups of students and "increasing divergence between those who are on positive trajectories as compared to those on negative trajectories" (Petersen et al., 1991, p. 104). For many youths, adolescence is a time of growth and positive development (Petersen et al., 1991). For some, however, this period of self-definition and experimentation is marked by disengagement from school and increasingly negative outcomes (Eccles et al., 1991; Petersen et al., 1991).

One of the central developmental tasks of adolescence is the formation of a student's attachment to school and educational aspirations. Research on motivation and achievement has found that during adolescence there is a general decline in students' interest in school, academic motivation, and school attachment (Eccles and Midgley, 1989; Petersen et al., 1991). There has been little research, however, on the extent to which differences in school performance and experiences during adolescence are related to later school outcomes. When viewed as the educational trajectories of adolescents, the school career paths of dropouts and graduates in the Fall River school system provide strong evidence that during this period we see an increasing divergence in students' school performance and engagement—trends, moreover, that differ by whether students drop out or graduate as well as whether they graduate in the bottom or the top two-thirds of the graduating class.

What factors influence the ability of youths to cope successfully with the dramatic changes of adolescence? We can begin to gain insight into this question by looking at the findings of the Fall River study on the impact of school transitions.

Development does not occur in isolation. It emerges from and is shaped by a student's experiences at home, at school, in the community, and with peers, as well as by the interrelationships among these domains. For students in the Fall River public school system, the transitions to middle school and to high school were defining events. School transitions are difficult periods for youths. These school moves, as I discussed in Chapter 5, involve multiple changes in a student's role, and in the size and complexity of a youth's physical and academic environment. At each of these transitions a student's subsequent persistence and success in the new institution are dependent upon whether he or she can successfully adapt, form positive attachments, and begin to identify with the social and academic community in which the pupil has become a new member. In previous chapters, I documented that there was a wide variance in the ability of students in the Fall River cohort to maneuver both the transition to middle school and to high school. Most youths experienced moderate grade declines following these school moves. Some, however, encountered substantial difficulty following these school transitions.

There are several alternative explanations for why some students would encounter greater difficulty than others when making the move to middle level schools and high schools. One explanation is that students differ in their ability to cope with the stresses and academic and social challenges of these moves. Students from educationally disadvantaged backgrounds may have fewer supports and may receive less guidance maneuvering the stresses of school adjustment. A student's home educational environment may play an important role in determining the degree to which he or she receives support in coping with the new educational and social demands of middle school and of high school. For example, Dale Blyth and Roberta Simmons found that the degree to which parents supervised their child's education was associated with differences in academic and adjustment difficulties following the move to junior high school (Blyth and Simmons, 1987).

Youths will differ in the resources they bring to school. They may also differ in their vulnerability to school transition stress. Students from low socioeconomic backgrounds are more likely to be coping with multiple stresses during adolescence—a factor that may negatively impact a child's capacity to maneuver school transitions (Dornbusch et al., 1991; Felner et al., 1981). Similarly, lower performing students may be less facile in adjusting to changes in teaching style and changes in the organization of classroom learning. Students who are already having difficulty in school and those who are showing signs of disengagement from school may also be more likely to withdraw when faced with the stresses of adjustment (Tinto, 1987).

These explanations for differences in the ability of youths to maneuver school transitions could be characterized as ecological explanations for school transition stress. An ecological explanation would posit that the grading and organizational arrangements of schools will have important influences on students' outcomes because school transitions create critical junctures during which differences in the resources and attributes that they bring to school become important determinants of their subsequent persistence. The greater the extent of ecological change students must face during these school moves, the more differences among students in their coping abilities and vulnerability to stress will create variance in these students' outcomes.

In Chapter 5, I noted that Eccles, Midgley, and their colleagues have challenged the assumption that grade declines associated with school transitions are solely caused by ecological stress (Eccles et al., 1991). These researchers studied the effect of differences in the educational practices and environments of elementary and middle schools by following a large sample of students as they moved from elementary school in the sixth grade to junior high school in the seventh grade (Feldlaufer et al., 1988). Eccles and her colleagues found that junior high school teachers were more likely to rely on educational techniques—including public evaluation of students' work, the use of whole class rather than small group instruction, and more rigorous grading procedures—which highlighted and encouraged comparisons of students' abilities, rather than emphasizing individual task mastery and progress. Teachers in junior high school math classrooms placed greater emphasis on discipline and less emphasis on student participation. In addition, students perceived junior high school teachers as less supportive than their elementary school instructors.

This comparative study of differences in elementary and junior high school math classrooms found that changes in classroom practices had strong impacts on a variety of student outcomes, including achievement in math, attitudes toward learning, and motivation in school. For example, students' interest in math and the extent to which they thought math was important declined when they moved from elementary school teachers whom they characterized as supportive to junior high school teachers whom they characterized as less supportive. On the other hand, when students moved from teachers they characterized as less supportive to those they characterized as more supportive—a much less common experience—their interest in math and the value they placed on math increased. In addition, Eccles and her colleagues found that lower-performing students were much more vulnerable to differences in teaching style than were higher performing students: "By the end of the junior high school year, the confidence that the low achieving students who had moved from high to low efficacy teachers had in their own performance and competence had declined dramatically" (Eccles et al., 1991, p. 536).

In sum, an alternative explanation for school transition stress posits that grade declines can largely be attributed to the effect of the educational practices and environments of elementary and middle level schools (Eccles et al., 1991; Feldlaufer et al., 1988; Midgley et al., 1989). At-risk students according to this perspective encounter greater difficulty during the first year in a middle level school because of a "stage environment" mismatch between the developmental needs of adolescents and the practices of secondary schools. As at-risk students move into middle school and high school, their interactions with school personnel become more anonymous and less supportive, their in-class experiences become less engaging and rewarding, and they receive direct messages in terms of track placement regarding their relative position in their school. For students who are already at the margin academically and who face a greater risk maneuvering the ecological stresses of the school moves, it is not surprising that they would encounter substantial difficulties following school transitions. The messages that school systems are sending lower-performing youths at a time in their development when they are using that information to form a sense of themselves and to define their roles, would work to decrease their motivation and increase the likelihood that they would feel out of step and isolated from that school community. In comparison, students who do well in school receive messages as they move into middle school and junior high school that would promote positive self-identity and increase their attachment to school.

Previous research has largely focused on how overall school climate and the environment of the classroom influence a student's attitudes, behavior and school attachment (Eccles et al., 1991; Eccles and Midgley, 1989; Lipsitz, 1984). My findings on the impact of grade retention suggest that specific school policies may also directly influence a student's school attachment. I find that students who are overage for grade face an increased risk of dropping out regardless of whether or not they experienced a grade retention in elementary or in middle school. A developmental perspective emphasizes that school policies and practices determine the educational environment in which learning occurs and the social context in which development occurs. This perspective, then, provides an important insight into why students who are overage for grade may face an increased risk of dropping out. A grade retention may increase a student's chances of dropping out if that student learns less than if he or she had been promoted. A grade retention also changes a student's relative position in school and sends clear messages to that youth regarding his or her educational capacities. During adolescence, when students are using these messages to form a conception of themselves in relation to their peers, being older than other students in the class may have important influence on youths' assessments of themselves as well as their decisions regarding their education and affiliations.

In this section, I have drawn upon research in adolescent development to suggest one interpretation of the findings of this study. As students move into middle school, they enter a period where they begin to assess the extent to which they feel in step with and part of the day-to-day life of school. There is an emerging consensus that during this period, students' school experiences will have a greater impact on their achievement and school membership than at any point during their school career (Linn and Songer, 1991; Midgley et al., 1989). Tinto's theory of school withdrawal, discussed previously, also tells us that those students who begin to feel out of step, who are not integrated, and who feel that membership is not consistent with their goals and values are much more likely to withdraw. Tinto's theory of school withdrawal applies equally well to persistence in college, to a student's success in middle school, or even in a later occupation. Research on adolescent development, however, provides critical insights into why it is during middle school, rather than later in high school, that we would begin to see the school career paths of late grade dropouts and graduates become defined.

Clearly, the contextual influence of classroom environments and school policy on a student's development paths are not the sole determinant of dropouts' poor school performance and disengagement from school. There is little evidence, for example, that the deterioration in the school performance of early grade dropouts can be linked to changes in their school environment. I also found that the average attendance of late grade dropouts began to decline in the sixth grade among both students who made the transition to middle school and those who remained in their grammar school in the sixth grade.

At the same time, the Fall River study provides evidence that the divergent career paths of late grade dropouts and graduates are not simply a natural and unavoidable consequence of adolescence. My findings on the impact of both school transitions and grade retention suggest that, in looking for ways to reduce school dropout, school systems could look to their own policies and practices that affect the way that these students experience school. This section has identified three important ways that school policies may influence the course of students' school careers. First, how we choose to organize and structure school transitions will determine the number, magnitude, and nature of changes that students must cope with following these school moves. Second, how we choose to teach in, organize, and structure middle school and high school environments will determine the extent to which a student's experiences in school promote or inhibit positive self-identity and engagement in school. And, third, how we choose to react to students' difficulties in school may play an important role in establishing their relative position and forming the direction of their day-to-day experiences in school during adolescence. What, then, does this analysis imply for the development of dropout prevention policies and programs?

THE TWO DROPOUT PROBLEMS

In the next chapter, I discuss in detail the policy implications of my findings regarding the impact of school transitions and grade retention. In this section, I discuss how we can use the findings of the Fall River study to develop a broader framework for thinking about the nature of the problem that school systems face and the development of policy approaches for improving the chances that students will stay in school.

The first contribution that the Fall River study makes to our understanding of school dropout is that school systems with high dropout rates may face two quite different dropout problems that call for two very different policy responses. The first problem, characterized by the school career paths of early grade dropouts in this study, is that of youths who encounter substantial difficulties early on in their school career and whose school performance and engagement deteriorate quite rapidly as they move through middle school.

The second dropout problem, characterized by trends in the school career paths of the majority of dropouts in this study, is that of students who are at the margin between dropping out and going on to graduate in the bottom third of their class. In the context of research in adolescent development, this second dropout problem is that of students who are the most vulnerable by virtue of their personal attributes, situational characteristics or school experiences, to experiencing difficulty during school transitions and disengagement from school during adolescence. For these youths, the path to dropping out may best be portrayed as the educational course of students who experience the greatest difficulty traversing those academic and developmental hurdles that are normally stressful for even the most capable of students.

In sum, the school career paths of students in the Fall River cohort, suggest that differences in outcomes could be linked to differences in both early school performance and school performance and experiences during adolescence. This finding has important implications for the timing and focus of dropout prevention initiatives as well as for an understanding of the underlying causes of school dropout. One of the most important implications of this study may be that it asks educators to shift their focus away from identifying student attributes which predict school dropout to an investigation of why and how some students are more vulnerable than others.

Much of the previous research on school dropout has focused on identifying the characteristics of students and their schools that predict school dropout. In Chapter 4, I found that we would not have identified that majority of late grade dropouts in this study as highly at risk of dropping out on the basis of their fourth-grade school performance. This finding is, indeed, contrary to what many who work in schools believe. Teachers and school administrators have often told me that they can walk into a fourth-grade class and identify the dropouts. Studies have also found that we can predict with some accuracy who will drop out on the basis of early performance and family background (Lloyd, 1983). Are these teachers and researchers just plain wrong? The answer is no. But with the exception of classrooms in the poorest and most blighted areas of inner cities, how many fourth-grade teachers would identify the middle half of their class as likely dropouts? My guess is a teacher would identify the bottom ten to twenty percent of her class as having difficulty early on. She would also most likely identify the most able students as the sure graduates. In both cases, as we found in Chapter 4, she would probably be correct. But, in school systems with high dropout rates, the middle of the fourth-grade class is also highly at risk.

If the Fall River data set had contained more detailed information on the family background, home educational environment, and ability of students, I would most likely have been able to obtain better predictions of school outcomes. But, a sole emphasis on the predictive power of family background has, I would argue, veiled important differences in the manner in which the attributes that students bring to school interact with the institutional characteristics of that school. For high-risk students, the question appears to be: Why do these students encounter such significant problems early on in their school careers? For students at the margin, the question is: Why do some students have greater difficulty than others maneuvering school transitions or the stresses of adolescence? As I discussed in the previous section, students from disadvantaged backgrounds may encounter greater difficulty following school transitions because they may have fewer resources to draw upon to help them maneuver the stress of these school moves. Students from disadvantaged backgrounds may also encounter greater difficulty because they are more likely to be placed in lower tracks or to be retained in grade. Thus, a simple focus on the predictive power of family background may miss important temporal differences in the manner in which students' family backgrounds influence performance in school and the degree to which school systems have the capacity to influence the direction of students' careers. Consider the following three dropout stories that were told in a recent issue of *Catalyst*, an educational newsletter that reports on the progress of Chicago school reform:

The first student is Sammy Burkes who, at age 15, "was dropped from Chicago Vocational High School because he had missed too many days of school. 'I was avoiding fights' he says, 'There were a lot of gangs and they would pick on anyone who wasn't with them.' Sammy got a letter informing him he was no longer enrolled, and a list of alternative schools and programs for dropouts."

The second student is Taheshia Covington who "was put out of Corliss High School. . . . Two weeks before her sixteenth birthday, she was told to leave. 'I was put on probation and I got into another fight, so they put me out at the end of February.' . . . she doesn't want to go back to Corliss because she feels 'they don't like me there.' "

And the third student is Matthew Beck who, at 19, "hopes to graduate from Orr Community Academy in June after five years in high school. He spent his freshman year goofing off and he's paying for it now." The Lighthouse Program Matthew participates in "serves students who have failed classes, are likely to drop out, or have dropped out." (Selinker and Martin, 1992, pp. 2–3)

These students' stories illustrate the extent to which this study has provided new insights into the dynamics of school withdrawal and new directions for dropout prevention. Taheshia's substantial disengagement from school, and her conflicts with other students as well as with school authorities, would suggest that marginal changes in the structure and policies of schools would not, most likely, address the causes of her disengagement and her poor school performance. For students like Taheshia a range of policies aimed at early intervention, intensive services, and the creation of alternative learning environments may be the most appropriate policy response. At the high school level, Whelage and others have documented the success of alternative schools, like the one Taheshia is enrolled in, in creating efficacious school environments for high-risk youth (Whelage et al., 1989).

Sammy and Matthew's stories, however, clearly confirm the findings of this study regarding the importance of the transition to high school for students. In large urban school systems, the high school is a scary, often infamous environment where students, and especially males, face very real fears about their safety. Sammy's withdrawal from school most likely reflects a lack of educational support and guidance at home. It also reflects the extent to which school transitions create critical junctures in students' school careers. To what extent would Sammy's school career have been different if the high school was organized into smaller, more supportive, and less ecologically challenging environments? Would he have been better able to maneuver this school transition, rather than to withdraw, if staff and faculty members were actively responsible for and engaged in contacting students?

The second contribution of the Fall River study is that it suggests two specific directions for dropout prevention policies aimed at this middle group of students. The first direction is to identify and create alternatives to those school policies and practices, such as grade retention, that may attenuate or inhibit a student's school attachment. The second direction is to introduce programs and policies that may better facilitate and promote the personal and social development of at-risk adolescents. In essence, the second direction for dropout prevention is to create more effective schools for young adolescents in both middle school and in high school (Lipsitz, 1984). A starting place is to intervene to facilitate the transitions to both middle school and to high school.

The next chapter discusses several alternative approaches to reducing the stress of school transitions. I have not recommended that school systems eliminate these school moves for two important reasons. The first reason is that this recommendation is impractical. During the past several decades, the elementary, middle school, and high school grade configuration has emerged as the most common grade organization in U.S. school systems. For example, from 1979 to 1989, the number of middle schools increased from 2,080 to nearly 8,000 (U.S. Department of Education, 1991). During this time period the number of junior high schools serving grades 7 and 8 or grades 7 to 9 decreased from 7,750 to 4,687, while the number of elementary schools declined from 60,000 to 50,756.

The second reason I do not recommend eliminating school transitions is that these school moves play an important role in students' personal, social, and academic development.[2] In successfully maneuvering the transition to middle school and to high school, students develop new problem-solving, coping, and adaptation skills. They experience increased autonomy and learn to choose and form new attachments in more heterogeneous environments. The skills that students develop following school transitions and the role that these moves play in their personal and social development may provide an important foundation that will then enable students to more successfully cope with the next important move. Indeed, transitions play an important role in development across the life course. There is the transition to middle school, to high school, to work, to college, and to a variety of adult roles. Each of these transitions involves movement into environments that offer greater levels of complexity, diversity, and autonomy. The ability of students to meet these new challenges will shape the direction of their life course. The failure to acquire these coping resources or the extent to which difficulties following these school moves inhibit positive development may, as we found in this study, have long-term implications for continued progress.[3] Indeed, an important question raised by this study is: How does the failure of students to successfully maneuver a school change affect their ability to meet the next larger and more complex transition?

In the cases outlined above, we found that Sammy withdrew from school while Matthew learned that he could overcome his mistakes and, by participating in school, could find a supportive environment and alternative ways of meeting his goals. How will these different experiences and, in particular, Sammy's failure to successfully maneuver this school change affect Sammy and Matthew as they enter the job market—a transition that has been portrayed as increasingly complex and fraught with difficulty (Grant Foundation Commission on Work, Family and Citizenship, 1988)? Neither Sammy's family nor his school intervened to facilitate his development. Sammy may have lost more than a high school diploma in the process.

The finding that school transitions are critical periods for students offers a concrete direction for dropout prevention policy. As I noted in Chapter 1, many of the important debates around dropout prevention policy are questions regarding the timing of intervention. Should dropout prevention activities be focused on the middle school or the high school? Should dropout prevention be early intervention? My analysis suggests that school systems must begin to think about several different intervention points for different groups of youths. In particular, students who are educationally and socially disadvantaged may face a greater risk to their development throughout their school career—whether it be differences in their early school performance, their ability to successfully maneuver school transitions, or difficulty during adolescence. The school career paths of late grade dropouts clearly illustrate that raising students' early school performance to the point that their average grades and attendance are not different from their classmates will not necessarily ensure their continued progress in school if they will later be vulnerable to experiencing difficulty following school transitions. Similarly, I have provided new empirical evidence that dropout prevention must begin in the middle school years. I have also found that the ability of students to adapt and form positive attachments in high school may be as critical for their persistence. In summation, the third major contribution of this study is that the most appropriate question is not when is the best time to intervene, but what kinds of intervention are needed over the course of a student's school career, and for whom?

SUMMARY

The premise of this research was that an understanding of the manner in which poor school performance and disengagement develop over the course of a student's school career would provide a base of knowledge to guide the development of dropout prevention efforts. I find that Fall

River has a high dropout rate because there are a group of students whose poor early school performance and disengagement from school places them highly at risk of dropping out. Fall River also has a high dropout rate because a high proportion of students who are at the margin will experience substantial disengagement from school during adolescence. Reducing dropout rates, then, will require developing policies aimed at both of these groups. For high risk youths, the first and most appropriate policy response must be early intervention aimed at increasing early school performance and in reducing the chances that students will be retained in school in the early grades. Simply restructuring school transition will not adequately address the academic and engagement problems of students who are substantially disengaged from school. Nor may reducing rates of grade retention in middle school and high school address the problems of teenage parents.

The school career paths of late grade dropouts suggest, however, that students' school career path is not solely formed early in their school career. Adolescence, or the middle school years, emerges as another important period in the formation of students' development. While youths' experiences during adolescence will be shaped by their early school performance, this study, as well as an emerging body of evidence on the role of social context in determining developmental trajectories, suggests that a student's experiences during adolescence are critical in determining persistence. In particular, my findings regarding the impact of school transitions and grade retention suggest that marginal changes in how school systems choose to teach in, organize, and structure middle school and high school environments may have an important influence on determining the proportion of this middle group who will drop out.

NOTES

1. In this section, I draw upon descriptions of the development changes that occur during adolescence and of the implication of these changes for students' identity formation and school attachment in Elliot and Feldman (1990); Entwistle (1990); Harter (1990); Linn and Songer (1991); Petersen and Stemmler (1991); Petersen and Epstein (1991); and Smetana et al. (1991).

2. In Bronfenbrenner's influential work on the ecology of human development, transitions are both a "consequence and an instigator of development processes." Indeed, Bronfenbrenner defines human development as the process "through which the growing person acquires a more extended, differentiated, and valid conception of the ecological environment, and becomes motivated and able to engage in activities that reveal the properties of, sustain, or restructure that environment at levels of similar or greater complexity in form and content" (Bronfenbrenner, 1979, p. 27).

3. Garbarino (1982) notes that students from disadvantaged families face risks

to their development both because of the quality of their participation and because of the absence of participation and interaction. Thus, when a student withdraws from or becomes substantially disengaged from school, rather than learns to cope, that act becomes a threat to development.

Chapter 8

Policy and Research Implications

In the previous chapter I argued that the findings of this study, in the context of research on the role of school experiences in shaping development processes, can be used to develop a new framework for thinking about the nature of school dropout in systems with high dropout rates. To briefly summarize, I argue that, for an important group of dropouts, the individual manifestations of school leaving and the academic processes that lead to school withdrawal can be linked to, and are influenced by, aspects of the policies, organization, and structures of schools. The conclusion of this research is that school systems can look to their own policies for ways that promote or inhibit attachment across students' school careers. Perhaps the best way to illustrate the implications of this framework for policy is to end this book with a discussion of the policy implications of my findings regarding the impact of both school transitions and grade retention.

SCHOOL TRANSITIONS

One of the questions that motivated this study was: Are there critical points in students' school careers during which intervention may reduce the chances of early school leaving? The school transitions from both elementary to middle school and from middle school to high school emerge as critical junctures for youths. There is also some evidence, from an evaluation of the School Transitional Environment Project, that intervention following the school move to high school may be effective in stemming grade losses and in decreasing the chances that students will drop out. I discuss the results of this evaluation later in this chapter.

Program Models

This section presents an array of program models to facilitate school transitions. These programs range from expanding orientation activities, to the more extensive approach of school restructuring. Unfortunately, few of the options that I discuss in this section have been systematically evaluated, nor is there sufficient evidence to gauge the comparative effectiveness of alternative approaches. At the end of this section, I discuss several questions that arise when choosing among program options. Perhaps the most important policy question is: Why do some youths encounter greater difficulty than others following school transitions?

An ecological explanation for school transition stress posits that youths encounter difficulty because of the complexity and scope of change that they encounter following these school moves. At-risk youths, as I discussed in Chapter 7, may experience greater difficulties for two reasons. First, lower performing students may be less capable of adapting to new academic demands and teaching styles. Second, students who are educationally disadvantaged at home may possess fewer coping resources and supports to assist them in overcoming adjustment difficulties. This explanation for school transition stress would argue for interventions that increase social and academic support and reduce the extent of ecological change that students are exposed to following these school moves. Three general program models that fall under this rubric are: orientation programs; remediation and summer transition programs; and cluster programs.

Orientation Programs. Orientation programs have long been the model used by colleges to facilitate this transition (Tinto, 1987). The typical college model is a week or several days of an orientation period at the beginning of the first term. The purposes of orientation sessions are to provide information for students; to allow students extra time to become acquainted with the physical environment of the campus; and to enable students to form social attachments before they are faced with the beginning of classes and the arrival of upperclassmen.

Many middle schools, junior high schools, and high schools currently employ some form of orientation or introductory activities, including orientation periods; information or visiting sessions during the last year in elementary or middle level schools; and buddy, or mentoring, programs whereby an arriving student is paired with an upperclassman (Capelutti and Stokes, 1991; Epstein and MacIver, 1990). Over half of middle schools currently use information sessions (Epstein and MacIver, 1990). The remaining practices are much less common.

Orientation activities are a low cost intervention designed to reduce ecological stress by increasing a student's knowledge of the new middle school or high school, dispelling myths and anxieties in the process. The college orientation model goes one step further than those currently being used in secondary schools by providing a transition period, as well as information.

An enhanced version of an orientation period is a program that combines a transition period with academic enrichment. Summer transition programs with academic contents are often used by exam and advanced placement high schools to prepare students for the greater academic demands of accelerated programs. The Mackey Mosaic Program, developed by former Boston public school principal Diana Lam, provides an exemplary program model for improving the transition to middle school. In this program, entering middle grade students participated in a two-week, four hour per day, transition program. The program included orientation activities for students and their parents; life skills activities; and a curriculum designed to introduce students to the interdisciplinary, cooperative learning approach that was used in the middle school (Massachusetts Advocacy Center, 1986).

Targeted Remediation Programs and Summer Transition Programs. A second approach that has gained popularity at the college level is to provide targeted academic support during the first year of college for those students who may encounter academic difficulties meeting the new demands of college environments (Tinto, 1987). These programs were developed primarily out of concern that minority students were being placed in disadvantaged positions in college because of deficiencies in their prior academic training.

At the middle school and high school level, targeted academic support programs may include placing students in an extra class period to help develop study skills; providing extra counseling and social support; and providing tutoring and supplemental academic support such as help with writing or basic math skills. The WAVE program, discussed later in this section, is a variant of this approach.

The Summer Training and Education Program (STEP) is a summer remediation and life skills program for at-risk youth. The STEP program provides two summers of remediation, work experience, and life skills training for 14- and 15-year-old disadvantaged youth. STEP also includes a school year support component aimed at providing a bridge between the first and second summer of STEP. This program was designed to reduce the chances that students would drop out by stemming learning losses that poor students experienced during the summer months. Participants in STEP must be eligible for the Summer Youth Employment and Training Program and are identified as educationally at risk of dropping out.

STEP was evaluated in a large-scale randomized experiment conducted in five cities. The program was also later replicated in over one hundred cities in fifteen states. The evaluation of STEP found that the program was effective in stemming learning losses (Walker and Vilella-Velez, 1992). Unfortunately, achievement gains did not translate into better performance during the school year, nor did participation increase a student's chances of graduating from high school.

The Fall River study lends further evidence to the proposition that if programs such as STEP are to be successful, they must be linked to and affect a student's day-to-day experiences in school (Grannis, 1991; Walker and Vilella-Velez, 1992). The failure of STEP to produce long-term gains may not mean that the appropriate conclusion is to end the program. Rather, modifying STEP to address school transitions may provide an important means by which local agencies could retain and build on the successful elements of STEP while increasing its potential efficacy. STEP, through the use of proven remediation techniques such as Computer Assisted Instruction, did produce impressive gains in student achievement. On average, participants' reading and math achievement was about one-half of a grade level higher at the end of the summer than the achievement scores of students who held regular summer youth jobs.

A modified version of STEP would include targeting the intervention to 14- and 15-year-olds who are making the transition to high school; linking the program to a student's entering school; and creating an ongoing, in-school program. Examples of effective ongoing support may include a clustering arrangement or the use of a special class approach, such as WAVE in Schools, discussed below. In sum, STEP offers the opportunity to combine both a transition program with an academic content with a school year support model. At the same time, STEP offers students Summer Youth Employment and Training Jobs, an introduction to work and employment skills, and an intensive life skills component.

Cluster Programs. Orientation activities and summer programs assume that we can reduce adjustment difficulties and increase a student's ability to adapt to the academic and social setting of new schools by getting a youth over the initial hurdles of adjustment. Cluster programs, on the other hand, are designed to provide ongoing support by either reducing the size of a student's environment or by providing a base of support. Three models of cluster programs are: Schools within Schools; Advisory Periods; and Special Classes.

Schools Within Schools. The School Transitional Environment Project—another STEP—was designed to ease the transition to high school by increasing peer and teacher support and by providing a stable environment for youths. Participants in STEP were assigned to the same home room and academic classes in a limited geographic area of the high school. Teachers met as a group, with a counselor, on a regular basis.

In addition, STEP expanded the home room teacher's role to include counseling (Felner et al., 1981).

Felner et al. evaluated the effect of STEP on a student's academic adjustment to high school (Felner et al., 1981). This evaluation compared ninth-grade and later outcomes of sixty-five youths who were randomly chosen to participate in the program with those of 120 control youths. The control group was matched by eighth-grade characteristics. These researchers found that participants in STEP had significantly higher GPAs and attendance at the end of ninth grade. In addition, a followup study found that participants in the one-year program had markedly lower dropout rates than controls (Felner and Adan, 1988). In the followup study, the dropout rate for participants was 21 percent compared to a dropout rate for the control youths of 43 percent.

This school-within-school, or house model, was recently adopted by the New York City public schools as the cornerstone of its newest dropout prevention initiative, Project Achieve (Grannis, 1991; Public Education Association, 1990). In Project Achieve, ninth- and tenth-graders will be organized into houses that will integrate staff and academic personnel. The effectiveness of this model will be assessed through an ongoing evaluation.

Advisory Periods and Special Classes. In one study of secondary schools, over one-quarter of teachers reported that they see more than 150 students a day, while 46 percent reported that they see between 100 and 150 students a day (Corcoran, 1990). These high student-teacher ratios mean that teachers have very little personal contact with students. Unless students are able to overcome the odds, most will have very little day-to-day contact with an adult in the school who is attentive to their progress. Advisory periods have emerged as one approach toward increasing the level of personal contact between students and teachers.

In advisory periods, students meet in a small group every day or on a regular basis, with a teacher, administrator, or counselor. The purpose of these sessions, as opposed to the announcement and general record-keeping tasks of homerooms, is to deal with students' individual needs, discuss topics of importance to the students, and provide a regular source of contact with an adult (Carnegie Council on Adolescent Development, 1990; Muth and Alvermann, 1992). Advisory periods, then, expand a teacher's role to include guidance and monitoring.

The Work Achievement Values and Education Program (WAVE in Schools) is an approach to advisory periods that combines both social support with a more intensive life skills component. WAVE currently operates in over one hundred high schools nationwide (WAVE, 1992). High school students in WAVE meet together in a class with no fewer than twenty students for one class period a day. The central focus of the WAVE model is a participatory curriculum that includes lessons in life and employability skills. The goal of WAVE is to build students' self-esteem and interpersonal skills, as well as to increase attachment to school by providing a supportive community. An important component of the WAVE model is teacher training in the WAVE curriculum, in participatory techniques, and in methods to create supportive environments within classrooms.

The WAVE model is currently designed as a four-year intervention, although many schools operate the program for less than four years. Schools most commonly operate WAVE in the first two years of high school. WAVE is targeted at at-risk students who are recommended for the program. An early evaluation of WAVE found that the dropout rate for participants in the program was lower than that of other students in the school, even though WAVE students were recommended for the program because they were identified as at-risk of dropping out. WAVE in Schools is currently undergoing a more rigorous and extensive evaluation.

Each of the program models discussed so far is targeted at both reducing the extent of ecological change students are asked to cope with following school transitions and increasing academic and social support for students in their new school. None of these programs change how students spend their time, how students are organized for instruction, or how teachers teach in their classrooms. If students encounter difficulties following school transitions because the organizational arrangements and pedagogical practices of middle schools and high schools do not meet their developmental and educational needs, then the solution is to adopt programs and policies that better meet the needs of adolescents. This approach, sparked by the Carnegie Foundation on Adolescent Development's influential report, entitled *Turning Points*, has provided the basis for a growing movement to restructure middle schools (Carnegie Council on Adolescent Development, 1990).

School Restructuring. School restructuring has become a catchword that may mean many different things to many different educators. In this section, I discuss several alternative approaches to scheduling, grouping, and teaching students in major academic subjects. I limit myself to approaches that were included in *Turning Points* which have been successfully implemented in restructured middle schools, and which have been promoted by school organizations and educators as essential components of such efforts (Carnegie Corporation on Adolescent Development, 1990; Illinois State Board of Education, 1992; Muth and Alvermann, 1992; MacIver and Epstein, 1991).

Four important components of restructured schools are: (1) the creation of smaller learning environments by organizing students into cluster programs or schools-within-schools; (2) the reorganization of instruction using interdisciplinary teams of teachers, flexible block scheduling, and more flexible grouping arrangements; (3) the introduction of instructional techniques, such as collaborative or continuous progress learning approaches that are task-oriented, allow for heterogeneous grouping, and have been shown to increase students' engagement in the learning process; and (4) the provision of support for students through the use of teacher-based guidance and advisory periods (Massachusetts Advocacy Center, 1988; Muth and Alvermann, 1992). These more comprehensive approaches to reducing grade declines and increasing a student's adaptive capacity following school transitions combine efforts to decrease ecological stress with changes in the educational environments of middle school classrooms.

Two of the centerpieces of restructured educational environments are the use of interdisciplinary team teaching and flexible block scheduling. Teachers on an interdisciplinary team are assigned the same group of students. These teams are usually comprised of a science teacher, a social studies teacher, and a language arts teacher. Ideally, teachers on a team are provided common planning time in order to share information about students, and to coordinate activities and instructional programs across subjects (Muth and Alvermann, 1992). The interdisciplinary focus of team teaching aims to increase a student's engagement in learning by making it easier for students to integrate learning across subjects.

An important component of interdisciplinary team teaching is flexible block scheduling (Muth and Alvermann, 1992). Flexible block scheduling, as opposed to the rigidity of the traditional forty-five-minute period, allows teachers on the team the flexibility to meet a range of instructional needs. Instruction is arranged within an academic block of time that may be composed of four or five periods. Within a block, teachers on a team can choose to divide time differently from day to day and from student to student. The interdisciplinary team approach, when combined with clustering across age groups, also allows teachers to teach a range of abilities. In particular, the use of flexible grouping across grade levels may provide an important alternative to grade retention and may allow students to learn at different paces (Massachusetts Advocacy Center, 1986).

A third essential component of restructured schools is the use of educational techniques that increase a student's participation in learning, which focus on task mastery rather than ability/self-assessment, and which allow for heterogeneous grouping of students. Continuous-progress models, collaborative and cooperative learning approaches, and whole language instruction are often cited as examples of alternatives to the use of whole-class instruction (Carnegie Council on Adolescent Development, 1990; Slavin, 1987). The key elements of these approaches are the use of small group instruction; flexible grouping arrangements in which a student's group membership may be short-term and may vary widely from subject to subject or activity to activity; and the use of heterogeneous grouping arrangements. Many of these approaches have been documented to be effective in improving the academic achievement of students (Slavin, 1987).

One example of cooperative learning is the Team Accelerated Instruction approach (TAI) (Carnegie Council on Adolescent Development, 1990). In TAI, students are grouped into teaching teams and home teams. Teaching teams are groups of students who are performing at the same level. Teaching teams are provided with materials and instruction directed at their level of ability. Students are also grouped into home teams, composed of students of different ability levels. Home teams work together on problems and provide peer tutoring. Students are then graded on their individual progress and on home team performance. Evaluations of TAI and other cooperative learning programs have found that these approaches provide benefits for students across a range of ability levels. For example, one large evaluation of TAI showed that "TAI students consistently show a 2-to-1 ratio in achievement gains over control students" (Carnegie Council on Adolescent Development, 1990, p. 51).

Taken together, the elements of restructured schools provide the most comprehensive approach to promoting positive development and increasing the school engagement of students. Can school-wide restructuring approaches provide an alternative to the current organizational arrangement and educational practices of middle schools and, possibly, high schools? This brings us back to the question of which model or models provide the most effective and feasible approaches to facilitating school transitions.

This section has presented an array of possible program models. When choosing among these, educators must decide among issues of targeting, the duration and scope of interventions, and the potential feasibility.

Program Issues

Targeting. I have described several approaches that are targeted specifically at students who are doing poorly in school, such as the WAVE in Schools and School Transitional Environment Program, and approaches that invoke school-wide change, such as advisory periods. Several issues arise when thinking about whether to choose programs that are targeted specifically at students who may be at risk of experiencing school transition stress. On the one hand, programs such as advisory periods or expanded orientation activities provide extra support but may not provide enough intervention to adequately address the needs of students who are highly at risk of experiencing difficulty following school transitions. On the other hand, broad based programs may be more effective in producing changes in a student's day-to-day relationships in school. School-wide reform may be more likely to become integrated into the school environment and to gain widespread support among teachers. Targeted dropout prevention efforts have traditionally encountered difficulty because they are often seen as peripheral and as providing noneducational, supplemental support services; a lack of integration that fundamentally undermines their potential efficacy (Grannis, 1991; Massachusetts Advocacy Center, 1988; Public Education Association, 1990; Whelage et al., 1992).

Finally, targeting requires that school systems accurately identify which students are most at risk of experiencing difficulty following school transitions. In this study, I found that those students for whom difficulty following school transitions were defining events were not necessarily those who were doing the most poorly in school before the school move. As I discussed in Chapter 7, students who are performing very poorly in school and who are substantially disengaged from school may need more intensive intervention than that which would be provided by any of the program models described in this section. Such efforts may, however, provide critical intervention for more marginal students. The implication of this finding is that programs that target the most highly at-risk pupils run the risk of targeting the wrong intervention at the wrong group. This study has not addressed the question: Which students are most at risk of experiencing difficulty maneuvering school transitions? Investigating this question, however, is of critical policy significance.

The Duration and Scope of Intervention. The program models discussed in this section also vary in the duration and scope of intervention. Orientation and summer transition programs are premised on the assumption that we can address school transition stress by getting students over the initial hurdles of adjustment. Programs such as the WAVE in Schools model provide ongoing support but do not change the structure of schools or the educational environment of classrooms. School-restructuring approaches are premised on the assumption that difficulty following school transitions arises from both ecological stress and a mismatch between the educational practices of schools and the needs of adolescents. How much intervention is needed following school transitions? Answering this question will require that we develop a better understanding of why some students encounter more difficulty than others following these school moves. Answering this question will also require that we conduct evaluations and demonstrations of many of the policy approaches discussed in this section. The results of Felner's evaluation of the School Transition Environment Project did find that cluster programs may be an effective intervention at the high school level. This evaluation, however, was based on a small sample and has not been replicated on a larger scale.

Feasibility. A final question that arises when choosing among program options is which can provide feasible alternatives to our current practice. School-wide restructuring approaches clearly provide the most comprehensive alternative. They are also the most costly and require the greatest amount of effort, time, training, and commitment on the part of school administrators and teachers to transform the educational environments of middle schools. There are many examples of middle schools that have successfully implemented comprehensive school reform. The question, however, is to what extent can these approaches be successfully implemented in the rule rather than the exception?

There is some evidence that many of the elements of school restructuring are being introduced in middle schools. For example, Douglas MacIver and Joyce Epstein found that when middle level principals were asked to identify which practices among a list of twenty-two were currently in place or were being considered for the future, principals most often cited that they were planning on implementing or increasing the use of advisory periods; interdisciplinary teams of teachers; the provision of common planning time for interdisciplinary teams; the use of cooperative learning approaches; and greater parental involvement in schools (MacIver and Epstein, 1991).

The increasing prevalence of these practices is partly due to the efforts of groups such as the National Middle School Association and foundations such as the Carnegie Foundation and the Edna McConnell Clark Foundation to actively disseminate information on and promote these model practices. The extent to which middle level practitioners are willing to consider these more extensive restructuring approaches also suggests that these alternatives may better meet the needs of both students and teachers. For example, the Chicago Teacher's Union recently established the Quest center. The purpose of the Quest center is to provide information and to assist teachers in implementing many of the restructuring reforms.

The level of support school-restructuring efforts have received from middle school teachers and administrators is promising. There is less evidence that school-restructuring approaches could provide feasible alternatives in the larger, more departmentalized environments of high schools. This does not mean that approaches such as cluster programs, schools-within-schools, or interdisciplinary team teaching would not be effective interventions at the high school level. It may suggest that high schools are more difficult to reform.

In sum, the Fall River study provides strong evidence that intervening during school transitions may provide an efficacious use of dropout prevention resources. As is illustrated in this discussion, the question becomes: What would such an intervention look like? Designing such interventions requires us to resolve issues of targeting, scope, duration, and feasibility. Many of the program approaches discussed in this section may provide important means of reducing dropout rates. Critical next steps, then, lie in investigating which students are most at risk of experiencing difficulty following these school moves, developing a fuller understanding of why students encounter difficulty, and establishing which program options provide the most effective and feasible alternatives in both middle schools and in high schools.

GRADE RETENTION

The Fall River study was designed to extend our analysis of early school leaving to middle school and early high school. One of the purposes of collecting longitudinal data on the pre-high school experiences of students is that such data allow us to more adequately address the question: Is there evidence that school policies regarding tracking, discipline, and grade retention hurt youths' chances of graduating from high school? In this study I have examined the association between grade retention and school dropout. This section presents the results of my analysis in the context of the trend toward tougher promotion policies in school systems, the increase in retention rates in the 1980s, and the debate over the effects of these policies. In this section, I argue that reducing rates of grade retention will require a two-tiered approach. The first approach is to pursue efforts to reduce the incidence of grade retention in the early grades. The second approach is to provide preventive intervention and to develop alternatives to grade retention in the middle grades and in high school.

The Policy Context

The proportion of youths who are promoted from one year to the next is largely determined by school systems' promotional policies and by the attitudes of teachers and principals regarding the benefits of retention. The past two decades have witnessed a dramatic shift in these promotional policies. During the 1970s, the prevailing philosophy was that social promotion was most beneficial to youths (Rose et al., 1983). Policies of social promotion came under sharp criticism during the standard-raising movement of the 1980s. The movement to raise standards in schools, discussed in Chapter 1, pointed to declines in the achievement of American students as evidence that such lenient policies as social promotion had caused a dilution of standards and a decline in the quality of American education. As A Nation At Risk argued, "Our society and its educational institutions seems to have lost sight of the basic purpose of school and of the high expectation and disciplined effort needed to attain them" (National Commission on Excellence in Education, 1983, pp. 5–6).

The educational movement of the 1980s ushered in several important policy initiatives. One of most important changes that occurred in the past decade was a dramatic shift in the attitudes of teachers and educators toward retention. During the 1980s, many school systems drafted strict promotional policies, often tied to scores on curriculum-referenced or basic skills tests. For example, in 1983, in an effort to "restore meaning" to the Boston public school diploma, the Boston School Committee passed a new Student Promotion Policy that required 85 percent attendance in each quarter, passing grades in coursework, and a pass on curriculum-referenced tests for promotion (Massachusetts Advocacy Center, 1986).

This shift in school policies toward retention often resulted in sharp increases in rates of retention. For example, in the Atlanta public schools, the implementation of minimum competency testing in 1981 resulted in a fourfold increase in the percentage of first-graders retained in grade (Rose et al., 1983). In 1981, the Atlanta public schools retained 18 percent of first-graders. Similarly, in 1980, the District of Columbia retained 32 percent of primary grade students under its newly instituted "student progress plan" (Rose et al., 1983).

Perhaps the most dramatic indicator of the impact of the standard-raising movement was the rise in the proportion of youths who were overage for grade. From 1970 to 1978, during the decade of social promotion, the percentage of 14-year-olds who were enrolled below their modal grade level (ninth grade) decreased from 23.1 to 19.2 percent (Shepard and Smith, 1989). From 1978 to 1989, the percentage of 14-year-olds who were enrolled below their modal grade level increased from 19.2 to 32 percent.[1]

In Chapter 1, I noted that one of the reasons that dropout rates re-emerged on the educational agenda was the concern that standard-raising reforms, and in particular these shifts in promotional policies, would exacerbate the academic and engagement problems of at-risk youths. Opponents of grade retention cited research evidence that non-promotion is an ineffective means of remediating poor school performance. Opponents have also cited high dropout rates among retained youth as evidence that grade retention places students at risk of early school leaving. One of the purposes of this study was to begin to sort out the extent to which grade retention may improve, impede, or have no effect on a student's school progress by controlling for differences in the grades and attendance of students as early as the fourth grade. As I noted in Chapter 6, the Fall River data set does not contain detailed information on students' abilities, home environments, motivation in school, or measures of teachers' attitudes toward retention. This lack of detailed information on differences among students did constrain my ability to fully identify the causal relationships between grade retention and school dropout. Nevertheless, this study provides the strongest evidence to date that students who are retained in grade face an increased risk of dropping out.

After a decade of get tough promotion policies, many school systems are reviewing the impact of these policies and are searching for alternatives. Boston, Chicago, Minneapolis, and New York, along with many other school districts, have recently revised or revoked their promotional policies.[2] These changes in policies have been motivated by research evidence. They were also motivated by school systems' own experience. For example, in 1990, the chancellor of New York's public schools revised that city's strict promotional policy, citing evidence that dropout rates among those retained were higher than among youth with comparable reading levels, even though those youth who were retained under the policy received special services (New York City Board of Education, 1988). The New York policy, which required retention of fourth- and seventh-graders who scored more than a year and a half behind grade level on the Gates test of reading comprehension, contributed to New York's high rates of retention. In 1988, more than 40 percent of New York City's public school students were overage for their grade by the time they entered high school (PINS Advisory Committee, 1988).

The stricter promotion policies that were enacted during the 1980s were motivated by the legitimate concern that students should not be allowed to pass through the school system performing well below their grade level. Our experiences with these policies are now leading many to conclude that the goal of ensuring minimum competency cannot be met by implementing policies that harm youths' chances of graduating and which do not, as the literature suggests, produce improvements in school performance and attachment to school. Simply revoking these policies will not, however, resolve the retention/promotion controversy. Most youths do not experience a grade retention because of a score on a standardized test. Students are most often retained in kindergarten and first grade. In middle school and in high school, moreover, students are most often retained in grade because they are doing very poorly in school. Reducing the incidence of grade retention while ensuring that youths attain a minimum level of basic skills will require investments in both preventive efforts and in the development of alternatives to retention at the middle and high school levels. My analysis of the impact of grade retention and, specifically, of the effects of being overage for grade, have implications for policies toward both early grade retention and the development of approaches toward grade retention in middle schools and high schools.

Early Grade Retentions

Many of the testing policies implemented in the 1980s were directed at readiness testing in kindergarten and first grade. The increased use of readiness testing in the early grades and an escalation in the academic demands of kindergarten have contributed to high rates of retention (Shepard and Smith, 1988). Eleven percent of students in the Fall River cohort were retained in either kindergarten or first grade. Rates of early grade retention of this magnitude or higher are not uncommon in school systems. For example, in 1989, the Chicago public schools retained close to 9 percent of children in the first grade, by far the highest proportion of youth retained in any grade (Easton and Storey, 1990). In 1988, the Boston public schools retained close to 5 percent of children in kindergarten and close to 17 percent of children in the first grade (Massachusetts Advocacy Center, 1989).

There is an emerging body of evidence that kindergarten and early grade retentions provide few long-term academic or emotional benefits to students (Mantzicopoulos et al., 1992; Schultz, 1989; Shepard and Smith, 1986; 1988). In addition, I find that students who experienced early grade retentions dropped out at higher rates even when controlling for differences in the grades and attendance of retained and promoted youths as late as middle school; in part because students who are overage for grade may face an increased risk of dropping out. If these findings are robust, then early grade retentions would place youths at a higher risk of early school leaving, even if they had short-term positive benefits.

The lack of evidence that early retentions are a valid or necessary educational tool suggests that reducing the incidence of retentions in the early grades would be an efficacious use of dropout prevention resources. This task, however, will not be easy. Early intervention programs have documented success in improving students' early school performance and in reducing the likelihood that a student will be retained in grade (Dryfoos, 1990; Natriello et al., 1991). Reducing rates of grade retention in the early grades will also require concerted efforts to educate primary grade teachers regarding the influence of early retentions on students' later school outcomes. Despite research evidence to the contrary, there is strong and widespread belief among teachers that early grade retention has both short- and long-term benefits (Smith and Shepard, 1987; Tompchin and Impara, 1992). In addition, reducing rates of grade retention in the early grades may require school systems to address issues regarding changes in the academic demands and content of early grade curriculums; changes that have led to an increasing focus on skills mastery in kindergarten and first grade. For example, Mary Smith and Lorrie Shepard, in their analyses of changes in early grade education, argue that increases in the academic demands of kindergarten and first grade have resulted in dramatic increases in retention in the early grades. For example, from 1979 to 1989, the proportion of seven-year-olds who were enrolled below their modal grade level (second grade) increased from 14.2 to 22.5 percent.[3]

Middle School and High School Retentions

Retention in the early grades is largely based upon a teacher's assessment of a student's "readiness" for school. Middle school and high school retentions, on the other hand, are primarily the result of students' failing several or all of their courses. If there is a lesson to be learned from our experiences with promotional policies over the past two decades, it may be that neither social promotion nor grade retention alone adequately serve the needs of youths who are doing poorly in school.

Research on grade retention has found that promotion with remediation provides more short-term academic benefits to youths than either retention alone, retention with remediation, or promotion alone (Karweit, 1991; Smith and Shepard, 1989). The results of the Fall River study lend additional support to the conclusion that promotion with remediation is the appropriate alternative. If being older than their classmates places students at risk of dropping out, then nonpromotion policies that attempt to redress the impact of grade retention with remediation or special services would not fully mitigate the impact of that retention. Indeed, this more rigorous analysis is consistent with the experience of the New York public schools, which found that retained youths dropped out at high rates even when students were provided with costly special services (PINS Advisory Committee, 1988).

Three policy approaches to providing both alternatives to and prevention of retention at the middle school and high school level are the use of alternative grouping and grade arrangements; the provision of remedial and supplemental instruction; and the use of alternative classrooms and programs.

Alternative Grouping Arrangements. Advocates of school restructuring argue that the use of alternative grouping and instructional practices in middle schools provides critical alternatives to grade retention. In particular, multigrade and multiability classrooms allow students to progress at their own pace. The use of small group instructional approaches, interdisciplinary team teaching, and flexible block scheduling, described in the previous section, also enhance the ability of teachers to meet a range of instruction needs in classrooms and to teach more heterogeneous groups of students (Massachusetts Advocacy Center, 1990). One example of multigrade arrangements are classrooms that combine two or more grade levels within one classroom. For example, students may be assigned to fourth/fifth grade rather than to fourth grade alone. The National Coalition of Advocates for Students argues that such arrangements reduce grade retentions because students have more time to learn at their own pace and because teachers have more time to work with individual students. As the NCAS argues:

Retention, in the traditional sense, does not occur in multi-age classes because at least half of the students are expected to remain in the class at the end of each school year rather than be promoted to the next set of grade levels. Because teachers have a second or third year with students, they feel less pressure to retain them if they have not yet achieved a determined set of skills. (National Coalition of Advocates for Students, 1991, p. 165)

Another approach to more flexible grouping arrangements is to allow teachers on teams or across classrooms to use flexible grouping arrangements across subjects. A variant of this approach is used at the high school level in school systems that do not retain students in high schools. For example, high school students in the Fall River public schools are not officially retained in grade although they may retake courses they have failed. Thus, students in the school system may be retaking freshman year English at the same time that they are taking sophomore year English. At the middle school level, grouping approaches that allow students to participate in several different grade levels with remedial support in order to master material may be an effective alternative. While these alternatives are promising, there has been no evaluation of the extent to which alternative grading or organizational arrangements provide effective alternatives to retention or the extent to which more flexible grouping arrangements are feasible in schools that have not undertaken large-scale school restructuring.

Remediation and Preventive Interventions. Any serious effort to reduce rates of grade retention must include a focus on the provision of remediation or preventive tutoring in the middle grades. We know much about the effectiveness of alternative approaches to remediation in the early grades (Natriello et al., 1991; McPartland and Slavin, 1990; Slavin, 1987). Unfortunately, we know very little about effective remediation techniques, and especially of preventive interventions, in the middle and upper grades (MacIver, 1991; McPartland and Slavin, 1990). Remedial efforts in the middle grades have not been studied or developed as widely as those of earlier grades primarily because most remediation monies are targeted at the elementary grades. In addition, those remediation efforts that currently take place in middle school have tended to focus on more intensive interventions rather than on prevention.

Most middle level schools provide some form of remediation for students. In one survey, over 60 percent of middle level schools reported that they provide pull-out programs in reading or English and 51 percent reported pull-out programs in math (Epstein and MacIver, 1990). Pull-out programs refer to supplemental remedial activities, often based on diagnostic evaluation of basic skills deficiencies, which take students out of class to provide remediation. These programs are usually funded with Chapter 1 compensatory education funding. In addition, over half of middle level schools reported using summer school or before and after school coaching classes to provide remediation.

While most middle level schools provide some remediation activities, school systems devote fewer resources to remediation in middle school and high school than to remediation activities in the elementary grades. The majority of Chapter 1 and state compensatory education funding is directed at the elementary grades (Children's Defense Fund, 1988; McPartland and Slavin, 1990). For example, the Children's Defense Fund found that in 1987 less than half of the states provided state compensatory education or remediation to the middle grades either for remediation activities or for summer school (Children's Defense Fund, 1988). Partly because of these limited resources, schools most often target remediation activities in the middle grades at the provision of services for students with more severe skills deficiencies than at the provision of preventive services (Epstein and Salinas, 1990).

Two approaches to preventive remediation are the use of tutoring and the use of special class approach to remediation. A variety of tutoring approaches have been found to be effective in improving student performance. These include peer and cross-age tutoring as well as the use of adult mentors as tutors (Carnegie Council on Adolescent Development, 1990; Massachusetts Advocacy Center, 1990; Slavin, 1987). Cross-age and peer tutoring have also been shown to be beneficial for the students who are the tutors as well as for the students who are being tutored. Cross-age and peer tutoring, moreover, has the advantage of being able to take place during the school day, perhaps during an elective period. MacIver, in a review of remedial approaches in the middle grades, argues strongly for in-school tutoring. In particular, MacIver argues that the extra subject period, or elective approach, to remediation is a particularly promising approach to providing preventive intervention (MacIver, 1991; MacIver and Epstein, 1991). The provision of remediation through an extra subject period avoids the attendance problems of before and after school coaching classes, and may be less stigmatizing than the traditional pull-out approach to remediation.

Alternative Classroom and Programs. A third programmatic alternative to grade retention in middle school and in high school is the use of special programs or alternative schools to provide conditional promotions with special services. As I noted in Chapter 6, students who are overage for grade and who become eligible to leave school when they are still in middle school are very likely to drop out. One interpretation of this association is that there is a large discouragement effect of being overage for grade. Another interpretation is that students who fail grades in late middle school are very likely making the decision to drop out and are giving up on school. In either case, students who are substantially disengaged from school and who are failing grades, particularly in late middle school, may need more intensive intervention. Programs that create alternative learning environments within middle level schools, high schools, or alternative schools may be effective in meeting the special educational and motivational needs of adolescents who are overage for grade.

One exemplary program model is the Boston RECAP program. RECAP is a promotional alternative for students who are substantially disengaged from school and who will not be promoted to high school. In RECAP, students sign a contract agreeing that they will meet promotion, behavior, and attendance standards. Students who meet these standards are allowed to attain two promotions in one year, once in January and once in July. RECAP advocates, who are staff members from the school, maintain day-to-day contact with students to ensure that they are in attendance. Students are also provided with special supplemental support services such as tutoring after school. In addition, participants in RECAP earn school credit for community service. The program has documented success in the number of students who are promoted (Massachusetts Advocacy Center, 1986).

A final preventive approach to retention are school transition programs. In this study, I found that it was largely following school transitions, and in particular following the transition to high school, that many students encountered severe academic difficulty. It is not surprising, then, that rates of grade retention are extremely high during the first year of high school in school systems that employ high school retention. For example, in 1988, almost one-quarter of Boston public school students were retained in their freshman year of high school in 1988 (Massachusetts Advocacy Center, 1989). Next to kindergarten and first-grade retention, the incidence of grade retention is highest in the ninth and tenth grades (Shepard and Smith, 1989). Thus, programs that are directed at facilitating school transitions and at reducing a student's academic difficulties following these school moves may also be placed under the rubric of retention prevention.

This section has discussed several approaches to reducing rates of grade retention and to reducing the likelihood that students who are retained will drop out. In middle level schools and in high schools, efforts to reduce the incidence of grade retention include the development of alternatives to retention (such as the use of more flexible, non-grade specific scheduling or organizing students into multiage and multigrade classrooms) and the provision of preventive interventions (such as the provision of tutoring, special help classes, and summer school sessions). Efforts to reduce grade declines and decrease academic and adjustment difficulties following school transitions may also be an important approach to prevent retention, particularly at the high school level. Finally, programs such as RECAP are designed to reduce the likelihood that students who have been retained in grade or who are overage for grade will decide to leave school by providing alternatives to nonpromotion.

The practice of retaining students who are doing poorly in school has become increasingly controversial. In this context, it is striking that there are few clear policy alternatives to retention. Investment in preventive services services and alternatives to promotion through the use of Chapter 1 funding, state compensatory education funds, or dropout prevention monies, would fill an important gap in services for at-risk youths. A first step is to develop and test alternative remediation, instructional strategies, and broader restructuring approaches for their effectiveness in reducing the use of retention.

CONCLUSION

The Fall River study was designed to address an important gap in research on school dropout. Along the way, this study has provided several new insights into the nature of the dropout population. I have developed a conceptual foundation for understanding the manner in which school policies and practices may influence the direction of students' school careers. I have also identified two areas for intervention. The first is to develop programs and policies to facilitate the transitions to middle level schools and high schools. The second is to develop initiatives aimed at reducing rates of both early and late grade retention. This study has also provided several new directions for research.

Research in adolescent development is only just beginning to examine the extent to which the developmental trajectories of students vary across youths and the degree to which these differences can be linked to differences in later outcomes. In this and the preceding chapter, I have suggested several hypotheses for why students who are doing poorly in school and those who are educationally and economically disadvantaged would face a greater risk to their development as they move through middle school and into high school. I have also suggested several alternative explanations for how experiences, such as being retained in grade or having difficulty following a school transition, may pose barriers to school membership.

More rigorous explication of how these and other aspects of the policies and organization of schools influence behavior is exigent. Alternative explanations for adjustment difficulties following a school move would, for example, lead to quite different program models. One explanation is that students vary in their ability to cope with school transition stress by virtue of their personal or situational characteristics. This ecological explanation would argue for programs such as the School Transition Environment Project which increase peer and teacher support and provide a smaller and more stable physical environment. A second explanation for why some students would encounter greater difficulties than others following these school moves is that the policies and practices that students encounter in these new schools treat youths differently. If dropouts' difficulties following school transitions can be attributed to the impact of pedagogical practices, aspects of tracking, or the attitudes of teachers, then more substantial changes in in-class instruction and classroom organization would be called for. And finally, some students may show greater declines in their average grades because transitions are natural gateposts during which those who are moving toward dropping out of school use as an exit point. This final explanation would suggest that intervention to ease the stress of school transitions would do little to address the cause of their disengagement.

Regardless of which specific program options a school system chooses, policy initiatives to reduce the incidence of grade retention or to intervene following school transitions will most certainly require a revision of the approach to dropout prevention that was most often taken during the 1980s. When asked about the factors that lead students to drop out of school most school administrators cite behavior problems and problems with the home environments of children as the primary causes of school leaving (Hyle et al., 1991). In the previous chapter, I argued that the results of the Fall River study challenge educators to develop a new conception of the nature of school dropout—one that is strongly influenced by a student's experiences in school. This chapter presented a wide range of program models and alternative policy approaches aimed at reducing the stress of school transitions and the use and impact of grade retention. Almost every one of these approaches takes as its starting place changing specific school policies, teachers' attitudes, and the nature of a student's day-to-day interactions with teachers and the school. Few of these programs have been adopted on a widespread scale or have been recognized as central components of dropout prevention.

The promise of this study is that school systems have the capacity to influence the nature of school transitions, the policies that govern schools, and how students are organized for instruction. These results, however, challenge educators to refocus dropout prevention initiatives and to direct resources toward programmatic and policy changes in schools, rather than on the provision of ancillary services. These initiatives include experimenting with alternative ways of organizing students for instruction within and across classrooms. They include changing the policies and practices that govern how school systems respond to students' academic and engagement problems. And, they include taking steps to reduce the anonymity and bureaucracy of large urban schools. This discussion of policy implications leads to the conclusion that reinvigorating and restructuring the education of adolescents in both middle level schools and high schools must be the centerpiece of dropout prevention initiatives in the decade ahead.

NOTES

1. There is no precise national estimate of the cumulative incidence of grade retention. We can, however, obtain rough estimates of the incidence of grade retention by examining the percentage of a cohort who are enrolled below their modal grade level in any given year. The October Current Population Survey provides information on school enrollment by grade and age and, thus, provides a source for estimating the cumulative incidence of retention. In this chapter, I report information on the percentage of 14-year-olds who are overage for grade. A more precise measure of the incidence of retention in a given age range would correct for the proportion of students who began their education overage for grade. For example, in the years 1979–1981, 8.6 percent of 16-year-olds were enrolled below their modal grade level (first grade). I use a three-year average to correct for year-to-year fluctuations often occurring in the Current Population Survey. Eight years later, at 14 years old, 28.9 percent of these cohorts were enrolled below their modal grade level (ninth grade). The difference between these two numbers gives us a rough estimate of the percentage of youths who experienced at least one grade retention from the first to the eighth grade. Thus, we can estimate that, in the years 1987 to 1989, roughly 20.4 percent of 14-year-olds had experienced at least one grade retention during this grade span. This estimate does not include kindergarten or high school retentions (U.S. Bureau of the Census, Current Population Reports, Series P–20, *School Enrollment: Social and Economic Characteristics of Students* [Washington, D.C.: U.S. Government Printing Office, various years]).

2. In 1992, the Minneapolis public schools suspended its 1984 policy of using kindergarten testing to determine readiness for the first grade (*Education Week*, April 29, 1992, p. 1). In 1991, the Boston public school superintendent's task force reviewed Boston's tracking and retention policies and recommended widespread changes in both areas (*Boston Globe*, July 1, 1991, 14:1; May 30, 1991, 23:6; September 30, 1991, sec. A, 8:3). For information on Chicago public schools' promotional policies, see Easton and Storey (1990).

3. Increases in the proportion of students who are overage for grade in the second grade are partly attributable to an increase in early grade retentions and partly to increases in the age of entry into kindergarten (Shepard and Smith, 1988). Data on the proportion of youth who are overage for grade were obtained from the October Current Populations Survey (U.S. Bureau of the Census, Current Population Reports, Series P–20, *School Enrollment: Social and Economic Characteristics of Students* [Washington, D.C.: U.S. Government Printing Office, various years]).

Appendixes

Appendix 1-A
Comparing Measures of the National Dropout Rate
Chapter 1 discussed three commonly used measures of the national dropout rate: (1) the number of graduates compared to the population 17 years of age in a given year; (2) the number of public high school graduates compared with public school ninth-grade enrollment four years earlier; and (3) the percentage of 18- and 19-year-olds with a high school diploma or equivalency degree. This appendix describes how each measure is calculated and briefly discusses the advantages and disadvantages of each.

One of the most commonly used measures of the national dropout rate is to compare the number of students who graduated from regular elementary and secondary schools each year with the population 17 years of age. The number of graduates in each year is obtained from the National Center for Education Statistic's Common Core of Data. The population 17 years of age is estimated from the October Current Population Survey. NCES's Common Core of Data includes: the Biennial Survey of Education in the United States; Statistics of State School Systems; and the Fall Statistics of Public Elementary and Secondary Schools. The number of graduates is adjusted to include estimates for private schools. Ungraded pupils are not included.

The number of graduates as a percentage of the population 17 years of age in each year is an estimate of uninterrupted completion, since youth who never failed a grade would be approximately 17 years of age at the beginning of their senior year. If there are not large year-to-year fluctuations in the population, or large year-to-year fluctuations in the proportion of youth who are "held back" and graduating late, this measure would capture noninterrupted completion with some degree of accuracy.

Another method of estimating the national dropout rate is to compare the number of graduates from public high schools in a given year with the number of students enrolled in public high schools four years earlier. Both the number of graduates from public high schools and the number of graduates in any given year is collected by the National Center for Education Statistics in their Common Core of Data. Private high schools, who report lower dropout rates, are not included (Bryk and Driscoll, 1988). Comparing the number of public high school graduates to the number of ninth-graders four years earlier is an intuitively appealing measure of uninterrupted completion in public high schools. This statistic, however, may not provide a very reliable measure of the national dropout rate. The measure is not corrected for transfers into and out of the public school system after the ninth grade. In addition, since the cohort is defined as the population at ninth grade, youth who left the school system prior to ninth grade are not included.

A third measure of the dropout rate can be obtained from the Current Population Survey. The Current Population Survey in October of each year asks survey participants their enrollment status in school, as well as their educational attainment. Youths who never failed a grade should turn 18 by the time they graduate from high school in June. Youths who graduate a year late would be 19 by the time they graduate from high school. The percentage of 18- to 19-year-olds who report a maximum educational attainment of four years of high school or greater in the October Current Population Survey provides an estimate of the percentage of youths who graduate by the time they are 19.

Statistics calculated from the Current Population Survey, unlike those calculated from NCES's Common Core of Data, also provide estimates of educational attainment by race, ethnicity, and gender. Two of the main limitations of the Current Population Survey arise specifically in calculating dropout rates for minority populations. The Current Population Survey does not distinguish between youths who completed their education in the United States and those who completed their education outside of this country and are immigrants. This is a particular problem in analyzing Hispanic dropout rates. In addition, the Current Population Survey has been criticized for undercounting minorities, particularly the inner city poor. In the case of the first problem we would overestimate the dropout rate from U.S. school systems. In the second case, we would underestimate the dropout rate for minorities. While neither of these problems would have a large effect on the overall dropout rate, they should be considered when looking at dropout rates for subgroups within the population.

A final source of information on dropout rates comes from the large longitudinal data surveys conducted by the National Center for Education Statistics, such as the High School and Beyond Survey. These data sets provide estimates of dropout rates among nationally representative samples for the grades included in the survey. For example, High School and Beyond did not include youths who dropped out previous to the spring of their sophomore year in high school. Dropout rates from High School and Beyond do not provide us with good measures of the national dropout rate. They do provide important information on how completion rates differ by student characteristics. The dropout rate for sophomores in High School and Beyond was 17.3 percent (Frase, 1989).[1] This measure is consistent with Current Population Survey data when dropout rates are calculated excluding youths who left school prior to the tenth grade. NCES's newest longitudinal survey, the National Educational Longitudinal Survey, will follow a cohort of eighth-graders. This new survey will provide much more detailed and accurate information about national dropout rates.

NOTE

1. This dropout rate from the High School and Beyond Survey of 17.3 percent is the dropout rate calculated at the third followup—post-high school. Most of the data that I report from the High School and Beyond Survey in this and later chapters are from the second followup—senior year—unless otherwise noted. Information on the dropout rate calculated from High School and Beyond's second and third followup of the sophomore cohort is from Frase (1989).

Appendix 1-B
Percentage Change in the Median Earnings of Young Adult Workers and Year-Round, Full-Time Workers Aged 20 to 29, 1972–1987

	EDUCATIONAL ATTAINMENT			
	< High School	High School Only	Some College	4 or more Years of College
MALE				
Total[a]	- 36.70	- 29.39	- 9.96	- 1.50
- Full-time/year-round[b]	- 31.11	- 27.20	- 15.85	- 4.25
White/Non-Hispanic	- 34.50	- 26.89	- 7.97	- 1.87
- Full-time/year-round	- 26.38	- 25.22	- 15.68	- 2.51
Black/Non-Hispanic	- 54.47	- 37.95	- 14.82	- 1.60
- Full-time/year-round	- 19.00	- 26.88	- 17.14	- 7.45
FEMALE				
Total	n/a	+ 89.64	+ 68.50	+ 14.32
- Full-time/year-round	- 10.90	- 9.40	- 8.30	- 2.60
White/Non-Hispanic	n/a	+102.78	+ 76.00	+ 19.38
- Full-time/year-round	- 2.50	- 9.30	- 8.40	- .20
Black/Non-Hispanic	n/a	+ 10.00	+ 28.70	- 15.55
- Full-time/year-round	- 3.30	- 3.74	+ 1.80	- 10.30

a. Total = percentage change in the median earnings of all workers (non students)
b. Full-time/year-round = percentage change in the median earnings of workers who worked full-time year-round.

Notes: n/a = median earnings in 1972 reported as zero. The average earnings of Hispanic males fell by 22.66 percent from 1972 to 1987 and for Hispanic male full-time year-round workers by 26.87 percent. The comparable figures for Hispanic females are a decrease of 3.50 percent in the earnings of full-time, year-round workers. Sample size reported in the March 1972 Current Population Survey was not adequate to report trends in Hispanic income by gender and educational attainment.

Source: Calculated from the March 1973 and March 1988 Current Population Surveys.

Appendix 3-A
Entered Sample Composition by Demographic Variables

	Middle School Drops	High School Drops	Grads	Transfers	Total
Female	33.33%	47.25%	60.06%	56.00%	52.84%
Place of Birth					
Fall River		73.38%	67.16%	76.90%	76.60%
United States (not Fall River)	6.83%	5.97%	5.70%	19.15%	
Azores/other		19.79%	26.87%	17.41%	4.26%
Nativity					
Born United States/ parents United States		58.33%	65.22%	89.36%	62.77%
Second-generation[a]		13.73%	15.84%	6.38%	13.69%
Foreign born/non-immigrant[b]		10.29%	9.01%	2.13%	8.68%
Immigrant[c]		17.65%	9.94%	2.13%	14.86%
Father's Occupation/Group					
Professional[d]		3.75%	18.90%	22.22%	14.49%
Skilled[e]		34.48%	36.08%	36.11%	35.51%
Unskilled[f]		41.25%	34.71%	22.22%	35.71%
Not employed or not in house[g]		20.63%	10.31%	19.44%	14.29%
Number of Siblings					
None		9.63%	12.42%	6.82%	11.05%
One		15.51%	29.30%	31.82%	24.86%
Two		25.67%	24.20%	20.45%	23.94%
Three		19.79%	16.56%	18.18%	18.05%
Four		10.70%	7.01%	13.64%	8.84%
Five or more		18.72%	10.51%	9.09%	13.26%

a. Second-generation = born United States, one or both parents born outside of the United States

b. Foreign born/non-immigrant = born outside of United States, entered school system in kindergarten.

c. Immigrant = born outside of United States, entered school system after kindergarten.

d. Professional includes= professional/managerial/technical: armed forces/protective service.

e. Skilled includes= sales/administrative support: farm/forestry/transportation: precision product/craft/repair

f. Unskilled includes = operators/assemblers: laborers: service

g. Not employed or not in house includes = home/unemployed/disabled: other: divorced/separated/deceased.

Appendix 4-A
Average Fourth-Grade Mean Academic Grades, Mean Social Grades, Attendance and Percentile Rank of Dropouts and Graduates by Grade of Dropout and Graduating Class Rank

	Average Fourth-Grade Mean Academic Grades		
	Mean	Standard Deviation	n
7th-9th Grade Drops	1.76	0.67746	90
10th-12th Grade Drops	2.26	0.81229	190
Bottom 1/3 Grads	2.27	0.74730	95
Mid 1/3 Grads	2.69	0.77558	119
Top 1/3 Grads	3.38	0.57711	136

	Average Fourth-Grade Mean Social Grades		
	Mean	Deviation	Standard n
7th-9th Grade Drops	2.82	0.39230	90
10th-12th Grade Drops	2.92	0.18626	190
Bottom 1/3 Grads	2.95	0.13677	95
Mid 1/3 Grads	2.95	0.20827	119
Top 1/3 Grads	2.99	0.15819	136

	Average Fourth-Grade Percentile Rank		
	Mean	Standard Deviation	n
7th-9th Grade Drops	0.254	0.19169	90
10th-12th Grade Drops	0.410	0.25771	190
Bottom 1/3 Grads	0.417	0.24207	95
Mid 1/3 Grads	0.554	0.25997	119
Top 1/3 Grads	0.777	0.18810	136

Attendance	Average Fourth-Grade Attendance		
	Mean	Standard Deviation	n
10th-12th Grade Drops	164	11.61351	144
Bottom 1/3 Grads	164	9.56674	77
Mid 1/3 Grads	164	12.54274	102
Top 1/3 Grads	168	6.68701	112

Appendix 4-B
Means, Standard Deviations, and Sample Sizes for Figures 4.1, 4.2, 4.3, 4.5, and 4.6

SECTION A

Average Mean Academic Grades from the Fourth to the Twelfth-Grade

| | Fourth-Grade Mean Academic Grades | | |
	Mean	Standard Deviation	n
Seventh	1.71	0.73108	23
Eighth	1.73	0.65737	34
Ninth	1.82	0.67595	33
Tenth	2.17	0.76734	64
Eleventh	2.28	0.81417	69
Twelth	2.33	0.86243	57
Bottom 1/3 Grads'	2.28	0.74730	95
Mid 1/3 Grads	2.69	0.77558	119
Top 1/3 Grades	3.38	0.57711	136
Transfers	2.27	0.86843	42

| | Fifth-Grade Mean Academic Grades | | |
	Mean	Standard Deviation	n
Seventh	1.54	0.76124	27
Eigth	1.70	0.82085	38
Ninth	1.77	0.74620	34
Tenth	1.99	0.72217	62
Eleventh	2.24	0.83744	74
Twelfth	2.18	0.81013	59
Bottom 1/3 Grads	2.17	0.68846	97
Mid 1/3 Grads	2.60	0.70873	127
Top 1/3 Grads	3.35	0.52357	139
Transfers	2.66	0.79629	43

| | Sixth-Grade Mean Academic Grades | | |
	Mean	Standard Deviation	n
Seventh	1.30	0.64464	29
Eighth	1.42	0.66537	40
Ninth	1.59	0.61842	34
Tenth	1.85	0.69481	71
Eleventh	1.87	0.75209	75
Twelfth	2.03	0.74688	60
Bottom 1/3 Grads	2.08	0.57537	97
Mid 1/3 Grads	2.52	0.55742	128
Top 1/3 Grads	3.18	0.51005	141
Transfers	2.42	0.82131	45

Appendix 4-B *(continued)*

	Seventh-Grade Mean Academic Grades		
	Mean	Standard Deviation	n
Eighth	1.04	0.65141	42
Ninth	1.22	0.75173	41
Tenth	1.67	0.80604	72
Eleventh	1.85	0.72898	77
Twelfth	2.03	0.72357	63
Bottom 1/3 Grads	2.04	0.60488	101
Mid 1/3 Grads	2.42	0.59336	133
Top 1/3 Grads	3.18	0.56103	144
Transfers	2.24	0.89224	47

	Eighth-Grade Mean Academic Grades		
	Mean	Standard Deviation	n
Ninth	1.25	0.77032	39
Tenth	1.70	0.65457	72
Eleventh	1.81	0.64504	72
Twelfth	1.99	0.62379	61
Bottom 1/3 Grads	2.03	0.56566	100
Mid 1/3 Grads	2.45	0.60374	132
Top 1/3 Grads	3.07	0.57170	144
Transfers	2.38	0.77460	50

	Ninth-Grade Mean Academic Grades		
	Mean	Standard Deviation	n
Tenth	0.69	0.83826	68
Eleventh	1.10	0.99733	68
Twelfth	1.14	0.84749	56
Bottom 1/3 Grads	1.39	0.60586	94
Mid 1/3 Grads	2.12	0.59867	124
Top 1/3 Grads	3.06	0.59503	142

	Tenth-Grade Mean Academic Grades		
	Mean	Standard Deviation	n
Eleventh	0.44	0.69498	67
Twelfth	0.80	0.75267	59
Bottom 1/3 Grads	1.11	0.56169	97
Mid 1/3 Grads	1.83	0.65053	126
Top 1/3 Grads	2.97	0.64023	143

Appendix 4-B *(continued)*

Eleventh-Grade Mean Academic Grades		
Mean	Standard Deviation	n
Twelfth	0.74	0.74335	57
Bottom 1/3 Grads	1.36	0.72426	100
Mid 1/3 Grads	1.98	0.64699	132
Top 1/3 Grads	2.80	0.73364	144

Twelfth-Grade Mean Academic Grades		
Mean	Standard Deviation	n
Bottom 1/3 Grads	1.74	0.83319	100
Mid 1/3 Grads	2.18	0.64445	132
Top 1/3 Grads	2.92	0.64170	144

SECTION B

Average Mean Social Grades from the Fourth to the Twelfth-Grade

Fourth-Grade Mean Social Grades		
Mean	Standard Deviation	n
Seventh	2.69	0.64387	23
Eighth	2.84	0.31575	34
Ninth	2.88	0.15115	33
Tenth	2.91	0.17293	64
Eleventh	2.91	0.16826	69
Twelfth	2.91	0.22140	57
Bottom 1/3	2.94	0.13677	95
Mid 1/3	2.95	0.20827	119
Top 1/3	2.99	0.15819	136
Transfers	2.95	0.12222	42

Appendix 4-B *(continued)*

	Fifth-Grade Mean Social Grades		
	Mean	Standard Deviation	n
Seventh	2.56	0.70541	27
Eighth	2.63	0.38259	38
Ninth	2.69	0.33101	34
Tenth	2.73	0.36652	62
Eleventh	2.76	0.52215	74
Twelfth	2.85	0.46308	59
Bottom 1/3	2.90	0.47445	97
Mid 1/3	3.00	0.36741	127
Top 1/3	3.26	0.35510	139
Tranfers	2.87	0.73721	43

	Sixth-Grade Mean Social Grades		
	Mean	Standard Deviation	n
Seventh	2.37	0.48095	29
Eighth	2.31	0.74953	40
Ninth	2.44	0.50713	34
Tenth	2.66	0.53145	71
Eleventh	2.60	0.56768	75
Twelfth	2.72	0.51710	60
Bottom 1/3	2.73	0.43458	97
Mid 1/3	2.99	0.46637	128
Top 1/3	3.38	0.34234	141

	Seventh-Grade Mean Social Grades		
	Mean	Standard Deviation	n
Eighth	2.14	0.76201	42
Ninth	2.20	0.71170	41
Tenth	2.67	0.57173	72
Eleventh	2.67	0.65525	77
Twelfth	2.83	0.60106	63
Bottom 1/3	2.86	0.46913	101
Mid 1/3	3.15	0.44359	133
Top 1/3	3.51	0.39444	144
Transfers	2.94	0.77228	47

Appendix 4-B *(continued)*

Eighth-Grade Mean Social Grades			
	Mean	Standard Deviation	n
Ninth	2.08	0.86172	39
Tenth	2.58	0.64946	72
Eleventh	2.50	0.64799	72
Twelfth	2.76	0.60629	61
Bottom 1/3	2.85	0.44466	100
Mid 1/3	3.07	0.53874	132
Top 1/3	3.50	0.37728	144
Transfers	2.98	0.64662	50

Ninth-Grade Mean Social Grades			
	Mean	Standard Deviation	n
Tenth	0.89	0.98552	68
Eleventh	1.35	1.01125	68
Twelfth	1.68	0.91950	56
Bottom 1/3	1.98	0.77212	94
Mid 1/3	2.62	0.68324	124
Top 1/3	3.32	0.50177	142

Tenth-Grade Mean Social Grades			
	Mean	Standard Deviation	n
Eleventh	0.72	0.96561	69
Twelfth	1.62	0.88153	58
Bottom 1/3	2.01	0.76676	96
Mid 1/3	2.68	0.65635	126
Top 1/3	3.44	0.53592	141

Eleventh-Grade Mean Social Grades			
	Mean	Standard Deviation	n
Twelfth	1.00	0.79164	56
Bottom 1/3	1.96	0.82168	100
Mid 1/3	2.53	0.72079	131
Top 1/3	3.28	0.67027	140

Twelfth-Grade Mean Social Grades			
	Mean	Standard Deviation	n
Bottom 1/3	2.06	0.74474	100
Mid 1/3	2.49	0.73075	132
Top 1/3	3.07	0.73348	142

Appendix 4-B *(continued)*

Average Attendance from the Fourth to the Twelfth-Grade

| | Fourth-Grade Attendance | | |
	Mean	Standard Deviation	n
Ninth	162	12.29945	27
Tenth	161	15.56860	52
Eleventh	167	8.87760	51
Twelfth	168	6.90281	41
Bottom 1/3	164	9.56674	77
Mid 1/3	164	12.54274	102
Top 1/3	168	6.68701	112
Transfers	166	7.42318	37

| | Fifth-Grade Attendance | | |
	Mean	Standard Deviation	n
Ninth	156	11.75004	28
Tenth	154	12.69229	51
Eleventh	154	10.66610	55
Twelfth	159	10.15524	42
Bottom 1/3	158	9.30749	74
Mid 1/3	158	9.13704	109
Top 1/3	161	6.90260	117
Transfers	161	7.27466	36

| | Sixth-Grade Attendance | | |
	Mean	Standard Deviation	n
Ninth	159	14.67136	28
Tenth	161	14.49601	58
Eleventh	163	10.74750	56
Twelfth	169	9.09784	45
Bottom 1/3	167	10.18995	78
Mid 1/3	168	8.88747	110
Top 1/3	171	8.30863	117
Transfers	168	8.47363	41

Appendix 4-B *(continued)*

	Seventh-Grade Attendance		
		Standard	
	Mean	Deviation	n
Ninth	150	26.25614	30
Tenth	157	15.87948	57
Eleventh	157	20.45091	58
Twelfth	164	11.39502	45
Bottom 1/3	165	11.36651	81
Mid 1/3	166	10.49301	114
Top 1/3	169	10.48350	116
Transfers	165	14.89524	43

	Eighth-Grade Attendance		
		Standard	
	Mean	Deviation	n
Ninth	139	29.39861	33
Tenth	148	17.61116	57
Eleventh	148	21.38543	57
Twelfth	158	15.93318	44
Bottom 1/3	162	13.07180	80
Mid 1/3	164	11.12688	113
Top 1/3	169	8.46669	120
Transfers	163	12.61714	46

	Ninth-Grade Attendance		
		Standard	
	Mean	Deviation	n
Tenth	110	43.56673	63
Eleventh	135	28.84600	66
Twelfth	153	15.77316	42
Bottom 1/3	155	17.12522	92
Mid 1/3	161	15.03309	124
Top 1/3	168	9.94792	141

	Tenth-Grade Attendance		
		Standard	
	Mean	Deviation	n
Eleventh	103	47.02886	69
Twelfth	146	19.08664	45
Bottom 1/3	154	15.93314	93
Mid 1/3	159	12.29351	126
Top 1/3	165	12.07351	143

Appendix 4-B *(continued)*

	Eleventh-Grade Attendance		
	Mean	Standard Deviation	n
Twelfth	131	28.62081	44
Bottom 1/3	154	15.10240	97
Mid 1/3	158	12.50535	132
Top 1/3	166	11.95072	144

	Twelfth-Grade Attendance		
	Mean	Standard Deviation	n
Bottom 1/3	152	23.38522	99
Mid 1/3	159	12.59246	133
Top 1/3	166	11.21222	143

Appendix 4-C
Logit Coefficients for Table 4.10

	P(Drop)			P(Drop 9th or later)		
	Coeff.	Mean	t-stat	Coeff.	Mean	t-stat
One	4.178	1.000		3.425	1.000	
Fourth-Grade						
Mean Academic Grade	-0.848	2.240	7.2	-0.686	2.345	5.52
Mean Social Grade	-0.944	2.602	1.89	-1.050	2.652	1.82
Attendance				-0.001	120.530	0.104
Retentions k-3	0.811	0.245	4.24	0.771	0.222	3.73
Census Tract						
% HS grads	-1.497	0.294	0.93	-1.949	0.297	1.11
% PA	7.596	0.203	2.75	7.669	0.202	2.58
% O/F/L	-3.517	0.372	2.07	-4.330	0.370	2.41
School quality	0.145	3.630	2.9	0.096	3.562	1.77
Female	-0.452	0.530	2.66	-0.373	0.549	2.0
# of siblings				0.109	1.950	2.09
Father skilled				0.960	0.253	2.11
Father unskilled				0.823	0.256	1.74
Father other				1.134	0.108	2.27
Immigrant k+				.617	0.101	1.72
Immigrant pre-k				-0.130	0.075	0.33
2nd-generation				-0.196	0.120	0.64
Missing Dummies						
Ac4	-3.957	0.112	2.67	-4.317	0.099	2.46
At4				-0.623	0.269	0.375
Census	0.233	0.0914	0.19	-0.158	0.089	0.11
Father occ.				1.394	0.284	2.77
Immigrant				0.348	0.228	0.97
Siblings				0.413	0.206	0.87
Log-likelihood	-422.57			-371.19		
Chi-square	191.30			160.16		
n	757			683		

Notes: Means reported are the means of the independent variable with missing values equal to zero so that Mean non-missing = (Mean missing / (1 - % missing). Missing values: dummy variable equal to 1 if the observation is missing for this variable, otherwise 0.

Appendix 5-A
Effect of Single Grade Mean Academic Grades on the Conditional Likelihood of Dropping Out Given Persistence to the Ninth, Tenth, and Eleventh Grades: Logit Coefficients for Tables 5.2 and 5.3

| | Probability Drop 9th or later | | |
	Equation 1	Equation 2	Means
One	3.92	4.305	1.00
Interaction Term			
Middle *Ac6	-.422	-.433	1.774
Other * Ac6	-.703	-.927	.042
Academic Grades			
Fourth (Ac4)	-.034	.099	2.345
Fifth (Ac5)	.015	.093	2.342
Sixth (Ac6)	-.204	-.181	2.237
Seventh (Ac7)	-.436	-.320	2.243
Eighth (Ac8)	-1.096	-.885	2.211
Attendance			
Fourth		.031	120.53
Fifth		-.015	118.66
Sixth		.012	130.17
Seventh		.004	130.16
Eighth		-.059	128.32
# Retentions		.777	.340
# School changes		.384	1.471
School quality		.048	3.562
Census Tract			
% HS grads		.804	.2965
% PA		.859	.2018
% O/F/L		-.327	.3701
Female		-.355	.549
# of siblings		.039	1.95
Father skilled		.275	.253
Father unskilled		.300	.256
Father other		.574	.108
Immigrant k+		.511	.101
Immigrant pre-k		.070	.075
2nd-generation		.071	.120
Missing Dummies			
Ac4	.304	1.02	.099
Ac5	.951	1.96	.070
Ac6	-2.096	-2.00	.047
Ac7	-1.294	-2.11	.007
Ac8	-.581	-.702	.019
At4		4.86	.269
At5		-3.01	.250
At6		.783	.220

Appendix 5-A *(continued)*

	Equation 1	Probability Drop 9th or later Equation 2	Means
At7		-1.09	.203
At8		-8.65	.195
Census		1.11	.089
Father Occ.		.969	.284
Immigrant		.336	.228
siblings		.559	.206
Log-likelihood	-331.36	-278.15	
Chi-square	239.82	346.24	
Pseudo-R^2	24.76	38.36	

		Probability Drop 10th or later	
One	3.155	.372	1.00
Interaction Term			
Middle *Ac6	-.412	-.450	1.82
Other * Ac6	-.595	-.795	.04
Academic Grades			
Fourth (Ac4)	.083	.262	2.40
Fifth (Ac5)	.144	.213	2.40
Sixth (Ac6)	-.157	-.207	2.30
Seventh (Ac7)	-.043	.018	2.31
Eighth (Ac8)	-.658	-.483	2.28
Ninth (ac9)	-1.175	-1.158	1.65
Attendance			
Fourth		.040	121.41
Fifth		-.018	119.42
Sixth		.008	131.56
Seventh		.015	131.45
Eighth		-.054	129.37
# Retentions		.754	.297
# School changes		.419	1.47
School quality		.034	3.55
Census Tract			
% HS grads		1.803	.299
% PA		8.203	.202
% O/F/L		-2.711	.372
Female		-.285	.56
# of siblings		.056	1.95
Father skilled		.320	.254
Father unskilled		.438	.258
Father other		.675	.106

Appendix 5-A *(continued)*

| | Probability Drop 10th or later | | |
	Equation 1	Equation 2	Means
Immigrant k+		.348	.090
Immigrant pre-k		.007	.075
2nd-generation		.031	.125
Missing Dummies			
Ac4	.336	.982	.093
Ac5	1.589	2.460	.064
Ac6	-2.567	-2.715	.039
Ac7	-1.289	-2.377	.008
Ac8	1.205	.878	.017
Ac9	-1.175	-2.115	.104
At4		6.580	.265
At5		-3.532	.246
At6		.394	.213
At7		3.417	.200
At8		-8.124	.195
Census		1.667	.084
Father Occ.		1.273	.280
Immigrant		-.0461	.228
siblings		.0867	.197
Log-likelihood	-278.829	-241.03	
Chi-square	259.62	335.22	
Pseudo R^2	31.78	41.02	

Appendix 5-A *(continued)*

	Equation 1	Equation 2	Means
		Probability Drop 11th or later	
One	2.479	-4.353	1.00
Interaction Term			
Middle *Ac6	-.5177	-.5796	
Other * Ac6	-1.5566	-.1845	
Academic Grades			
Fourth (Ac4)	.122	.225	2.46
Fifth (Ac5)	.251	.239	2.49
Sixth (Ac6)	.007	-.033	2.36
Seventh (Ac7)	-.008	.139	2.39
Eighth (Ac8)	-.348	-.257	2.35
Ninth (ac9)	-.531	-.563	1.77
Tenth (ac10)	-1.623	-1.673	1.52
Attendance			
Fourth		.099	122.30
Fifth		-.022	120.90
Sixth		-.004	132.07
Seventh		.003	132.58
Eighth		-.054	131.11
# Retentions		.163	.218
School changes		.319	1.444
School quality		.073	3.543
Census Tract			
% HS grads		2.028	.306
% PA		6.038	.202
% O/F/L		-2.489	.371
Female		-.284	.564
# of siblings		.032	1.887
Father skilled		.042	.256
Father unskilled		.227	.256
Father other		.751	.104
Immigrant k+		.126	.080
Immigrant pre-k		-1.028	.065
2nd-generation		.122	.126

Appendix 5-A *(continued)*

	Equation 1	Equation 2	Means
		Probability Drop 11th or later	
Missing Dummies			
Ac4	.778	.842	.09
Ac5	.169	-.130	.053
Ac6	-1.494	-.719	.04
Ac7	-.484	-1.092	.007
Ac8	1.428	1.466	.017
Ac9	-.864	-1.111	.109
Ac10	-2.184	-2.270	.111
At4		17.002	.262
At5		-4.103	.239
At6		-2.598	.214
At7		2.365	.197
At8		-8.279	.191
Census		2.010	.075
Father Occ.		.815	.271
Immigrant		-.560	.228
siblings		.408	.175
Log-likelihood	-194.844	-170.502	
Chi-square	246.50	296.16	
Pseudo R^2	38.84	46.48	

Notes: Means reported are the means of the independent variable with missing values equal to zero so that Mean non-missing = (Mean missing) / (1- % missing).

Missing values. Dummy variable equal to 1 if the observation is missing values for this variable; otherwise 0.

Appendix 6-A
Effect of Grade Retentions Controlling for Background Variables, Fourth-Grade Mean Academic Grades and Attendance: Logit Coefficients for Tables 6.2, 6.3, 6.4, and 6.5

| | Logit Coefficients and T-statistics for Probability Drop | | | | | | |
	Equation 1		Equation 2		Equation 3		Means
One	-3.03	(2.34)	-1.173	(.844)	4.75	(1.62)	
Retentions							
# Retentions	1.27	(7.48)	.900	(4.99)	.802	(4.18)	.354
Academic Grades							
Fourth (Ac4)			-.723	(5.79)	-.089	(.49)	2.24
Fifth (Ac5)					-.149	(.76)	2.25
Sixth (Ac6)					-1.007	(5.65)	2.14
Attendance							
Fourth					.019	(1.46)	109.60
Fifth					-.023	(1.76)	`148.10
Sixth					-.020	(1.62)	117.76
# School changes	.450	(3.04)	.498	(3.22)	.518	(3.12)	1.40
School quality	.088	(1.70)	.098	(1.83)	.107	(1.86)	3.63
Census Tract							
% HS grads	-.340	(.20)	-.652	(.38)	-1.24	(.68)	.293
% PA	6.323	(2.30)	7.54	(2.60)	6.76	(2.15)	.203
% O/F/L	-3.243	(1.86)	-3.48	(1.91)	-4.82	(2.45)	.372
Female	-.530	(3.01)	-.460	(2.53)	-.352	(1.79)	.53
# of siblings	.119	(2.30)	.099	(1.86)	.050	(.89)	1.76
Father skilled	.846	(1.91)	.839	(1.83)	.707	(1.40)	.230
Father unskilled	.865	(1.91)	.744	(1.59)	.788	(1.55)	.231
Father other	1.21	(2.50)	1.018	(2.02)	.952	(1.73)	.098
Immigrant k+	.482	(1.46)	.336	(.95)	.300	(.79)	.118
Immigrant pre-k	-.092	(.25)	-.104	(.28)	`.083	(.20)	.069
2nd-generation	-.152	(.50)	-.235	(.74)	.025	(.07)	.108
Missing Dummies							
Ac4			-1.20	(2.44)	.305	(.41)	.112
Ac5					1.05	(1.07)	.075
Ac6					-2.49	(3.11)	.049
At4					2.73	(1.27)	.335
At5					-3.87	(1.83)	.321
At6					-3.76	(1.79)	.293
Census	1.14	(.91)	.899	(.679)	-.585	(.40)	.091
Father occ.	1.61	(3.29)	1.40	(2.74)	1.37	(2.46)	.352
Immigrant	.013	(3.88)	.0468	(.14)	.222	(.60)	.273
Siblings	.752	(2.04)	.676	(1.79)	1.28	(2.45)	.283
Log-likelihood	-404.64		-385.10		-348.19		
Chi-square	227.16		266.24		340.06		
n	757		757		757		

Appendix 6-A *(continued)*

	Equation 4		Equation 5		Equation 6		Means
			Logit Coefficients and T-statistics for Probability Drop				
One	-4.823	(1.65)	4.75	(1.62)	-6.48	(1.52)	
Retentions							
# Retentions							.354
Retentions = 1	.851	(3.50)			.139	(.45)	.219
Retentions > 1	1.522	(2.97)			.002	(.00)	.065
Retention k-3			.802	(3.77)			.222
Retention 4-6			.801	(2.07)			.136
Age Grade 7					.071	(3.64)	144
Academic Grades							
Fourth (Ac4)	-.094	(.514)	-.0895	(.489)	-.099	(.53)	2.24
Fifth (Ac5)	-.144	(.74)	-.149	(.76)	-.146	(.74)	2.25
Sixth (Ac6)	-1.068	(5.65)	-1.068	(5.65)	-1.057	(5.55)	2.14
Attendance							
Fourth	.019	(1.45)	.019	(1.47)	.024	(1.81)	109.60
Fifth	-.023	(1.74)	-.023	(1.76)	-.023	(1.76)	148.10
Sixth	-.020	(1.64)	-.020	(1.62)	-.020	(1.62)	117.76
# School changes	.513	(3.09)	.518	(3.10)	.513	(3.06)	1.40
School quality	.108	(1.88)	.107	(1.86)	.112	(1.93)	3.63
Census Tract							
% HS grads	-1.274	(.69)	-1.245	(.68)	-1.25	(.68)	.293
% PA	6.75	(2.15)	6.77	(2.15)	6.42	(2.01)	.203
% O/F/L	-4.84	(2.46)	-4.82	(2.45)	-4.72	(2.35)	.372
Female	-.352	(1.80)	-.352	(1.80)	-.296	(1.48)	.53
# of siblings	.049	(.85)	.050	(.89)	.052	(.91)	1.76
Father skilled	.710	(1.40)	.708	(1.40)	.668	(1.29)	.230
Father unskilled	.787	(1.54)	.788	(1.54)	.797	(1.52)	.231
Father other	.945	(1.72)	.952	(1.73)	.911	(1.64)	.098
Immigrant k+	.304	(.80)	.300	(.78)	.292	(.75)	.118
Immigrant pre-k	.091	(.22)	.083	(.20)	-.030	(.07)	.069
2nd-generation	.027	(.08)	.025	(.07)	-.03	(.08)	.108
Missing Dummies							
Ac4	.284	(.38)	.305	(.41)	.070	(.09)	.112
Ac5	1.09	(1.10)	1.05	(1.07)	1.08	(1.07)	.075
Ac6	-2.50	(3.12)	-2.49	(3.11)	-2.59	(3.16)	.049
At4	2.69	(1.25)	2.73	(1.27)	3.54	(1.63)	.335
At5	-3.82	(1.82)	-3.87	(1.83)	-3.89	(1.83)	.321
At6	-3.79	(1.80)	-3.76	(1.79)	-4.05	(1.89)	.293
Census	-.620	(.42)	-.585	(.39)	-.520	(.35)	.091
Father occ.	1.38	(2.46)	1.38	(2.46)	1.48	(2.59)	.352
Immigrant	.219	(.59)	.221	(.60)	.33	(.87)	.273
siblings	1.27	(2.42)	1.27	(2.45)	1.18	(2.17)	.283
Log-likelihood	-348.42		-348.19		-341.39		
Chi-square	339.60		340.06		353.66		
n	757		757		757		

Appendix 6-A *(continued)*

	Logit Coefficients and T-statistics for Probability Drop 10th or Later						
	Equation 1		Equation 2		Equation 3		Means
One	-2.306	(1.66)	-.942	(1.47)	.997	(.27)	
Retentions							
# Retentions	1.137	(6.38)	.865	(4.48)	.622	(2.60)	.297
Academic Grades							
Fourth (Ac4)			-.513	(3.90)	.180	(.78)	2.40
Fifth (Ac5)					.157	(.65)	2.40
Sixth (Ac6)					-.563	(2.04)	2.30
Seventh (Ac7)					.001	(.00)	2.31
Eighth (Ac8)					-.443	(1.74)	2.28
Ninth (Ac9)					-.844	(4.32)	1.65
Attendance							
Fourth					.049	(2.84)	121.41
Fifth					-.017	(1.01)	119.42
Sixth					.018	(1.02)	131.56
Seventh					.015	(1.00)	131.45
Eighth					-.040	(2.88)	129.37
Ninth					-.023	(3.05)	129.62
# School changes	.434	(3.17)	.443	(3.18)	.398	(2.16)	1.47
School quality	.057	(1.01)	.066	(1.15)	.089	(1.24)	3.55
Census Tract							
% HS grads	-1.788	(.99)	-2.00	(1.08)	-1.881	(.87)	.299
% PA	5.168	(1.72)	5.789	(1.85)	6.183	(1.67)	.202
% O/F/L	-3.613	(1.93)	-3.604	(1.89)	-6.441	(2.64)	.372
Female	-.380	(1.99)	-.337	(1.72)	-2.46	(1.00)	.56
# of siblings	.126	(2.36)	.111	(2.03)	.058	(.85)	1.95
Father skilled	.862	(1.76)	.847	(1.69)	.436	(.76)	.254
Father unskilled	1.018	(2.05)	.913	(1.81)	.561	(.96)	.259
Father other	1.144	(2.15)	1.016	(1.88)	.577	(.89)	.106
Immigrant k+	-.050	(.13)	-.119	(.30)	.437	(.88)	.09
Immigrant pre-k	-.207	(.55)	-.187	(.49)	-.167	(.32)	.075
2nd-generation	-.058	(.19)	-.114	(.36)	.020	(.05)	.125

Appendix 6-A *(continued)*

	Equation 4		Equation 5				Means
					Logit Coefficients and T-statiistics for Probability Drop 10th or later		
Missing Dummies							
Ac4			-.820	(1.49)	.587	(.58)	.093
Ac5					2.560	(1.98)	.064
Ac6					-2.750	(2.25)	.039
Ac7					-2.60	(1.74)	.008
Ac8					.873	(.75)	.017
Ac9					-2.71	(4.13)	.104
At4					8.10	(2.83)	.265
At5					-3.526	(1.31)	.246
At6					2.06	(.67)	.213
At7					2.894	(1.15)	.20
At8					-5.799	(2.50)	.19
At9					-2.398	(2.03)	.145
Census	.025	(.02)	-.173	(.12)	-1.39	(.79)	.084
Father occ.	1.63	(3.08)	1.49	(2.74)	1.31	(2.02)	.28
Immigrant	.301	(.80)	.329	(.89)	-.015	(.03)	.23
Siblings	-.05	(.13)	-.085	(.20)	.467	(.57)	.20
Log-likelihood	-344.21		-335.40		-239.43		
Chi-square	128.06		145.68		337.62		
n	642		642		642		

Appendix 6-A *(continued)*

	Equation 4		Equation 5		Means
	Logit Coefficients and T-statistics for Probability Drop 10th or later				
One	.989	(.27)	1.000	(.27)	
Retentions					
Retention ==1	.690	(2.28)			.207
Retentions >1	1.108	(1.84)			.044
Retention k-3			.621	(2.34)	
Retention 4-8			.627	(1.41)	.0997
Academic Grades					
Fourth (Ac4)	.176	(.76)	.180	(.78)	2.40
Fifth (Ac5)	.159	(.65)	.157	(.65)	2.40
Sixth (Ac6)	-.557	(2.02)	-.563	(2.03)	2.30
Seventh (Ac7)	.007	(.02)	.002	(.01)	2.31
Eighth (Ac8)	-.448	(1.76)	-.444	(1.74)	2.28
Ninth (Ac9)	-.844	(4.32)	-.845	(4.30)	1.65
Attendance					
Fourth	.048	(2.81)	.049	(2.84)	121.41
Fifth	-.017	(1.00)	-.017	(.99)	119.42
Sixth	.017	(.98)	.018	(1.02)	131.56
Seventh	.015	(1.02)	.015	(1.00)	131.45
Eighth	-.040	(2.88)	-.040	(2.88)	129.37
Ninth	-.023	(3.05)	-.023	(3.05)	129.62
# School changes	.400	(2.17)	.398	(2.13)	1.47
School quality	.092	(1.27)	.089	(1.23)	3.55
Census Tract					
% HS grads	-1.822	(.84)	-1.88	(.87)	.299
% PA	6.176	(1.66)	6.184	(1.67)	.202
% O/F/L	-6.378	(2.61)	-6.443	(2.63)	.372
Female	-.246	(1.00)	-.246	(1.00)	.56
# of siblings	.057	(.83)	.058	(.85)	1.95
Father skilled	.437	(.76)	.436	(.75)	.254
Father unskilled	.555	(.95)	.561	(.95)	.259
Father other	.570	(.88)	.577	(.89)	.106
Immigrant k+	.420	(.83)	.437	(.87)	.09

192

Appendix 6-A *(continued)*

	Logit Coefficients and T-statiistics for Probability Drop 10th or later				
	Equation 4		Equation 5		Means
Immigrant pre-k	-.160	(.31)	-.166	(.32)	.075
2nd-generation	.024	(.06)	.020	(.05)	.125
Missing Dummies					
Ac4	.585	(.58)	.587	(.58)	.093
Ac5	2.62	(2.01)	2.56	(1.96)	.064
Ac6	-2.76	(2.27)	-2.75	(2.25)	.039
Ac7	-2.60	(1.74)	-2.60	(1.72)	.008
Ac8	.869	(.75)	.871	(.74)	.017
Ac9	-2.71	(4.12)	-2.71	(4.13)	.104
At4	8.02	(2.79)	8.10	(2.83)	.265
At5	-3.53	(1.32)	-3.533	(1.29)	.246
At6	2.01	(.65)	2.06	(.67)	.213
At7	2.99	(1.18)	2.89	(1.15)	.20
At8	-5.789	(2.50)	-5.80	(2.50)	.19
At9	-2.403	(2.03)	-2.397	(2.03)	.145
Census	-1.365	(.77)	-1.391	(.79)	.084
Father occ.	1.30	(2.01)	1.31	(2.02)	.28
Immigrant	-.005	(.01)	-.015	(.03)	.23
Siblings	.430	(.52)	-.467	(.56)	.20
Log-likelihood	-239.38		-239.43		
Chi-square	337.72		337.62		
n	642		642		

Notes: Means reported are the means of the independent variable with missing values equal to zero so tha
Mean non-missing = (Mean missing)/(1 - %missing). Missing values: dummy variable equal to 1 if th
observation is missing values for this variable; otherwise 0. T-statistics in parentheses

193

Appendix 6-B
Coefficient Estimates for Logit-Hazard of Dropping Out by Risk Period and Being Behind in Grade: Logit Coefficients for Table 6.7

	Equation 7		Equation 8	
One	1.95252	(1.55)	-.6082	(.33)
Age 17 (Period 2)	-.12729	(.63)	6.4146	(2.51)
Age 18 or 19 (Periods 3 & 4)	.16210	(.70)	6.7769	(2.63)
Below grade level				
One grade	.5365	(2.01)	.6176	(2.29)
Two or more	2.1119	(6.83)	2.1741	(6.60)
Period/Below grade level interactions				
below 1 * age 17	.1174	(.28)	-.2427	(.55)
below 2 * age 17	-1.1523	(1.99)	-2.1521	(3.37)
below 1 * age 18/19	-.2016	(.48)	-.4415	(1.01)
below 2 * age 18/19	-1.1527	(1.88)	-1.9065	(2.91)
Academic Grades				
Sixth (Ac6)	-.9162	(8.64)	-.8516	(5.44)
Sixth (Ac6)* Per 2-4			.2312	(.97)
Eighth (Ac8)*Per 2-4			-.7708	(3.94)
Attendance				
Sixth (At6)	-.0126	(1.63)	.0022	(.19)
Sixth (At6)* Per 2-4			-.0115	(.70)
Eighth (Ac8)* Per 2-4			-.0219	(2.78)
# School changes	.1970	(2.07)	.1518	(1.54)
Immigrant k-3	.0598	(.18)	.0147	(.04)
Immigrant 4-8	.4528	(1.37)	.6840	(1.95)
Missing Dummies				
Sixth (Ac6)	-1.7867	(4.36)	-1.2928	(2.31)
Sixth (Ac6)* Per 2-4			-.2908	(.32)
Eighth (Ac8)*Per 2-4			-.9933	(1.43)

Appendix 6-B *(continued)*

	Equation 7		Equation 8	
Sixth (At6)	-1.6939	(1.33)	.7706	(.42)
Sixth (At6)* Per 2-4			-2.7431	(.99)
Eighth (Ac8)* Per 2-4			-2.5194	(1.88)
Log-likelihood	-641.46		-617.02	
Chi-square	328.10		376.98	
n	1568		1568	

Notes: See endnotes Appendix 6-A.
Sixth (Ac6) * Per 2-4 = Interaction term =1 * Ac6 if risk period 2 or risk period 3. Immigrant k-3 = 1 if youth immigrated to the school system in kindergarten to third grade. Immigrant 4-8 = 1 if youth immigrated to the school system in fourth to eighth grade.

Bibliography

Abrahamse, Allan; Morrison, Peter A.; and Waite, Linda J. (1988) *Beyond Stereotypes: Who Becomes a Single Teenage Mother?* Santa Monica, Calif.: Rand Corporation.

Adler, Mortimor Jerome. (1982) *The Paideia Proposal.* New York: Macmillan.

Alexander, Carryall, and Pallas, Aaron. (1984) "Curriculum Reform and School Performance: An Examination of the 'New Basics'." *American Journal of Education* 92: 391–420.

Alpert, Geoffrey, and Dunham, Roger. (1986) "Keeping Academically Marginal Youths in School: A Prediction Model." *Youth and Society* 17, 4: 346–361.

Bachman, Jerald G.; Green, Swayzer; and Wirtanen, Ilona D. (1971) *Dropping Out—Problem or Symptom? Youth in Transition.* Vol. 3. Ann Arbor, Mich.: Institute for Social Research, University of Michigan.

Barro, Stephen, and Kolstad, Andrew. (1987) *Who Drops Out of High School? Findings from High School and Beyond* (Report No. CS 87–397c). Washington, D.C.: U.S. Department of Education, National Center for Education Statistics.

Bastian, Ann, et al. (1986) *Choosing Equality: The Case for Democratic Schooling.* Philadelphia, Pa.: Temple University Press.

Becker, Henry Jay. (1987) *Addressing the Needs of Different Groups of Early Adolescents: Effects of Varying School and Classroom Organizational Practices on Students from Different Social Background and Abilities* (Report No. 16). Baltimore, Md.: Center for Research on Elementary and Middle Schools, Johns Hopkins University.

Blyth, Dale A., and Simmons, Roberta G. (1987) *Moving into Adolescence: The Impact of Pubertal Change and School Context.* Hawthorne, N.Y.: Aldine De Gruyter.

Blyth, Dale A.; Simmons, Roberta G.; and Bush, Diane. (1978, July) "The Transition into Early Adolescence: A Longitudinal Comparison of Youth in Two Educational Contexts." *Sociology of Education* 51: 149–162.

Blyth, Dale A.; Simmons, Roberta G.; and Carlton-Ford, Steven. (1983) "The Adjustment of Early Adolescents to School Transitions." *Journal of Early Adolescence* 3: 105–120.

Borus, Michael E., and Carpenter, Susan A. (1983) "A Note on the Return of Dropouts to High School." *Youth and Society* 14, 4: 501–507.

Boston Public Schools, Office of Research and Development. (1986) *A Working Document on the Dropout Problem in Boston Public Schools.* Boston, Mass.: Boston Public Schools.

Boyer, Ernest L. (1983) *High School: A Report on Secondary Education in America.* New York: Harper and Row.

Bronfenbrenner, Urie. (1979) *The Ecology of Human Development.* Cambridge, Mass.: Harvard University Press.

Brooks-Gunn, Jeanne. (1991) "How Stressful is the Transition to Adolescence for Girls?" In *Adolescent Stress: Causes and Consequences,* edited by Mary Ellen Colten and Susan Gore. New York: Aldine De Gruyter: 131–150.

Bryk, Anthony S., and Driscoll, Mary Erina. (1988) *The High School as Community: Contextual Influences and Consequences for Students and Teachers.* Madison, Wis.: National Center on Effective Secondary Schools, University of Wisconsin, Madison.

Bryk, Anthony S., and Thum, Yeow Meng. (1989) "The Effect of High School Organization on Dropping Out: An Exploratory Investigation." *American Educational Research Journal* 26, 3: 353–383.

Burtless, Gary. (1990) "Introduction and Summary." In *A Future of Lousy Jobs: The Changing Structure of U.S. Wages,* edited by Gary Burtless. Washington, D.C.: The Brookings Institution: 1–30.

Byrnes, Deborah A. (1989) "Attitudes of Students, Parents, and Educators Toward Repeating a Grade." In *Flunking Grades: Research and Policies on Retention,* edited by Lorrie A. Shepard, and Mary Lee Smith. London: Falmer Press.

Cameron, Stephen V., and Heckman, James J. (1991) "The Nonequivalence of High School Equivalents" (Working Paper No. 3804). Cambridge, Mass.: National Bureau of Economic Research.

Capelluti, Jody, and Stokes, Donald. (1991) *Middle Level Education: Programs, Policies and Practices.* Reston, Va.: National Association of Secondary School Principals.

Carnegie Council on Adolescent Development. (1990) *Turning Points: Preparing American Youth for the 21st Century.* New York: Carnegie Corporation of New York.

Catterall, James S. (1985) *On the Social Costs of Dropping Out of High School.* Stanford, Calif.: Stanford Education Policy Institute.

———. (1986, November) *School Dropouts: Policy Prospects, Policy Issues.* Charlestown, W. Va.: Policy and Planning Center, Appalachia Educational Laboratory.

Children's Defense Fund. (1988) *Making the Middle Grades Work.* Washington, D.C.: Children's Defense Fund.

Cohen, Deborah. (1992, February 19) "Learnfare Fails to Boost Attendance, New Study Finds." *Education Week* 11, 22: 1.

College Entrance Examination Board. (1983) *Academic Preparation for College: What*

Students Need to Know and Be Able to Do. New York: College Entrance Examination Board.

Combs, Janet, and Cooley, William W. (1968) "Dropouts: In High School and after High School." *American Educational Research Journal* 5, 3: 343–363.

Comer, James. (1986) Foreword Note in Bastian, Ann, et al. (1986) *Choosing Equality: The Case for Democratic Schooling.* Philadelphia, Pa.: Temple University Press.

Committee for Economic Development. (1987) *Children in Need: Investment Strategies for the Educationally Disadvantaged.* New York: Committee for Economic Development.

Corcoran, Thomas B. (1990) "Schoolwork: Perspectives on Workplace Reform in Public Schools." In *The Contexts of Teaching in Secondary Schools: Teachers' Realities,* edited by Milbrey W. McLaughlin, Joan E. Talbert, and Nina Bascia. New York: Teachers College Press.

Crockett, Lisa J.; Petersen, Anne; Graber, Julia; Schulenberg, John E., and Ebata, Aaron. (1989, August) "School Transitions and Adjustment During Early Adolescence." *Journal of Early Adolescence* 9, 3: 181–210.

Dornbusch, Sanford M.; Mont-Reynaud, Randy; Ritter, Philip L.; Chen, Zengyin; and Steinberg, Laurence. (1991) "Stressful Events and Their Correlates among Adolescents of Diverse Backgrounds." In *Adolescent Stress: Causes and Consequences,* edited by Mary Ellen Colten and Susan Gore. New York: Aldine De Gruyter.

Dryfoos, Joy G. (1990) *Adolescents at Risk: Prevalence and Prevention.* New York: Oxford University Press.

Duncan, Greg, and Hoffman, Saul. (1989, October) "Teenage Underclass Behavior and Subsequent Poverty: Have the Rules Changed?" Paper prepared for the conference on *The Truly Disadvantaged.*

Easton, John Q., and Storey, Sandra. (1990) *June 1989 Grade Retention in Chicago Public Elementary School.* Chicago, Ill.: Chicago Panel on Public School Policy and Finance.

Eccles, Jacquelynne S.; Lord, Sarah; and Midgley, Carol. (1991) "What Are We Doing to Early Adolescents? The Impact of Educational Contexts on Early Adolescents." *American Journal of Education* 99, 4: 521–542.

Eccles, Jacquelynne S., and Midgley, Carol. (1989) "Stage-Environment Fit: Developmental Appropriate Classrooms for Young Adolescents." In *Research on Motivation in Education,* vol. 3, edited by R. E. Ames and C. Ames. New York: Academic Press.

Eckstrom, R. B.; Goertz, M. S.; Pollack, J. M.; and Rock, D. A. (1987) "Who Drops Out of High School and Why? Findings from a National Study." In *School Dropout: Patterns and Policies,* edited by Gary Natriello. New York: Teachers College Press.

Edelman, Marian Wright, and Howe, Harold II. (1985) *Barriers to Excellence: Our Children at Risk.* Boston, Mass.: National Coalition of Advocates for Students.

Elliot, Glen R., and Feldman, Shirley S. (1990) "Capturing the Adolescent Experience." In *At the Threshold: The Developing Adolescent,* edited by S. Shirley Feldman and Glen R. Elliot. Cambridge, Mass.: Harvard University Press.

Ellwood, David, and Crane, Jonathan. (1990) "Family Change among Black Americans: What Do We Know?" *Journal of Economic Perspectives* 4, 4: 65–84.

Ellwood, David and Rodda, David. (1991) *The Hazards of Work and Marriage: The Influence of Male Employment on Marriage Rates*. Working Paper # H–90–10. Cambridge, Mass.: Malcolm Wiener Center for Social Policy, Kennedy School of Government, Harvard University.

Entwistle, Doris R. (1990) "Schools and the Adolescent." In *At the Threshold: The Developing Adolescent*, edited by S. Shirley Feldman and Glen R. Elliot. Cambridge, Mass.: Harvard University Press.

Entwistle, Doris R., and Alexander, Karl L. (1992, February) "Summer Setback: Race, Poverty, School Composition, and Mathematics Achievement in the First Two Years of School." *American Sociological Review* 57: 72–84.

Epstein, Joyce L., and MacIver, Douglas. (1990) *Education in the Middle Grades: National Practices and Trends*. Columbus, Ohio: National Middle School Association.

Epstein, Joyce L., and Salinas, Karen Clark. (1990) *Promising Practices in Major Academic Subjects in the Middle Grades* (Report No. 4). Baltimore, Md.: Center for Research on Effective Schooling for Disadvantaged Students, Johns Hopkins University.

Farrell, Edwin. (1990) *Hanging In and Dropping Out: Voices of At-Risk High School Students*. New York: Teachers College Press.

Feldlaufer, Harriet; Midgley, Carol; and Eccles, Jacquelynne. (1988) "Student, Teacher, and Observer Perceptions of the Classroom Environment before and after the Transition to Junior High School." *Journal of Early Adolescence* 8, 2: 133–156.

Felner, Robert D., and Adan, Angela M. (1989) "The School Transitional Environment Project: An Ecological Intervention and Evaluation." In *14 Ounces of Prevention: A Casebook for Practitioners*, edited by Richard Price, et al. Washington, D.C.: American Psychological Association.

Felner, Robert D.; Ginter, Melanie; and Primavera, Judith. (1982) "Primary Prevention During School Transitions: Social Support and Environmental Structure." *American Journal of Community Psychology* 10, 3: 277–290.

Felner, Robert D.; Primavera, Judith; and Cauce, Ana M. (1981) "The Impact of School Transitions: A Focus for Preventive Efforts." *American Journal of Community Psychology* 9, 4: 449–459.

Fenzel, L. Mickey. (1989, August) "Role Strains and the Transition to Middle School: Longitudinal Trends and Sex Differences." *Journal of Early Adolescence* 9, 3: 211–226.

Fenzel, L. Mickey, and Blyth, Dale A. (1986) "Individual Adjustment to School Transitions: An Exploration of the Role of Supportive Peer Relations." *Journal of Early Adolescence* 6: 315–329.

Fernandez, Roberto; Paulsen, Ronnelle; and Hirano-Nakanishi, Marsha. (1989) "Dropping Out among Hispanic Youth." *Social Science Research* 18: 21–52.

Fine, Michelle. (1985, Fall) "Dropping Out of High School: An Inside Look." *Social Policy*: 43–50.

———. (1987) "Why Urban Adolescents Drop Into and Out of Public High

Schools." In *School Dropout: Patterns and Policies*, edited by Gary Natriello. New York: Teachers College Press.

————. (1991) *Framing Dropouts: Notes on the Politics of an Urban Public High School*. Albany, N.Y.: State University of New York Press.

Finn, Chester. (1987, Spring) "The High School Dropout Puzzle." *Public Interest* 87: 3–22.

Firestone, William A., and Rosenblum, Sheila. (1988) "Building Commitment in Urban High Schools." *Educational Evaluation and Policy Analysis* 10, 4: 285–299.

Frase, Mary J. (1989) *Dropout Rates in the United States: 1988* (NCES 89–609). Washington, D.C.: U.S. Department of Education, National Center for Education Statistics, U.S. Government Printing Office.

Fullerton, Howard N. (1987, September) "Labor Force Projections: 1986–2000." *Monthly Labor Review* 110, 9: 19–29.

————. (1991, November) "Labor Force Projections: The Baby Boom Moves On." *Monthly Labor Review* 114, 11: 31–44.

Garbarino, James. (1980) "Some Thoughts on School Size and Its Effects on Adolescent Development." *Journal of Youth and Adolescence* 9, 1: 19–31.

————. (1982) *Children and Families in the Social Environment*. Hawthorne, N.Y.: Aldine De Gruyter.

Goldstein, Naomi. (1991) *Why Poverty Is Bad for Children*. Dissertation Series. Cambridge, Mass.: Malcolm Wiener Center for Social Policy, Kennedy School of Government, Harvard University.

Goodlad, John I. (1983) *A Place Called School: Prospects for the Future*. New York: McGraw-Hill.

Gottredson, Gary D. (1988) *You Get What You Measure, You Get What You Don't: High Standards, High Test Score, More Retention in Grade* (Report No. 29). Baltimore, Md.: Center for Research on Elementary and Middle Schools, Johns Hopkins University.

Grannis, Joseph. (1991) "Dropout Prevention in New York City: A Second Chance." *Phi Delta Kappan* 73, 2: 143–149.

Grant Foundation Commission on Work, Family and Citizenship. (1988) *The Forgotten Half: Non-College Youth in America*. New York: William T. Grant Foundation.

Grissom, J. B., and Shepard, L. A. (1989) "Repeating and Dropping Out of School." In *Flunking Grades: Research and Policies on Retention*, edited by Lorrie A. Shepard, and Mary Lee Smith. London: Falmer Press.

Gross, Beatrice, and Gross, Ronald. (1985) *The Great School Debate: Which Way for American Education?* New York: Simon and Schuster.

Hammack, Floyd Morgan. (1987) "Large School Systems' Dropout Reports: An Analysis of Definitions, Procedures and Findings." In *School Dropouts: Patterns and Policies*, edited by Gary Natriello. New York: Teachers College Press.

Harter, Susan. (1990) "Self and Identity Development." In *At the Threshold: The Developing Adolescent*, edited by S. Shirley Feldman and Glen R. Elliot. Cambridge, Mass.: Harvard University Press.

Hauser, Stuart, and Bowlds, Mary Kay. (1990) "Stress, Coping, and Adapta-

tion." In *At the Threshold: The Developing Adolescent*, edited by S. Shirley
Feldman and Glen R. Elliot. Cambridge, Mass.: Harvard University Press.

Hayes, Cheryl (ed.). (1987) *Risking the Future: Adolescent Sexuality, Pregnancy and
Childbearing*. Washington, D.C.: National Academy Press.

Henderson, Valanne L., and Dweck, Carol S. (1990) "Motivation and Achievement." In *At the Threshold: The Developing Adolescent*, edited by S. Shirley
Feldman and Glen R. Elliot. Cambridge, Mass.: Harvard University Press.

Hess, G. Alfred. (1991) *School Restructuring, Chicago Style*. Newbury Park, Calif.:
Corwin Press.

Hill, C. Russell. (1979) "Capacities, Opportunities and Educational Investments:
The Case of the High School Dropouts." *Review of Economics and Statistics*
61: 9–20.

Hirsh, Barton, and Rapkin, Bruce. (1987) "The Transition to Junior High School:
A Longitudinal Study of Self-Esteem, Psychological Symptomatology,
School Life and Social Support." *Child Development* 58: 1235–1243.

Hodge, Robert W. (1981) "The Measurement of Occupational Status." *Social
Science Research* 10: 396–415.

Holmes, Thomas C. (1983) "The Fourth R: Retention." *Journal of Research and
Development in Education* 17, 1: 1–6.

———. (1989) "Grade Level Retention Effects: A Meta-Analysis of Research
Studies." In *Flunking Grades: Research and Policies on Retention*, edited by
Lorrie A. Shepard, and Mary Lee Smith. London: Falmer Press.

Holmes, Thomas C., and Matthews, Kenneth M. (1984, Summer) "The Effects
of Nonpromotion on Elementary and Junior High School Pupils: A Meta-
Analysis." *Review of Educational Research* 54, 2: 225–236.

Howe, Harold II. (1985) "Giving Equity a Chance in the Excellence Game." In
The Great School Debate: Which Way for American Education? edited by Beatrice Gross and Ronald Gross. New York: Simon and Schuster.

Howell, Frank M., and Frese, Wolfgang. (1982, Spring) "Early Transitions into
Adult Roles: Some Antecedents and Outcomes." *American Educational
Research Journal* 19, 1: 51–73.

Hyle, Adrienne E.; Bull, Kay S.; Salyer, Keith; and Montgomery, Diane. (1991)
"School Dropouts: What Agenda Do Administrators See for Dealing with
the Problem?" Paper presented at the Annual Meeting of the American
Educational Research Association. Chicago, Ill.

Illinois State Board of Education. (1992) *Illinois Middle-Level School Assessment: A
Look at the State-of-the-Art Practices*. Springfield, Ill.: Illinois State Board of
Education.

Jackson, Gregg B. (1975, Fall) "The Research Evidence of the Effects of Grade
Retention." *Review of Educational Research* 45, 4: 613–635.

Johnson, Clifford M.; Sum, Andrew; and Weill, James. (1988) *Vanishing Dreams:
The Growing Economic Plight of America's Young Families*. Washington, D.C.:
Children's Defense Fund.

Karweit, Nancy L. (1991, May) *Repeating a Grade: Time to Grow or Denial of Opportunity* (Report No. 16). Baltimore, Md.: Center for Research on Effective
Schooling for Disadvantaged Students, Johns Hopkins University.

Kaufman, Philip; McMillian, Marilyn; and Whitener, Summer. (1991) *Dropout
Rates in the United States: 1990*. Washington, D.C.: U.S. Department of

Education, National Center for Education Statistics, U.S. Government Printing Office.

Kmenta, Jan. (1986) *Elements of Econometrics*. New York: Macmillan.

Kolstad, A. J., and Owings, J. A. (1986) *High School Dropouts Who Change Their Minds about School*. Paper presented at the annual meeting of the American Educational Research Association, San Francisco, Calif.

Kutscher, Ronald E. (1991) "New BLS Projections: Findings and Implications." *Monthly Labor Review* 114, 11: 3–12.

Lee, Valerie and Ekstrom, Ruth B. (1987) "Student Access to Guidance Counseling in High School." *American Educational Research Journal* 24, 2: 287–310.

Lerman, Robert I. (1972) "Some Determinants of Youth School Activity." *Journal of Human Resources* 7, 3: 366–383.

Linn, Marcia C. and Songer, Nancy Butler. (1991) "Cognitive and Conceptual Change in Adolescence." *American Journal of Education* 99, 4: 379–417.

Lipstiz, Joan. (1984) *Successful Schools for Young Adolescents*. New Brunswick, N.J.: Transaction Books.

Lloyd, Norman Dee. (1978) "Prediction of School Failure from Third Grade Data." *Educational and Psychological Measurement* 38: 1193–1200.

McDill, Edward L.; Natriello, Gary; and Pallas, Aaron. (1986) "A Population at Risk: Potential Consequences of Tougher School Standards for Student Dropouts." In *School Dropouts: Patterns and Policies*, edited by Gary Natriello. New York: Teachers College Press.

MacIver, Douglas J. (1991) *Helping Students Who Fall Behind: Remedial Activities in the Middle Grades* (Report No. 22). Baltimore, Md.: Center for Research on Effective Schooling for Disadvantaged Students, John Hopkins University.

MacIver, Douglas, and Epstein, Joyce L. (1991) "Responsive Practices in the Middle Grades: Teacher Teams, Advisory Groups, Remedial Instructions, and School Transition Programs." *American Journal of Education* 99, 4: 587–622.

McKinley, L. Blackburn; Bloom, David E., and Freeman, Richard B. (1990) "The Declining Economic Position of Less Skilled American Men." In *A Future of Lousy Jobs: The Changing Structure of U.S. Wages*, edited by Gary Burtless. Washington, D.C.: The Brookings Institution: 31–76.

McLanahan, Sara. (1985) "Family Structure and the Reproduction of Poverty." *American Journal of Sociology* 90, 4: 873–902.

McLanahan, Sara, and Bumpass, Larry. (1988) "A Note on the Effect of Family Structure on School Enrollment." In *Divided Opportunities: Minorities, Poverty and Social Policy*, edited by Sandefur and Tienda. New York: Plenum Press.

McPartland, James M., and Slavin, Robert E. (1990) *Policy Perspectives: Increasing Achievement of At-Risk Students at Each Grade Level*. U.S. Department of Education, Office of Educational Research and Improvement, Policy Perspective Series. Washington, D.C.: U.S. Government Printing Office.

Maddala, G. S. (1986) *Limited-Dependent and Qualitative Variables in Econometrics*. New York: Cambridge University Press.

Mann, Dale. (1986) "Can We Help Dropouts: Thinking about the Undoable."

In *School Dropouts: Patterns and Policies*, edited by Gary Natriello. New York: Teachers College Press.

Mantzicopoulos, Panayota, and Morrison, Delmont. (1992) "Kindergarten Retention: Academic and Behavioral Outcomes Through the End of Second Grade." *American Educational Research Journal* 29, 1: 182–198.

Mare, Robert D. (1980) "Social Background and School Continuation Decisions." *Journal of the American Statistical Association* 75: 295–305.

Massachusetts Advocacy Center. (1986) *The Way Out: Student Exclusion Practices in Boston Middle Schools*. Boston, Mass.: Massachusetts Advocacy Center.

———. (1988) *Before It's Too Late: Dropout Prevention in the Middle Grades*. Boston, Mass.: Massachusetts Advocacy Center.

———. (1989) "Non-promotion and Dropout Data: 1986–87, 1987–88." Boston, Mass.: Massachusetts Advocacy Center.

———. (1990) *Locked In/Locked Out: Tracking and Placement Practices in Boston Public Schools*. Boston, Mass.: Massachusetts Advocacy Center.

Midgley, Carol; Feldlaufer, Harriet; and Eccles, Jacquelynne. (1989) "Student/ Teacher Relations and Attitudes towards Mathematics before and after the Transition to Junior High School." *Child Development* 60: 981–992.

Muth, Denise K., and Alvermann, Donna M. (1992) *Teaching and Learning in the Middle Grades*. Needham Heights, Mass.: Allyn and Bacon.

National Coalition of Advocates for Students. (1991) *The Good Common School: Making the Vision Work for All Children*. Boston, Mass.: National Coalition of Advocates for Students.

National Commission on Excellence in Education. (1983) *A Nation at Risk: The Imperative for Educational Reform*. Washington, D.C.: U.S. Government Printing Office.

Natriello, Gary; McDill, Edward L.; and Pallas, Aaron. (1991) *School Disadvantaged Children: Racing Against Catastrophe*. New York: Teachers College Press.

Neilsen, Arthur and Gerber, Dan. (1979) "Psychosocial Aspects of Truancy in Early Adolescence." *Adolescence* 14: 313–326.

Newmann, Fred M. (1989) "Reducing Student Alienation in High Schools: Implications of Theory." In *Dropouts from School: Issues, Dilemmas, and Solutions*, edited by Lois Weis, Eleanor Farrar, and Hugh G. Petrie. Albany, N.Y.: State University of New York Press: pp. 153–180.

New York City Board of Education, Office of Educational Assessment. (1988) *A Follow Up Study of the 1982–1983 Promotional Gates Students*. New York: New York City Board of Education.

Niklason, Lucille. (1984, October) "Non-Promotion: A Pseudoscientific Solution." *Psychology in the Schools* 21: 485–499.

Oakes, Jeannie. (1985) *Keeping Track: How Schools Structure Inequality*. New Haven, Conn.: Yale University Press.

———. (1992) "Can Tracking Research Inform Practice? Technical, Normative and Political Considerations." *Educational Researcher* 21, 4: 12–21.

OERI Urban Superintendents Network. (1987) *Dealing with Dropouts: The Urban Superintendents' Call to Action*. Washington, D.C.: U.S. Government Printing Office.

Overman, Monica. (1986, April) "Student Promotion and Retention." *Phi Delta Kappan* 67: 609–13.

Petersen, Anne, and Epstein, Joyce L. (1991) "Development and Education across Adolescence: An Introduction." *American Journal of Education* 99, 4: 373–378.

Petersen, Anne C.; Kennedy, Robert; and Sullivan, Patricia. (1991) "Coping with Adolescence." In *Adolescent Stress: Causes and Consequences*, edited by Mary Ellen Colten and Susan Gore. New York: Aldine De Gruyter.

Petersen, Anne C., and Stemmler, Mark. (1991) "Development Psychology: An Exciting Transition in the Field." *Educational Researcher* 20, 8: 26–27.

PINS Advisory Committee. (1988) *Promotional Policies and Children in New York City Schools*. New York: New York City's Chancellor's Office and Board of Education.

Pittman, Robert B., and Haughwort, Perri. (1987, Winter) "Influence of High School Size on Dropout Rate." *Educational Evaluation and Policy Analysis* 9, 4: 337–343.

Public Education Association. (1990) *Restructuring Neighborhood High Schools: The House Plan Solution*. New York: Public Education Association.

Reich, Carol, and Young, Vivienne. (1975) "Patterns of Dropping Out." *Interchange* 6, 4: 6–15.

Roderick, Melissa. (1991) *The Path to Dropping Out among Public School Youth: Middle School and Early High School Experiences* (Dissertation Series #D–91–2). Cambridge, Mass.: Malcolm Weiner Center for Social Policy, Kennedy School of Government, Harvard University.

Rose, Janet S.; Medway, Frederic; Cantrell, V. L.; and Marus, Susan H. (1983) "A Fresh Look at the Retention-Promotion Controversy." *Journal of School Psychology* 21: 201–211.

Rumberger, Russell W. (1983) "Dropping Out of High School: The Influence of Race, Sex and Family Background." *American Educational Research Journal* 20, 2: 199–220.

———. (1987) "High School Dropouts: A Review of Issues and Evidence." *Review of Educational Research* 57, 2: 101–121.

Rumberger, Russell W.; Ghatak, Rita; Poulos, Gary; Ritter, Philip L.; and Dornbusch, Sanford. (1990, October) "Family Influences on Dropout Behavior in One California High School." *Sociology of Education* 63: 283–299.

Rutter, Michael; Maughan, Barbara; Mortimore, Peter; and Ouston, Janet. (1979) *Fifteen Thousand Hours: Secondary Schools and Their Effects on Children*. Cambridge, Mass.: Harvard University Press.

Sandefur, Gary; McLanahan, Sara; and Wojtkeiwicz, Roger A. (1989) *Race, Ethnicity, Family Structure and High School Graduation* (Discussion Paper 893–89). Madison, Wis.: Institute for Research on Poverty, University of Wisconsin, Madison.

Schulenberg, John E.; Asp, C. Elliot; and Petersen, Anne C. (1984) "School for the Young Adolescent's Perspective: A Descriptive Report." *Journal of Early Adolescence* 4, 2: 107–130.

Schultz, Tom. (1989) "Testing and Retention of Young Children: Moving from Controversy to Reform." *Phi Delta Kappan*.

Selinker, Michael, and Martin, Michelle. (1991, June). "Dropout Prevention:

Falling Through Cracks." *Catalyst: Voices of Chicago School Reform* 3, 9: 1–5.

Shaw, Lois. (1982, June) "High School Completion for Young Women: Effects of Low Income and Living with a Single Parent." *Journal of Family Issues* 3, 2: 147–163.

Shepard, Lorrie, and Smith, Mary Lee. (1986) "Synthesis of Research on School Readiness and Kindergarten Retention." *Educational Leadership* 44: 78–86.

———. (1988) "Escalating Academic Demand in Kindergarten: Counterproductive Policies." *Elementary School Journal* 89, 2: 135–145.

———. (1989) "Introduction and Overview." In *Flunking Grades: Research and Policies on Retention,* edited by Lorrie A. Shepard and Mary Lee Smith. London: Falmer Press.

Silvestri, George, and Lukasiewicz, John. (1991) "Occupational Employment Projections." *Monthly Labor Review* 114, 11: 64–94.

Simmons, Robert G.; Black, Ann; and Zhou, Yingzhi. (1991) "African American versus White Children and the Transition into Junior High School." *American Journal of Education* 99, 4: 481–520.

Sizer, Theodore R. (1984) *Horace's Compromise: The Dilemma of the American High School.* Boston, Mass.: Houghton Mifflin.

Slavin, Robert E. (1987, October) "Making Chapter 1 Make a Difference." *Phi Delta Kappan* 69: 110–119.

Smetana, Judith G.; Yau, Jenny; Restrepo, Angela; and Braeges, Judith L. (1991) "Conflict and Adaptation in Adolescence: Adolescent-Parent Conflict." In *Adolescent Stress: Causes and Consequences,* edited by Mary Ellen Colten and Susan Gore. New York: Aldine De Gruyter.

Smith, Mary Lee, and Shepard, Lorrie A. (1987, October) "What Doesn't Work: Explaining Policies of Retention in the Early Grades." *Phi Delta Kappan* 69, 2: 129–134.

Spencer, Margaret Beale, and Dornbusch, Sanford. (1990) "Challenges in Studying Minority Youth." In *At the Threshold: The Developing Adolescent,* edited by S. Shirley Feldman and Glen R. Elliot. Cambridge, Mass.: Harvard University Press.

Stedman, Lawrence C., and Smith, Marshall S. (1983) "Recent Reform Proposals for American Education." *Contemporary Education Review* 2, 2: 85–104.

Steinberg, Laurence; Blinde, Patricia Lin; and Chan, Kenyon S. (1984, Spring) "Dropping Out among Language Minority Youth." *Review of Educational Research* 54, 1: 113–132.

Steinberg, Laurence; Greenberger, Ellen; Garduque, Laurie; and McAuliffe, Sharon. (1982) "High School Students in the Labor Force: Some Costs and Benefits to Schooling and Learning." *Educational Evaluation and Policy Analysis* 4, 3: 363–372.

Sum, Andrew; Fogg, Neal; and Taggart, Robert. (1988) *Withered Dreams: The Decline in the Economic Fortunes of Young, Non-College Bound Educated Male Adults and Their Families.* Paper prepared for the William T. Grant Foundation Commission on Family, Work, and Citizenship.

Sum, Andrew, and Johnson, Cliff. (1987) *Declining Earnings of Young Men: Their Relation to Poverty, Teen Pregnancy and Family Formation* (Adolescent Pregnancy Prevention Clearinghouse). Washington, D.C.: Children's Defense Fund.

Task Force on Education for Economic Growth. (1983) *Action for Excellence: A Comprehensive Plan to Improve Our Nation's Schools*. Denver, Colo.: Education Commission of the States.

Thornburg, Hershel D., and Jones, Randy M. (1982) "Social Characteristics of Early Adolescents: Age versus Grade." *Journal of Early Adolescence* 2, 3: 229–239.

Tidwell, Romeria. (1988) "Dropouts Speak Out: Qualitative Data on Early School Departures." *Adolescence* 23, 92.

Tinto, Vincent. (1987) *Leaving College: Rethinking the Causes and Cures of Student Attrition*. Chicago, Ill.: University of Chicago Press.

Toby, Jackson, and Armor, David D. (1992) "Carrots or Sticks for High School Dropouts?" *Public Interest* 106: 76–90.

Tompchin, Ellen M., and Impara, James C. (1992) "Unraveling Teachers' Beliefs about Grade Retention." *American Educational Research Journal* 29, 1: 199–223.

Twentieth Century Fund. (1983) *Report of the Twentieth Century Fund Task Force on Federal Elementary and Secondary Education Policy*. New York: Twentieth Century Fund.

U.S. Bureau of the Census. (1991 and various years) *Educational Attainment in the United States* (Current Population Reports, Series P–20). Washington, D.C.: U.S. Government Printing Office.

———. (1991 and various years) *School Enrollment—Social and Economic Characteristics of Students: October 1989* (Current Population Reports, Series P–20, No. 452). Washington, D.C.: U.S. Government Printing Office.

U.S. Department of Education, National Center for Education Statistics. (1991) *Digest of Education Statistics*. Washington D.C.: U.S. Government Printing Office.

U.S. General Accounting Office. (1986) *School Dropouts: The Extent and Nature of the Problem*. Washington, D.C.: U.S. Government Printing Office.

Voydanoff, Patricia, and Donnelly, Brenda W. (1990) *Adolescent Sexuality and Pregnancy*. Newbury Park, Calif.: Sage Publications.

Waite, Linda J., and Moore, Kristin A. (1978) "The Impact of an Early First Birth on Young Women's Educational Attainment." *Social Forces* 56, 3: 845–864.

Walker, Gary, and Vilella-Velez, Frances. (1992) *Anatomy of a Demonstration: The Summer Training and Education Program (STEP) from Pilot Through Replication and Postprogram Impacts*. Philadelphia, Pa.: Public/Private Ventures.

WAVE in Schools. (1992) "Request for Proposals to Evaluate a Nationwide Dropout Prevention Model." Washington, D.C.: Wave in Schools.

Weber, James M. (1986) *The Role of Vocational Education in Decreasing the Dropout Rate*. Columbus, Ohio: National Center for Research in Vocational Education, Ohio State University.

Weber, James M., and Sechler, Judith A. (1986) *Vocational Education and the Retention of At-Risk Youth*. Columbus, Ohio: National Center for Research in Vocational Education, Ohio State University.

Weiss, Lois; Farrar, Eleanor; and Petrie, Hugh. (1989) Introduction. *Dropouts from School: Issues, Dilemmas, and Solutions*. Albany, N.Y.: State University of New York Press.

Wheelock, Anne, and Dorman, Gayle. (1988) *Before It's Too Late: Dropout Prevention in the Middle Grades*. Boston, Mass.: Massachusetts Advocacy Center.

Whelage, Gary F., and Rutter, Robert A. (1986) "Dropping Out: How Much Do Schools Contribute to the Problem?" In *School Dropouts: Patterns and Policies*, edited by Gary Natriello. New York: Teachers College Press.

Whelage, Gary G.; Rutter, Robert A.; Smith, Gregory; Lesko, Nancy; and Fernandez, Ricardo. (1989) *Reducing the Risk: Schools as Communities of Support*. Philadelphia, Pa.: Falmer Press.

Whelage, Gary; Smith, Gregory; and Lipman, Pauline. (1992) "Restructuring Urban Schools: The New Futures Experience." *American Educational Research Journal* 29, 1: 51–93.

Willett, John B., and Singer, Judith D. (1991) "From Whether to When: New Methods for Studying Student Dropout and Teacher Attrition." *Review of Educational Research* 61, 4: 407–450.

Wilson, William Julius (with Robert Aponte and Kathryn Neckerman). (1987) *The Truly Disadvantaged*. Chicago, Ill.: University of Chicago Press.

Index

About the Author

MELISSA RODERICK is an Assistant Professor at the School of Social Service Administration at the University of Chicago where she teaches courses in social policy, program evaluation, and quantitative analysis. She is interested in the social and academic development of adolescents and the determinants of successful transitions to work and adulthood. Her research focuses on the influence of school organization, policies, and practices on student outcomes, and issues in urban education and youth policy. She is currently studying curriculum tracking in high schools.